The United States and the
Spanish Civil War

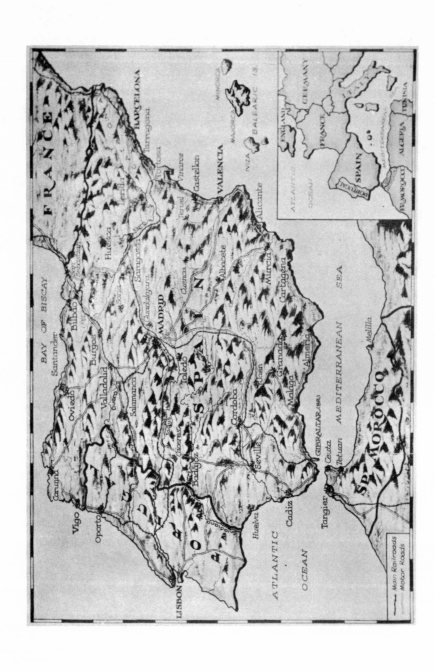

Main Railroads
Motor Roads

THE UNITED STATES
and the
SPANISH CIVIL WAR

by
F. Jay Taylor

1971

OCTAGON BOOKS
New York

Reprinted 1971
by special arrangement with Twayne Publishers, Inc.

OCTAGON BOOKS
A Division of Farrar, Straus & Giroux, Inc.
19 Union Square West
New York, N. Y. 10003

Library of Congress Catalog Card Number: 76-159232

ISBN-0-374-97849-2

Printed in U.S.A. by
NOBLE OFFSET PRINTERS, INC.
NEW YORK 3, N. Y.

For

Evelyn and Terry

Preface

In July 1936 international tensions were rendered more complex by the outbreak of the Spanish Civil War. Not only did this conflict seem to develop in some respects into an irreconcilable struggle among the forces of democracy, fascism, and communism, but it also became a dress rehearsal for the Second World War. In retrospect, however, the Spanish episode represented but one phase in the attempt of the dictators to extend their influence and power in Europe. It is an ugly memory in the minds of thoughtful democrats because the Western democracies permitted the Republic of Spain, for all its shortcomings, to be destroyed by fascist aggression. This abdication of responsibility in Spain has often troubled the conscience of the West.

In the United States, the Spanish Civil War was one of this generation's most impassioned political and religious controversies. Catholics and Protestants, liberals and conservatives, rightists and leftists — all expressed clashing views, championing either one or the other of the protagonists in Spain. American opinion became inflamed in an almost unprecedented manner. The issue was hotly debated — from the pulpit, in the halls of Congress, on college campuses, in the editorial columns of the press, and through every agency designed to influence public opinion. Even today, when considerations of world strategy seem to demand that the Western nations carefully reconsider the strategically placed Iberian peninsula, the political air is still full of the years' accumulation of heated arguments about the Franco regime.

Now, with the re-emergence of Spain in the political consciousness of the United States, it is appropriate to examine American reaction to the ordeal of the Spanish Civil War. The plan of this book has neither been to confine the study to an interpretation of American public opinion nor to restrict it to a discussion of official policy. Rather than treat these aspects of the subject individually, an attempt has been made to blend

7

them together to give a broad survey of American attitudes toward the civil war in Spain.

Some well-informed observers have contended that the position adopted by the United States during the Spanish War constituted the gravest error of American foreign policy during the Roosevelt Administration. Despite the correctness or falsity of this contention, the total complex of American reactions to the war marked a decisive step in the retreat from isolation. Although American policy was officially that of neutrality, this was the first European crisis in two decades in which Americans felt a deep personal involvement. From 1936 to 1939 many segments of public opinion in the United States shifted from a position of indifference to the civil war in Spain to a realization that this conflict was inexorably connected with the greater battle of diplomacy and power politics. The attitudes in this country were not just attitudes toward a third-rate European power; they also involved questions that were to become increasingly important prior to the attack on Pearl Harbor. Many of the basic tenets of American foreign policy — neutrality, freedom of the seas, embargoes, and recognition — were involved, and none of them could be divorced from the broader area of American policy toward the totalitarian aggressors.

The present treatment of the subject, except for two chapters relating to the Spanish and the American backgrounds, is limited to the period from the outbreak of the war in July 1936 to the recognition of the Nationalist Government in April 1939. The principal sources are Congressional debates, diplomatic correspondence in the Department of State, the unpublished papers of Franklin D. Roosevelt, published memoirs and papers of leaders in the Roosevelt Administration, the records of the veterans of the Abraham Lincoln Brigade, newspapers, and periodicals. Although a wealth of source material is available, no secondary accounts of the relations between the United States and Spain during the Spanish Civil War have dealt with the subject in more than a cursory manner.

I am indebted for the assistance they have rendered in gaining access to source material to Dr. Bernard Noble and Dr. E. Taylor Parks of the Division of Historical Policy Research in the Department of State; to Dr. Herman Kahn, Director of the Roosevelt Library in Hyde Park, New York; to the staffs of the

Los Angeles Public Library, New York Public Library, Library of Congress, Claremont College Library, Tulane University Library, and to Librarian Sammy A. Dyson of Louisiana College.

My sincere appreciation goes to Professor Harold W. Bradley of Vanderbilt University, Professor Wendell H. Stephenson of the University of Oregon, Professors William R. Hogan and Fred C. Cole of Tulane University, Professors James Thrasher and Calvin Huckabay, Mr. Bruce Lowe, and Miss Wilda Hundley of Louisiana College, and Mr. George Williams of New Orleans for their friendly interest and assistance.

Generous grants-in-aid from the Carnegie Foundation for the Advancement of Teaching and the Louisiana College Faculty Research Fund helped with the research connected with this study. My special appreciation goes to President G. Earl Guinn and Dean H. M. Weathersby of Louisiana College for their encouragement and understanding in this regard.

To Dean John R. Hubbard of Newcomb College and Mr. Claude G. Bowers I am deeply indebted and grateful for their invaluable advice and many suggestions throughout the research and writing of this book.

I wish to express my gratitude to the editors of Bookman Associates for their thorough and intelligent editing of the manuscript. Finally, it need hardly be said that this book would never have been completed without the limitless encouragement and assistance of my wife, Evelyn.

F. JAY TAYLOR

Louisiana College
Pineville, Louisiana
September, 1955

Table of Contents

can policy — The attack on the *Kane* — American shipping and the war — Mediation proposals — Interests and motives of the European powers — The International Nonintervention Committee — Board of Munitions Control upholds American policy — American diplomatic officials in Spain maintain a neutral course — Fundamental characteristics of American policy — Failure of the moral embargo. Notes.

CHAPTER IV   LEGISLATING NEUTRALITY 75

Failure of the Nonintervention League — Disregard of the moral embargo — Planes for the Loyalists — Official concern — Spanish embargo resolution introduced in Congress — Congressional debate — The embargo becomes law — Reaction abroad — American reaction — Congress turns its attention to permanent neutrality — Debate over method — Final passage of the measure — Provisions concerning Spain — State Department issues regulations governing soliciting and receiving contributions for use in Spain — Proposed extension of the arms embargo to Germany and Italy — Congressional sentiment — Proposal acclaimed by the liberal press — Attitude of the State Department — The President intervenes — American policy remains unchanged. Notes.

CHAPTER V   THE EVASION OF NEUTRALITY 101

American volunteers in Spain — Attitude of the State Department — Legislation prohibiting enlistment — The Lincoln-Washington Battalion — Number of enlistments and casualties — Motives and interests of Americans fighting in Spain — Recruiting activities in the United States. Notes.

CHAPTER VI   THE GREAT DEBATE 117

Ideological warfare — Choice of nomenclature — Propaganda floods the United States — Reporting the Spanish conflict — Secular press — Catholic press — Hearst press — Bombing of civilians and open cities in Spain — Americans protest — Senator Borah's rebuke to fascism — Defense of Franco — Statements by Cordell Hull and Sumner Welles — Protestant open letter to the Catholic hierarchy — The Catholic reply — American relief activities — Organizations in the United States — Repatriation of American volunteers — Pro-Loyalist activity in Hollywood — Catholic humanitarian organizations support the Insurgents — Activities of the American Red Cross — The Presi-

My own impression is that with every surrender beginning long ago with China, followed by Abyssinia and then Spain, the fascist powers, with vanity inflamed, will turn without delay to some other country — such as Czechoslovakia — and that with every surrender the prospects of a European war grow darker.

CLAUDE G. BOWERS

July 20, 1937

Introduction

Dr. Taylor in his book, *The United States and the Spanish Civil War*, has made an honest effort to clarify the issue and the significance of the war in Spain. That war was not a civil war in the usual sense since Mussolini sent in an army of a hundred thousand, Hitler armed forces of forty thousand; both sent a great fleet of fighting planes, and for more than two years both crowded rebel ports with vessels unloading arms and ammunition to be used by their own armed forces for the extermination of democracy in Spain. Thus it was a war of aggression from without. Between twenty-five and thirty German and Italian Generals were in actual command in this peculiar "civil war," on which the apologists of fascism still insist.

Never have the instruments of propaganda been used so brazenly to confuse the public mind beyond the Spanish border. With unprecedented facilities for the dissemination of the truth, the falsehoods over the wire and radio had the effect of confusing or poisoning public opinion, especially in the United States.

When the rebel Generals, by prearrangements with Hitler and Mussolini for their military aid, plunged a peaceful people into a welter of blood, the purpose was to end the reforms of the Republic aimed at wiping out the lingering feudalism in the land and the raising of the status of the workers to that of human dignity. Since world opinion could not be mobilized for that purpose another explanation had to be found. Thus for months before the Generals turned traitors to their trust, and Hitler and Mussolini poured their infantry, artillery and planes into a peaceful land, a cynically dishonest propaganda campaign began to persuade the world that Spain was in a state of anarchy and that its Government, headed by Manuel Azaña, was a Communist set-up.

There was no "anarchy," as I know, since I personally went to the seat of the alleged troubles and found nothing.

There was nothing in the Government of Azaña that had the slightest relation to communism. He was a great statesman, a great thinker and political philosopher, and a militant democrat, known to everyone in Spain as an enemy of both communism and fascism. His Ministers were drawn exclusively from the conservative, republican and democratic parties with not even a pale pink Socialist among them, and certainly no Communists in any post. In the Cortes, with a membership of 470, there were fifteen ineffective Communists. No one whose brains would not rattle in a mustard seed would think of describing as communistic the Government against which the Axis Powers began to wage war. At that very time there were a hundred Communist members of the French Congress, but the French Government was not called a Communist government; there are far more Communists in the Italian Congress today, but no one calls the Italian Republic Communistic.

The war of the Spanish Generals and their Axis allies was begun not against a Communist government that did not exist but against the Spanish democracy, and for its extermination.

All the resourcefulness of high-powered propaganda, à la Goebbels, was concentrated on "communism," but inside Spain the propaganda was made against democracy. The rebel newspapers, with no exceptions, reeked with ridicule and denunciation of the "moribund democracies." All indecently assailed Churchill and Roosevelt while glorifying Hitler and Mussolini, and fervently hailing the "new order" proclaimed by Hitler.

It was clear to anyone on the ground that the purpose of the Axis and their rebel allies was the extermination of democracy in Spain as the first step toward an all-out war for the extermination of democracy in Europe. It is a sad commentary on human weakness that while the totalitarians made no secret of their purpose, we democrats did our best to cover it up.

We now know that World War II did not begin in Poland but in Spain in July 1936, and that the six months interval between the destruction of democracy in Spain and the all-out war of the Axis to exterminate it in Europe was but an armistice in the same war in which the shibboleths and banners, so familiar to us from 1939 to 1945, were first seen and heard on the battlefields of Spain.

Had the Spanish Republic, recognized by every democratic nation as the legal constitutional government, not been shamefully denied its right, under universally recognized international law, to buy arms and ammunition for its defense, the Loyalists would have prevailed. The strange denial of this right, so vigorously denounced by Henry L. Stimson, Secretary of State under Hoover, and Secretary of War under Roosevelt, unwittingly made the great democratic nations actual collaborationists of the Axis in its war to destroy the democracy of the Spanish people.

The most vicious thing was the creation, and the shameful, cynically dishonest use of the Nonintervention Pact, on the demand of the dreary character with the umbrella who brought "peace in our times" from Munich. The pretended purpose was to prevent the involvement of other nations and to permit the Spaniards to settle their own dispute, thus preventing the spread of the war. We followed with our embargo, on the assumption that the Nonintervention Pact would be impartially enforced. But within ten days after the Spanish Generals launched their war the Axis powers were violating the agreement with an incredible defiance — and the Nonintervention Committee looked upon their crime with complacency, without a word of protest, while concentrating on enforcement against the Spanish Republic, which alone had the right to buy arms and ammunition under international law. That is one of the blackest crimes against freedom in modern times.

Too late, we realized that our embargo, if continued on the books, would, in the language of Roosevelt in a speech toward the close, make us partisans of the aggressor: and too late, after democracy had been destroyed in Spain, Senator Pittman, the author of the embargo, told me that we had "made a mistake as to Spain"; and Sumner Welles has written that our policy as to Spain had been one of the darkest in the history of our international policies.

All this is water over the dam. Spain has its Fascist government, and there is no freedom of speech, no freedom of the press, no religious freedom. But we can at least refuse to join in the plan to suppress, distort, and mutilate the history of those days. History is the torch that is meant to illuminate the past to guard us against the repetition of our mistakes of other days. We cannot join in the rewriting of history to make it conform to our comfort and convenience. Lincoln never said a truer thing than when he warned that "we cannot escape history."

It is therefore reassuring that historians are delving into the records, so long under cover, to set forth the actual facts of the Spanish War. Dr. Taylor has made an honest and meticulous effort to find them. They fairly scream from the pages of Ciano's *Diary* and from the papers found in the archives of the defunct Nazi Government. The author has set forth his findings and observations clearly, courageously, and most readably. Others will no doubt continue to peer behind the once iron curtain of secrecy and record the truth. It will be through the accumulation of such documents that the attempt to "doctor" history will inevitably fail.

CLAUDE G. BOWERS

Chapter One

The Spanish Background

Following the victory of the Republican parties over the Monarchist forces of King Alfonso XIII in the municipal elections throughout Spain, the second Spanish Republic[1] was proclaimed on April 12, 1931. Two days later, the last of the Bourbon monarchs abdicated the Spanish throne and fled his kingdom to live in exile. Since the uncertain days of 1923, when the King had willingly allowed his country to be subjected to the rule of a military dictator, the Spanish Government had followed an uncertain course. King Alfonso assumed responsibility for the policies of General Primo de Rivera, who, as a member of the Spanish officer caste, served as virtual dictator until January 1930. During this period the Government was absolute and was supported by a large part of the Army, the Catholic Church, and the landowning aristocracy. The dictatorship of de Rivera achieved initial success and enjoyed increased popularity with the Spanish people after the Government had successfully concluded the Morocco dispute and decreased unemployment with a vast public works project. After 1926, however, de Rivera's popularity rapidly declined as he dispensed with the Constitution, abolished free elections, curtailed freedom of speech, and rigidly controlled the press.[2]

By January 1930 popular sentiment had so crystallized against the dictatorship that the Monarchy was in grave peril. The King had accepted the dictatorship and consequently was held responsible for the totalitarian policies of the Government. Realizing that the country was facing a revolution, King Alfonso dismissed de Rivera from the Government and commissioned General Dámaso Berenguer to form a new ministry with a civilian cabinet.[3] Even

21

this action did not quiet the unrest. Many of the liberal groups, jubilant over the ease with which a dictator had been deposed, felt that the King could be handled in the same manner. Revolutionary committees were formed throughout Spain, and certain segments of the Spanish people, especially the Catalans and the urban proletariat, were intractable throughout the remainder of 1930. In December, Berenguer resigned and the King succeeded in forming a makeshift cabinet headed by Admiral Don Juan B. Aznar. Only a few persons had the slightest degree of confidence in the new Government, and the Admiral was unable to bring any degree of stability to the country. The King tried various expedients — short of a general election — to placate the dissidents. He was unable to rally support to his cause, however, and revolutionary leaders throughout the country threatened open violence. In the face of such determined opposition, Alfonso agreed to hold municipal elections in order that the popular will of the people might be determined.[4]

The victory of the Republican-Socialist parties in the municipal elections of April 1931 forced the King into exile. Before leaving for France King Alfonso sadly told his subjects:

> The elections which took place Sunday have clearly shown me that I have lost the affections of my people. . . . I could have employed divers means to maintain the royal prerogative and effectively combat my enemies, but I wish resolutely to step aside from anything that might throw some of my countrymen against others in a fratricidal civil war. . . .
>
> I renounce none of my rights, for they are not so much my own as a trust committed to me by History, for which one day I shall have to render her a strict account. . . . I deliberately suspend the exercise of royal power and leave Spain, thus showing that I recognize her as the sole mistress of her destinies.[5]

Thus with the King disposed of, the way was now cleared for the new Provisional Government to consolidate its gains through the formulation of a new constitution. The elections to the Constituent Cortes in June 1931 resulted in an overwhelming victory for the Republicans and their Socialist allies. One reliable authority estimated that the left-wing Republican group elected 150 deputies, the right-wing Republican group just over 100, and the Socialists 115. The parties which had voted against the Republic elected 52 deputies, and of these, only about half were confirmed Monarchists.[6] Thus much of the country, especially the urban districts, turned against the King and was practically unanimous in pledging support to the new regime.

Although it was remarkable that the transition from monarchy to republic was a relatively peaceful affair, Spain, nevertheless, was seething with deep social unrest. During the next five and a half years the Spanish people were not only suffering from a vast economic depression but also from divisions into many mutually antagonistic groups. There were strong, almost rebellious, movements for local autonomy in Catalonia and the Basque Provinces, which were opposed by a strong centralist bloc. The core of this Castilian centralism was the Army, supported by the landowners and other conservative forces such as the Monarchists and the Catholic Church. The workers, peasants, and urban proletariat were divided into two sections — the Socialists and Anarcho-Syndicalists. The Socialists found their greatest strength among the urban proletariat and shipworkers, while Anarcho-Syndicalism was very strong among the landless laborers of the large estates. Although the Communists were active in Spain, they were not strong enough to exert any positive influence at that time.[7]

Another small but politically active group stood between the aristocracy and the lower classes. This faction, comprising the lower middle class of the towns, was composed primarily of small tradesmen and formed the basis of the Republican movement. Many intellectuals, teachers, and journalists sympathized with them, especially in their desire to draft a new constitution and in their hostility toward the clergy.[8]

Such confusion of thought and difference of opinion among the various parties made the task that lay ahead a very difficult one. The aristocratic classes were primarily concerned with their own interests and felt confident that they could successfully oppose any Leftist Government which might come to power. The peasants and other workers, inspired with revolutionary ideologies, expected the new Republic to ameliorate their depressed conditions. It was necessary that the Republicans, greatly weakened by fluctuations within their own ranks, maintain a balance of power between these two groups until the Republic could be firmly established and essential reforms passed. Thus one of the primary aims of the Republican group was to take the power from the aristocracy and establish a government controlled by the lower middle class and backed by a contented peasantry.[9]

The Constituent Cortes met in Madrid on July 14, 1931, and the deputies immediately began work on a new constitution.[10] Harmony among the various groups was strained on many occasions because the Republicans were not a single party but a coalition of many different parties, including Socialists, Radical Socialists, Leftist Republicans, Federalists, Radicals, Progressives, Catalans, and Gallegans.[11] Although these parties were pledged to the formation of a new Republic, many important differences prevented a unified course of action. This was to be an almost fatal weakness of the Republican movement during the next five years.

Work on the new constitution progressed satisfactorily during the first three months, and twenty-five articles were passed without undue dissension. But the twenty-sixth article, concerning the position of the Catholic Church and its relation to the new State, provoked a serious division and a crisis which seriously weakened the new Government. The Commission which formulated the original draft of the Constitution recommended that the Church be separated from the State, but gave it the position of a public corporation which would be allowed special privileges.[12] This new position of the Church might have been accepted by most Catholics, but a majority of the deputies were opposed to the plan and held that granting a special status to the Church was a recognition that the clergy had sovereign rights. In the debate that followed, an article was drawn up and adopted which stated that the Church was an association subject to the general laws of the country without special privileges. Also included within the Constitution were provisions which prevented religious orders, such as the Jesuits, from conducting educational activities and prohibited the allocation of all state funds to the clergy. During the next two years the Catholic hierarchy was further alienated by the passage of laws which recognized divorce, secularized all cemeteries, abolished the Corps of Army Chaplains, and permitted civil marriages.[13]

Although the Spanish people were predominantly Catholic, sentiment was significantly strong against the Church. The explanation for this can be found not only in the power and privilege of the Spanish Church, but also in the attitude of the Catholic hierarchy prior to the revolution in 1931. The Republic was born as a reaction against dictatorship and monarchy, but the hierarchy had been one of the strongest supporters of General de Rivera and the King, even to the point of identifying the cause of the Monarchy with that of Catholicism in the recently concluded elections.[14] Two weeks after the proclamation of the Spanish Republic, Dr. Pedro Segura, Cardinal-Archbishop of Toledo and Primate of Spain, issued a pastoral letter that contained several paragraphs which were interpreted as unfavorable to the new Government. Cardinal Segura began the letter by expressing "grateful remembrance of His Majesty King Alfonso XIII, who during his reign successfully preserved the ancient traditions of faith and piety of his ancestors." He spoke several times of "his fallen majesty" and stated that "the enemies of Jesus Christ are advancing." The two concluding paragraphs were perhaps the most provocative:

> In these moments of terrible uncertainty, every Catholic must measure the magnitude of his responsibilities and valiantly perform his duty. If we all keep our eyes fixed on higher interests, and sacrifice what is secondary to what is important; if we unite our forces and prepare to fight with perfect cohesion and discipline, without vain parade, but with faith in our ideals, with abnegation and the spirit of sacrifice, we shall be able to look at the future with tranquillity, confident of victory.

> If we remain 'quiet and idle'; if we allow ourselves to give way to 'apathy and timidity'; if we leave the road open to those who are attempting to destroy religion or expect the benevolence of our enemies to secure the triumph of our ideals, we shall have no right to lament when bitter reality shows us that we had victory in our hands, yet knew not how to fight like intrepid warriors, prepared to succumb gloriously.[15]

The Government immediately requested the Holy See to remove the Cardinal from his Archbishopric, and during the next three weeks many supporters of the Republic, fearing the hierarchy as an enemy, created disturbances throughout the country by destroying churches and convents.[16] In any event, it was probable that the new Government regarded the Church as a chief support and maintenance of reaction and wished to destroy its political power in Spain.

This anticlerical policy provided a formidable weapon to the opposition in its effort to recoup its political losses, and it took advantage of the missed opportunity of the Constituent Cortes to create a Republican party within the Church. Many parish priests were extremely poor and had voted for the Republic in the hope that the Church would receive additional moral and financial support. When the priests had their primary means of income taken away, it was only natural that they would become anti-Republican.

The total effect of the reaction against the Church, however, was not so severe as might have been anticipated. Although there were many laws enacted which were directed against it, this legislation was not rigidly enforced. The Republican-Socialist coalition in power at that time did not carry out the anticlerical measures with any particular zeal. The monastic orders, with the exception of the Jesuits, were allowed to remain and not more than a quarter of Jesuit property was confiscated. The seizure of remaining Church lands was postponed until October 1, 1933. When this date arrived, the Government was preparing for general elections in November and action was again postponed. As a result of these elections the Leftist Republicans were ousted from power, and forces more friendly to the Church regained control of the Government. It was not until after the Popular Front victory in the February 1936 elections that the old anticlerical laws were revived, but the Church did not feel the full brunt of the popular fury until after the outbreak of the civil war in July 1936. Article XXVI of the Constitution, which had never been rigidly enforced, was given new life, and the Spanish Government ordered those provisions pertaining to the Church be strictly adhered to.[17]

The question of autonomy had long been an explosive factor in Spanish political life. Many Catalans desired complete independence, but a majority, recognizing the opposition that would be encountered if independence were proclaimed, advocated that Catalonia be given the status of a local state within a federated nation. The Castilian centralist bloc, as symbolized by the Army, strongly opposed any measure of home rule for the Catalans. After the overthrow of the monarchy, however, some well-informed observers were of the opinion that this concession to Catalonia was a necessity if the Republic were to survive.[18] The question was debated in the Constituent Cortes, and an article was included in the Constitution which permitted local statutes to be adopted by the several regions within the general Constitution of the Spanish State. Under the terms of this article the local governments would hold power specifically granted them by the national government.[19]

On August 2, 1931, the people of Catalonia approved a local autonomy statute which was presented to the Cortes for approval. There was considerable opposition to the measure, not only among the forces of the Right, but by many Republicans who feared that if Catalonia were organized into a local state the union of the country might be endangered. Although there was strong opposition and threatened violence throughout the nation, the Cortes ratified the statute a year later and Catalonia was granted the powers of an autonomous state within the framework of the Spanish Constitution. This issue was very important because it was later demonstrated that the Republic had won in the Catalan people a strong and loyal body of supporters.[20]

The Basques likewise were vitally interested in home rule, but their efforts to obtain a position similar to that granted to the Catalans encountered greater opposition. The drafting of a Basque home rule statute was especially difficult because of the anticlerical attitude of the Government. The Basque people were devoutly Catholic, and the Basque deputies in the Cortes had strongly opposed any action which appeared hostile to the Church. A statute of autonomy was eventually adopted by the Basques, but it had not been approved by the Cortes when that body was dissolved in the autumn of 1933.[21]

Another serious problem confronting the Republic was the formulation of a program which would conciliate the workers, both rural and urban. If the Republicans had been able to raise wages and decrease unemployment, they could have won the support of the laboring classes. Unfortunately, however, the Republic was proclaimed during a national and international economic crisis which had produced a critical situation in Spain. Unemployment was widespread, agricultural prices had fallen, and much land had been withdrawn from cultivation. The new Government took definite steps to alleviate these conditions, especially in aiding the urban workers to obtain increased wages and shorter hours. This did not soothe the unrest throughout the rural districts, which continued to spread as the Republican Government failed to adopt any notable agrarian reforms. Many of the peasants had expected that the large estates would be expropriated and were disappointed when it became apparent that such action would be indefinitely postponed. Perhaps the primary reason for the delay of the Government was the disagreement between the Republicans and Socialists as to how the large estates were to be divided. The Republicans favored a plan whereby the lands would be divided into individual holdings, while the Socialists advocated that the estates be distributed to collective farming associations. The issue was bitterly debated because it involved the future of both parties, and each hoped to win the gratitude of the farmers for the reforms. The result was an agrarian law which was obviously a compromise and proved to be largely ineffectual.

The agrarian statute was passed in two parts in July and September 1932. This statute created an Institute of Agrarian Reform of twenty-one members, which received yearly appropriations from the State. It was the responsibility of this Institute, working through regional committees, to determine just what land was to be taken by the State and how it was to be settled. The broad outlines of the law provided that all estates over fifty-six acres not under cultivation by the owners were liable to seizure. Compensation was to be paid, but the value of the property was to be determined on the basis of taxation returns submitted by the owners. It was obvious that a majority of the landowners would stand to lose a large percentage of their property because for years they had been sending in fraudulent returns. Royal estates and those of persons convicted of conspiracy against the Republic were to be confiscated without indemnification.[22]

The agrarian statute applied only to Central and South Spain, which were the sections of the country where the large estates were most commonly found. In Catalonia and other provinces in the North, the chief land problem was not the huge estates, but the reverse. Here the farms were divided into extremely small holdings of land unsuited for profitable and efficient cultivation. No provisions were made to assist the northern families who had too little land or were burdened with excessive taxes. The administration of the agrarian reforms was carried out in a halfhearted manner, and the Government delayed in taking any immediate or effective action. The deadlock between the Socialists and Republicans over the division of the expropriated estates continued, and little was accomplished in the form of actual relief for the peasants. Thus another important segment of opinion — the landless laborers — was alienated by the Government when it failed to enact agrarian reforms. The large landowners, who were already hostile to the Republic, naturally resented the provisions of a law which meant their economic ruin, and they were determined to return to power by any means.[23]

Throughout much of the history of Spain, the Spanish Army had held a position of prime importance. The officers through their own political machine and their own press directly influenced members of the Cortes and monopolized a number of important positions. Spain was divided into eight military regions, each commanded by a high ranking Army officer who enjoyed a life of political influence and honors. The Army also had its own system of military courts which sat in judgment against all persons, civil and military, who attacked the Government, or in essence, all those who attacked the Army.[24]   The new Republican Government made many changes in this system. The military courts, in which the military had invaded the sphere of civil life, were abolished. The military regional system was discontinued and all officers of the Army were given a chance to resign or swear allegiance to the Republic. By such decrees the Government antagonized the most pampered of all Spanish services. Many officers chose to resign and soon a powerful clique developed which plotted the overthrow of the Republic.[25]

A survey of the political actions of the Republican Government does not present an accurate picture of the Spanish scene, for while the Cortes debated the reform measures, a succession of strikes, boycotts, acts of sabotage, and armed revolts were in constant progress throughout the country. On January 11, 1933, an event occurred which hastened the downfall of the Government. On that day a small armed uprising occurred in Casa Viejas which the police and civil guards repressed by particularly brutal methods. A wave of indignation which greatly lowered the Government's prestige swept the country. After a series of ministerial crises throughout the spring and summer, the President of the

Republic dissolved the Constituent Cortes and general elections were ordered for November.[26]

The elections held in November 1933 resulted in a Rightist victory which swept the existing regime out of office. This would seem to indicate that the Spanish people were turning against the Republic. An analysis of the election returns, however, indicates that the distribution of deputies in the new Cortes did not accurately represent the popular strength of the contending forces. The election law was formulated to favor two main groups in the Cortes. Since the electorate voted for lists of parties and candidates, those which presented a united front enjoyed an advantage over those which did not. In this election the Left, after two years of party strife, was disunited, while the parties of the Right were temporarily united because of their common hostility to the Government. Although the Right obtained twice as many seats as the Left, the votes cast for it were fewer than the total cast for the disunited parties of the Left.[27]

A new Government was formed, supported by the Right and Center, and it immediately launched a program intended to make amends to the Army, Church, and landowners for the hardships they had undergone during the previous administration. Laws pertaining to wages and hours of work were either repealed or allowed to lapse. Wages dropped to a new low, landlords dismissed many of their laborers, and the small number of grandees whose estates had been confiscated had them returned intact. Most of the political prisoners were granted amnesty and the ousted army officers were reinstated. Similar steps were taken in regard to the Church. Of great influence in clerical matters was a powerful new political organization, *Acción Popular,* headed by Gil Robles. This party was the political organ of the Catholic group *Acción Católica,* and its platform reflected the attitude of the Church. Primarily through its influence many of the anticlerical statutes were allowed to lapse through neglect, and the substitution of lay schools for religious schools was indefinitely postponed. The Jesuits continued teaching, the priests were paid two-thirds of their salaries for 1934, and negotiations were opened with the Vatican.[28] Thus the new Government, supported by the aristocracy, attempted to nullify the work of the previous regime.

These measures failed to bring any degree of stability to the country. The Government was still weak and ministerial crises were constantly recurring. The left wing of the Socialist party led by Largo Caballero provoked numerous strikes throughout the country which seriously hampered any economic recovery. While Spain was in this confused condition the activities of the Communists were on the increase. During the preceding decade the Communist party had been so insignificant in Spain that Primo de Rivera had not considered it worthwhile even to censor the Communist press. After the proclamation of the Republic Communist influence increased, but the recruiting of new members proved to be a difficult task because the large majority of the Spanish workers belonged to the Socialist, Anarchist, or Anarcho-Syndicalist parties. The Communists then began to infiltrate these parties, and aided by the extreme social unrest they were able to make considerable progress. One observer stated that communism might possibly have achieved a dramatic triumph at that time had it not been for the Moscow purge trials and a growing feeling that there was too much "Tsardom in Stalindom and too much Tsarist secret police in the G. P. U."[29] Communism appealed to many workers, however, and was becoming a factor of increasing importance. During the early days of the Republic the Communist party numbered perhaps no more than 1,000 members. In the June 1931 elections none of the eleven Communist candidates for the Cortes came close to election, and their combined vote totaled only about 60,000 in all of Spain. The freedom offered by the Republic and the unsettled conditions during the depression gave the Communists ample opportunities to build up their ranks. In the November 1933 election one Communist deputy was elected from Málaga; by October 1934 the party claimed 20,000 members and by February 1936, 35,000 members.[30]

In 1932 José Antonio Primo de Rivera, a son of the former dictator, founded the *Falange Española*. The Falangist program was little more than orthodox fascism, differing from the Italian model only in its respect for the Church. José de Rivera staunchly proclaimed that only a Fascist State could successfully combat the rising tide of communism. He promised that the glory of Spain would be heightened by the re-creation of a Spanish Empire through the acquisition of further territory in Morocco, the possible annexation of Portugal, and the extension of Spanish influence in South America. The Falangists believed in terrorism and violence, thus abandoning all idea of legal and peaceful solution for the many problems facing the people of Spain. During 1933 and until the elections of 1936 the Falange remained a party of small but growing influence. Later, after Franco's victory, it was to enjoy the same influence and prestige in Spain as did Mussolini's Fascist party in Italy.[31]

The Basques and Catalans soon discovered that the new Government was not in sympathy with any movement for local autonomy. The Basques had voted with Robles and the Right in the hope that some measure of home rule might be revived. But not only did the Government refuse to recognize any such measure; indeed, the Basques were subjected to additional taxes. The people of the Basque Provinces were then confronted with the choice of renouncing their aspirations for autonomy or joining forces with the Catalans and the anticlerical and revolutionary groups in other parts of Spain. That choice was made during the interval between the elections in February 1936 and the outbreak of civil war in July. In this final decision the Basques, with the exception of the Navarrese, placed liberty before religion and remained loyal to the Republic.[32] This loyalty was rewarded on October 1, 1936, when the Cortes of the Spanish Republic ratified a statute of autonomy for the Basque Provinces.[33]

Throughout 1934 Spain was continually beset with domestic strife, while open revolt was threatened by the Anarchists, Anarcho-Syndicalists, and the extreme left wing of the Socialist party. On October 5, 1934, the Socialists called a nationwide general strike. There were armed uprisings in Barcelona and Madrid, easily suppressed by the Government. Resistance in the Province of Asturias was more violent, and soon a full-scale civil war was under way in that area. This, however, was a short-lived revolt, soon crushed by the Government, using Moorish regular troops by order of General Francisco Franco, Chief-of-Staff.[34]

The armed uprising and its harsh suppression by Moorish troops made a deep impression upon the Spanish people. The *New York Times* reported that 3,000 Asturian miners had been killed and some 7,000 wounded.[35] Resentment was high on both sides and many persons were of the opinion that the revolt in Asturias was but a dress rehearsal for a greater struggle to follow. Supporters of the Right, in an effort to gain public approval of their policies, accused the Asturians of many atrocious crimes, including the burning of churches and the raping of nuns. Two correspondents of the *New York Times*, both of whom were in Spain at the time, disagreed as to the truth of these charges. W. P. Carney supported the charges against the miners,[36] while Mildred Adams reported that she could find no truth in the atrocity stories.[37] Gerald Brenan was of the opinion that such stories were spread by the Rightist press to produce a feeling that would sanction vengeance and reprisals against the Asturians.[38] Ambassador Claude G. Bowers, who was in Spain at the time, has stated that the reports of the atrocities by the Moors in Asturias were not incorrect. He added that one foreign correspondent went to the Asturias right after the revolt and brought a report to the Embassy which was "too horrible to publish."[39] Certainly one result of the revolt was that it served to unite the masses of poorly paid workers into a feeling of increased hostility toward the Government.

After the revolt of the miners was suppressed, the forces of the Right gained considerable confidence because the Left was virtually powerless and the Center was in the process of disintegration. By the fall of 1935, however, a reaction had set in and the Left gradually regained strength. The reprisals against the Asturian miners had created a movement of sympathy throughout the country and the revolt, although a military failure, turned into a moral and political success. It was increasingly apparent that the miners had gained their initial success because the working class parties had united. This created a feeling among the masses that their leaders should unite and establish a popular front against the Right.[40]

By this time the political situation was as complicated as it had been at any time since the proclamation of the Republic. During the preceding twelve months there had been no fewer than six cabinet crises and there seemed no hope for further progress. Portfolios were changing hands so frequently that it was difficult to tell from one day to the next who was in the cabinet. An appeal to the people appeared to be the only solution, and on January 7, 1936, the President of the Republic dissolved the Cortes and ordered general elections to be held throughout the country on February 16.

The elections resulted in a victory for the *Frente Popular*, a coalition of the forces of the Left. The indefiniteness of the political affiliations of a number of deputies made it impossible to group the returned members other than approximately. The *New York Times* estimated that the Popular Front elected 269 deputies; the Center 72; and the Right 132.[41] The Popular Front, with whom the responsibility for a new Government now rested, was an admixture of parties that included Socialists, 89 deputies; Republican Left, 84 deputies; Republican Union, 37 deputies; and Communists, 16 deputies.[42] The Right charged that the elections were disorderly and fraudulent and therefore not a true expression of the desires of the Spanish people. There were many conflicting reports as to the truth of these charges. Brenan stated that the elections were orderly, but that both sides did buy votes and exerted pressure to win support at the polls.[43] W. P. Carney cabled from Madrid that the election was a victory for the Socialists and Communists, but he did not report any irregularities in the voting.[44]

The electoral triumph of the Left confused rather than clarified conditions within the country which rapidly degenerated into a still more chaotic state. With the Government constantly harassed, a chronicle of official constitutional history of Spain during the five months intervening between the February elections and the outbreak of the war would be, as Arnold Toynbee noted, hardly worth recording.[45] A new Left-dominated Government was formed, but it was quickly evident that the country had entered a phase of revolutionary activity of violence and chaos. There were burnings of buildings, sweeping arrests, assassinations, attacks against the Church, armed clashes between forces of the Right and Left, strikes, and land riots, all of which kept the country in a constant state of turmoil. In many cases it was not even possible to determine which side had committed a crime.[46]

In the meantime, the power and influence of the Communists and Falangists increased far out of proportion to the number of their respective party members. Toynbee estimated that there were only 50,000 Stalinist Communists in Spain at the outbreak of the war; yet the Communists were largely responsible for rallying the forces of the Government once the revolt began.[47] The Communists were well schooled in the ways of Spanish revolution as they had taken an active part in the Asturian rebellion almost two years earlier.[48] A recent authority has written that by 1936 the Comintern in Spain was no longer represented by the small, insignificant group of Communist revolutionaries as it had been in

1931. Although its strength still did not challenge that of the Anarchists or Socialists, the Communist party was attracting a sizeable political following and was thoroughly capable of taking an active part in the politics of the Left.[49] Yet the rise to influence of the Falange was even more rapid and successful than that of the Communist party. Until the February elections in 1936, it had remained a small party of little prestige. Initially, the Church practically ignored it, but after the Popular Front victory the Falangists gained considerable support from Catholics who feared that Catholicism might be deliberately eradicated in a communist Spain.[50] These two foreign ideologies of fascism and communism also served as a point around which hostility could be crystallized. Every person fighting on the side of the Spanish Government could be described as "anti-fascist" no matter which party he might personally favor. On the other hand the supporters of General Franco were commonly known as "anti-communist."

The Falange and other extreme Right and Left wing organizations were not the only parties plotting counterrevolution in Spain. There were also groups of Army officers and Monarchists who wished to see the Leftist Republican Government overthrown. The Army was deeply grieved at the loss of prestige the military had suffered and was intent on regaining a position of prominence. The officers, through a secret society known as the *Unión Militar Española,* were plotting an armed revolution and were only waiting for a favorable opportunity to commence hostilities. Likewise, the Monarchists had never been reconciled to the Republic; and although they were a small group, they were very powerful and had strong financial support.[51]

The tension caused by strikes, riots, shooting affrays, violence against the Church, and extreme unrest throughout the country continued into the early summer of 1936. The outbreak of civil war seemed imminent. Because of a division within the Cortes among the various parties, the legislative branch of the Government was powerless to meet the rapidly approaching crisis. The President of the Republic, Don Manuel Azaña, was unable to find a minister who could form a cabinet strong enough to cope with this domestic disintegration. On July 13, 1936, José Calvo Sotelo, a leader of the militant Right forces, was the victim of assassination. Four days later the Army, after long and careful planning, revolted in Morocco, crossed to the mainland, and within the course of a week end enveloped Spain in civil war.[52]

Armed conflict thus became the culmination of a struggle that had slowly been gathering strength since the Republic was proclaimed in 1931. The fall of the Monarchy brought to power a Government supported by liberal and labor groups pledged to effect by democratic methods changes in the social and economic system which had condemned the masses to a life of misery, ignorance, and poverty. The campaign of reforms initiated by the Republic, however, threatened the privileges long enjoyed by the Army officers, large landowners, industrialists, and clergy. At the same time, the changes by the Government did not materialize fast enough for the workers in the rural and urban districts. Tension between these factions, which seriously weakened the central Government, thus reached a point where recourse to violence appeared as the only solution to the problem.

NOTES

1. The first Spanish Republic was proclaimed in 1873, but in 1875 the House of Bourbon was restored in the person of King Alfonso XII.

2. *New York Times,* April 11, 15, 19, 1931; Salvador de Madariaga, *Spain* (New York, 1943), pp. 290-93; E. Allison Peers, *The Spanish Tragedy* (New York, 1936), pp. 1-13.

3. General Primo de Rivera went to Paris where he died on March 16, 1930.

4. Madariaga, *Spain,* pp. 292-93.

5. *New York Times,* April 16, 1931.

6. Gerald Brenan, *The Spanish Labyrinth* (New York, 1943), pp. 232-33. Since there were so many parties, and their political affiliations with the Right, Left, and Center were not always easily determined, various authorities disagree as to the number of deputies elected by each side. The *Times* (London) reported on July 29, 1932, that the full official figures of these elections were never published. The *Times* correspondent in Madrid asked permission to examine the results but was refused.

7. Brenan, *Spanish Labyrinth,* pp. 229-30.

8. *Ibid.,* p. 231.

9. *Ibid.,* pp. 231-32.

10. The Constituent Cortes had the twofold purpose of drafting a new constitution and serving as the legislative branch of the government.

11. Madariaga, *Spain,* p. 300.

12. Brenan, *Spanish Labyrinth,* pp. 234-36.

13. Peers, *Spanish Tragedy,* pp. 62-72. See also Madariaga, *Spain,* pp. 309-10. For the text of the Spanish Constitution, see *Current History* (New York), XXXVI (June, 1932), 374-84, or *New York Times,* December 2, 1931.

14. Brenan, *Spanish Labyrinth,* 236.

15. *El Sol*, May 7, 1931, quoted in Peers, *Spanish Tragedy*, pp. 52-53. See also *Times* (London), May 8, 1931.

16. Brenan states that in six large towns alone (Madrid, Seville, Málaga, Granada, Murcia, Valencia), 102 churches and convents were completely destroyed. Brenan, *Spanish Labyrinth*, p. 236 n.

17. Madariaga, *Spain*, pp. 308-11.

18. Mildred Adams, *New York Times*, August 7, 1932, VI, 5.

19. *Current History* (text of the Spanish Constitution), XXXVI (June, 1932), 374-75.

20. For an excellent discussion on the rise of Catalan nationalism and the inauguration of home rule for Catalonia, see Arnold J. Toynbee, *Survey of International Affairs, 1937*, II (London, 1938), 23-36.

21. *Ibid.*, pp. 37-41; Madariaga, *Spain*, pp. 307-08.

22. Brenan, *Spanish Labyrinth*, pp. 244-45.

23. *Ibid.*, pp. 244-46; Peers, *Spanish Tragedy*, pp. 99-101.

24. Madariaga, *Spain*, pp. 311-12.

25. *Ibid.* See also Charles A. Thomson, "Spain: Issues Behind the Conflict," *Foreign Policy Reports* (New York), XII (January 1, 1937), 246-47.

26. Brenan, *Spanish Labyrinth*, pp. 246-60; Anita Brenner, Spanish correspondent for the *New York Times*, describes the situation in that paper's edition of September 24, 1933, VI, 6.

27. Brenan, *Spanish Labyrinth*, p. 265. A good analysis of the elections can be found in Peers, *Spanish Tragedy*, pp. 141-44. See also Anita Brenner's feature article on Spanish political conflicts in the *New York Times*, December 17, 1933, VIII, 2.

28. Madariaga, *Spain*, pp. 324-25; Peers, *Spanish Tragedy*, pp. 145-46.

29. Madariaga, *Spain*, p. 274.

30. David T. Cattell, *Communism and the Spanish Civil War* (Berkeley, 1955), pp. 20-21. This is the most comprehensive and authoritative book on the subject.

31. Brenan, *Spanish Labyrinth*, pp. 308-11. In a letter to the author (February 15, 1954) Claude G. Bowers, former United States Ambassador to Spain, stated that José Primo de Rivera was not a champion of the Church and in a speech announced that under any regime connected with him the Church would go along unhindered in its purely religious work, but he would not tolerate its interference in politics. Bowers added that he knew de Rivera well; that he was "a fine young fellow, with not good judgment;" that he organized the Fascist party "partly because he resented the monarchy. This because of the scurvy treatment of his father."

32. Toynbee, *Survey, 1937*, II, 40-41.

33. *Times* (London), October 3, 1936.

34. Brenan, *Spanish Labyrinth*, pp. 283-88. See also *New York Times*, October 7, 1934.

35. *New York Times*, October 10, 1934.

36. W. P. Carney was the only foreign correspondent of the *New York Times* who remained sympathetic toward the Spanish Nationalists throughout the course of the conflict.

37. *New York Times,* October 21, December 9, 1934.

38. Brenan, *Spanish Labyrinth,* p. 287.

39. Bowers to author, February 15, 1954.

40. Toynbee, *Survey, 1937,* II, 18-19.

41. *New York Times,* February 23, 1936. Peers gives the figures as Left, 256; Center, 52; and Right, 165. Peers, *Spanish Tragedy,* p. 190.

42. G. M. Ganthorne-Hardy, *A Short History of International Affairs, 1920-1939* (London, 1947), p. 428.

43. Brenan, *Spanish Labyrinth,* pp. 299-300.

44. *New York Times,* February 23, 1936.

45. Toynbee, *Survey, 1937,* II, 20.

46. *New York Times,* February 22, March 1, 1936; *Times* (London), March 14, April 15, May 30, June 13, 1936.

47. Toynbee, *Survey, 1937,* II, 23 n.

48. Brenan estimates that 60,000 Socialists and 9,000 Communists participated in the Asturian rebellion. Brenan, *Spanish Labyrinth,* p. 286 n. Another writer stated that the rebellion of 1934 was instigated by the Communist International with the aim of establishing the first Soviet Republic of Spain. Anthony T. Bouscaren, "The Spanish Republic Reviewed," *Catholic World* (New York), CLXX (October, 1949), 43-49.

49. Cattell, *Communism and the Spanish Civil War,* pp. 20-21.

50. Toynbee, *Survey, 1936,* p. 25.

51. Brenan, *Spanish Labyrinth,* pp. 310-11.

52. *New York Times,* July 17, 18, 21, 1936; *Times* (London), July 14, 16, 23, 1936. Some observers maintain that the rebellion was a spontaneous uprising primarily concerned with restoring order and stability out of general chaotic conditions which reached a peak in the assassination of Sotelo. It is possible, however, that Allison Peers was much closer to the truth when he wrote that this was "a revolution carefully planned and skillfully organized by able military leaders on a nation-wide scale." Peers, *Spanish Tragedy,* p. 211.

Other writers have placed emphasis on the international causes of the Spanish Civil War stressing outside Communist and Fascist influence. A recent study of the subject has disclosed, however, that the struggle "was primarily caused by the outburst of a long accumulation of internal conflicts rather than by the action of a foreign power." Cattell, *Communism and the Spanish Civil War,* p. viii.

Chapter Two

American Neutrality and Isolationism

The repercussions of the Spanish Civil War in the Americas were not as immediate as in Europe. In part, this was because of the vast distances involved and the hope that the New World could remain aloof from the entanglements of Europe should the war spread beyond Spanish borders. To localize the Spanish conflict a Nonintervention Committee was formed by the European states. The American nations, however, were not asked to participate in the activities of this Committee, nor did they appear particularly anxious to do so. There were also significant differences in degree of concern among the various American states. In such countries as Chile, Argentina, Uruguay, Paraguay, Cuba, and Mexico, there were considerable groups of recent immigrants from Spain; consequently the war was of immediate personal concern to many persons in those countries. Iberian immigration to the other Spanish-speaking American countries had not been nearly so great and there were fewer close personal ties to Spain. Nevertheless, there was a community of language and culture in all of Hispanic America which gave the war an interest to the population that it did not have in the non-Spanish nations.

The principal English or French-speaking American states — the United States and Canada — had few cultural ties with Spain, and individuals in those countries were moved by consideration of their own national interest or sympathy for one of the ideologies embraced by the factions in Spain. Although most of the American states did not want to become involved in European affairs, this

39

did not prevent a strong division of sentiment on ideological grounds. Perhaps the strongest feeling of sympathy for the Spanish Nationalists was to be found in Portuguese-speaking Brazil and French-speaking Quebec. This was in part due to the incipient Fascist organizations already in existence there plus a deep feeling of sympathy for the Spanish clergy. The strongest support for the Spanish Government was probably in Mexico, a fact explained in part by the Mexican revolution of 1910, which, like that in Spain, had been an uprising against the privileged position of the lay and ecclesiastical classes.[1]

In the United States the chief concern of the majority of people was to avoid any entanglement which might involve the nation in European strife. The context from which American opinions took life was still streaked with the hatred of war. This feeling was expressed very clearly by Representative Hamilton Fish (R-New York) when he stated that he wanted "to serve notice on the Democratic majority that while we are only talking about the civil war in Spain, horrible and bloody as it is, that the people back home are much more interested in our own safety and in keeping the United States of America out of all wars."[2] When the Spanish Civil War began, this country was perhaps more isolationist than at any time since the First World War. For several years after that struggle it was hoped by some American liberals that our tradition of isolation and aloofness from Europe had begun to weaken and that the United States might be willing to assume a more prominent role in the international community. Unfortunately, however, the aftermath of the conflict was disillusioning. The Senate rejected membership in the League of Nations and the World Court, while the preponderance of American opinion absolutely refused to subscribe to any political commitment beyond the Monroe Doctrine. Economic collapse accentuated internal domestic problems, and in 1930 the United States passed the highest tariff this country had ever known. A still further blow to international cooperation was dealt by the refusal of this country to consider currency stablization at the London Economic Conference in 1933.

In viewing the First World War in retrospect, the American people were determined that there should be no repetition of military involvement by the United States in a European war. The "revisionist" view of this conflict was accepted by many, who held that both sides, and not simply the Germans, shared in the "war guilt," and that the United States had been brought into the war by a combination of British propaganda and the American economic stake in an Allied victory. In 1935 Walter Millis wrote a best seller entitled *The Road to War,* which presented the United States' decision to enter the war in 1917 as a great tragedy.[3] There were also other books and magazine articles which drew attention to the part played by the munition makers in fomenting wars. Simultaneously the Nye committee made a lengthy investigation, during which the enormous profits of arms manufacturers were exposed. The picture of war as a horror into which the common people were drawn by banking and business interests was readily accepted by a large segment of the American people. This attitude was reflected in the public opinion polls which reported in October 1937 that 73 per cent of the voters believed that Congress should obtain consent in a national referendum before declaring war.[4] Representative Louis Ludlow (D-Indiana) in that same year introduced a proposed amendment to the Constitution which provided, except in cases of actual invasion, for a national referendum before a declaration of war could be made by Congress. It was only through strong Administration pressure that this amendment was defeated by the narrow margin of 21 votes in the House of Representatives.[5]

It must not be supposed that international relations were uppermost in the minds of the American people. The relative indifference in the United States to foreign affairs in general during the 1930's can be largely explained by the preoccupation of most persons with problems of unemployment and the vast economic depression that had gripped this country since 1929. At the time the Spanish War became prominent in the news, Franklin D. Roosevelt was preparing to place his record before the electorate after having given the American people almost four years of the New Deal. The President's strongest critics were those who condemned the free spending and "pump-priming" techniques of his Administration rather than his foreign policy. Later, Roosevelt's Supreme Court fight and attempted purge of certain Congressmen brought forth a new wave of criticism. In December 1936 neutrality was only the third most important issue facing the American people according to their own estimates, and it was not until May 1939 that neutrality replaced unemployment as the paramount issue concerning Americans.[6]

The disinterestedness which characterized the American approach to foreign affairs, however, should by no means be ascribed to ignorance. Long before the Spanish War began, most Americans were aware that the revision of national frontiers by force had begun. In 1931 Japan had invaded Manchuria, and in 1935 Mussolini had launched the Italian invasion of Ethiopia. The League of Nations failed to take effective action against either of the aggressors and its prestige was reduced to nothingness. The Nazi Government of Germany had alarmed the peoples and governments of Europe by the march into the Rhineland and other bold moves which kept Europeans in fear of an immediate general war. As Germany rearmed, so did her neighbors, and by 1936 an international armament race was in full swing. In Asia the spread of aggression was equally alarming. A militant Japan, after having defied the world in Manchuria, was ready for new conquests and in 1937 the Japanese war lords ordered the full-scale invasion of China.

Yet in spite of these threats to world peace the American people refused to become alarmed. Instead,

> most Americans felt secure enough and beguiled themselves with arguments supplied them in quantity by some of their most respected public figures: war is inherently evil and settles nothing in any case; being not immediately menaced, the first duty of Americans is to maintain their unique civilization and protect it from foreign contamination; the best way, therefore, to deal with Fascism and Nazism is to stay away from them and concentrate all efforts on the solution of national social and economic problems, so as to preserve intact the great stronghold of democracy.[7]

The notion was generally accepted that the European political system had sown the seeds for its own destruction in a series of never-ending wars. The United States had entered one of these wars to save the world for democracy, and yet with the rise of dictatorship and aggression as its aftermath Americans watched with bitter disillusionment.

There were some indications in the 1920's and early 1930's that the United States might drift from a policy of national isolation to a policy of acting in concert with other nations to preserve world peace. Although the United States did not join the League, the State Department worked as closely with that international organization as public opinion would allow. This country aided in the relief and rehabilitation of Europe after the First World War; it cooperated in an effort to maintain peace in the Pacific at the Washington Disarmament Conference, 1921-1922; it attempted to outlaw war as an instrument of national policy by signing the Kellogg-Briand Pact in 1928; and in 1931 its Secretary of State, Henry L. Stimson, led the world in an international condemnation of Japan after the invasion of Manchuria. The American people, however, felt secure behind the snug wall of neutrality and would never permit actual commitments to act with others to prevent hostilities for they were overwhelmingly opposed to any involvement in foreign quarrels. The dominant opinion was to leave the rest of the world to its own folly.

This feeling found expression in the neutrality legislation of 1935-1937.[8] Such a program, strongly supported by American public opinion, was designed to prevent a repetition of the disaster brought about by America's entrance into the First World War. These laws, sometimes described as "isolationism in action," were this country's answer to the dangers appearing abroad and an effort to ensure its neutrality by legislation. When suddenly in May 1935 the international situation threatened to erupt into world conflict as Mussolini sent his legions driving into Ethiopia, Congress, deeply involved in domestic problems growing out of the depression, hurriedly passed a Neutrality Act which was signed into law on August 31, 1935, by the President. This legislation provided that it would be unlawful for Americans to sell or transport munitions of war to either of the belligerents should the President proclaim the existence of a war. The act, when amended in 1936, forbade private loans and credits to nations engaged in war and prohibited American travel on ships of warring nations. The neutrality legislation did not specifically apply to civil wars, and consequently a delicate political and diplomatic problem was posed with the eruption of the Spanish War. This loophole was quickly closed on January 6, 1937, when Congress passed a joint-resolution placing an embargo on shipments of arms to Spain.

Since the acts passed in 1935 and 1936 were only of a temporary character, hearings were held in February 1937 for the purpose of bringing about passage of a "permanent" neutrality act. After considerable debate, the Neutrality Act of 1937 was passed by Congress on March 1. The new legislation retained the same provisions as the old, the main difference being that the President was given considerably more discretionary power. One new feature of the act, the so-called "cash and carry" plan, provided that nonmilitary commodities could be paid for upon delivery and taken away from American ports by the foreign buyer. It was not until the outbreak of the general war in Europe in the fall of 1939 that the Administration reversed its policy and repealed the arms embargo provisions of the act.[9]

Although Roosevelt was deeply concerned with domestic policies affecting his New Deal program, he was well-informed and fully aware of the inherent dangers of aggression in Europe. The President expressed his displeasure over the inflexible provisions of the 1935-1937 neutrality legislation, but there is no evidence that he disapproved of its general purpose. "He was merely echoing the popular sentiment," as one observer has noted, "when he declared that his Administration was 'definitely committed to the maintenance of peace and the avoidance of any entanglements which would lead us into conflict.' "[10] In August 1936 the President declared in a speech at Chautauqua, New York, that "we shun political commitments which might entangle us in foreign wars; we avoid connections with the political activities of the League of Nations. . . . We are not isolationist except in so far as we seek to isolate ourselves completely from war."[11] And throughout the Spanish Civil War, no new conclusions were reached with respect to American policy.

Roosevelt has been sharply criticized for a lack of Presidential leadership during these years. It must be remembered, however, that the conduct of foreign policy in a democracy presents a very difficult task, as the formulation of American policy must have the support of public opinion and at least the implied consent of Congress. Roosevelt was very conscious of public opinion and kept constantly in mind the domestic reactions to foreign policy. Even though he personally favored lifting the arms embargo in March 1939, it was not until November of that year, after the outbreak of war in Europe, that Congress would pass such legislation. No matter how much the President wanted to help the European democracies, he could not move alone.

Important foreign policy matters were rarely discussed at cabinet meetings.[12] Perhaps this was one of the methods used by Roosevelt to keep peace within his official family. Secretary of the Treasury Henry Morgenthau, Jr., a neighbor and personal friend of the President, probably saw more of him than any other cabinet officer. Morgenthau served Roosevelt in any capacity desired, and this included many delicate and important matters, such as Lend-Lease, which were entrusted to him rather than to Secretary of State Hull. Morgenthau was an outspoken critic of the State Department, referring to it as "an antiquated, unwieldly and inefficient institution, ill-equipped to arrive at clear and prompt decisions and therefore an obstructive rather than a contributing force."[13] Hull very bitterly resented this attitude and suspected Morgenthau of trying to take over the vital functions of the State Department. Secretary Hull has stated that Morgenthau "often acted as if he were clothed with authority to project himself into the field of foreign affairs and inaugurate efforts to shape the course of foreign policy in given instances . . . [and] from his earliest days in the Government . . . he seldom lost an opportunity to take long steps across the line of State Department jurisdiction."[14]

Another cabinet member who was critical of Hull and the State Department was Secretary of the Interior Harold L. Ickes. Ickes especially disapproved of American policy toward the Madrid Government during the course of the Spanish Civil War. This, perhaps, prompted Hull to remark that "he was often quite far to the left and hence frequently out of line with many of us."[15] Hull also noted that Ickes "was one of the three cabinet members[16] who at times undertook to interfere with other cabinet functions." Then, treating Ickes with more kindness than he displayed toward Morgenthau, he concluded that "he [Ickes] did not often interfere, and in cases concerning the State Department I credit him with honestly believing that he did so because of overlapping jurisdictions."[17] As a subsequent chapter will demonstrate, Ickes did make a definite effort to alter American policy during the course of the Spanish conflict but was unsuccessful.

Within the State Department Secretary Hull was not lacking in authority, and there were few who questioned his influence in the formulation of American foreign policy. Many people today believe that Roosevelt acted as his own Secretary of State and ignored Hull or bypassed the State Department.[18] More recent scholarship, however, denies this contention. Langer and Gleason have stated that fundamentally the two men were agreed on major policies. They point out that Roosevelt may have "lost patience with the Secretary's caution and deliberation" but he did not by-pass him. Hull was kept as fully informed "as the President's habits permitted" and "his views carried great weight with his chief."[19] Certainly in regard to the Spanish War, Hull's ideas usually prevailed, and he was primarily responsible for the refusal of the United States to alter its Spanish policy, even when Roosevelt indicated at one time that he might be willing to do so.[20]

Another high official within the State Department who enjoyed a much closer relationship with the White House than Hull was Assistant Secretary — later, Under Secretary — Sumner Welles. Hull bitterly complained that his Under Secretary went "to the President at times without my knowledge, . . . even attempting to secure a decision, again without my knowledge. . . . I could not repose the same confidence in him that I did in my other associates."[21] The close relationship between Roosevelt and Welles was especially noticeable during the Spanish crisis. The Roosevelt Papers at Hyde Park reveal considerable evidence that Roosevelt relied more on Welles than Hull for advice and information concerning American policy. Despite this fact, however, there is nothing in the record to suggest that personal differences between Hull and Welles had a decisive effect on American policy. As far as the Spanish Civil War was concerned the evidence would seem to indicate that Hull and Welles were very much in accord on American policy. Welles later wrote that "of all our blind isolationist policies, the most disastrous was our attitude on the Spanish Civil War."[22] As yet, however, this writer has not been able to find reliable evidence that Welles tried to persuade Hull or the President to alter American policy toward Spain.

The American Ambassador to France, William C. Bullitt, and our representative at the Court of St. James, Joseph P. Kennedy, were close observers of the war in Spain and no doubt exerted considerable influence on American policy. Kennedy has been described by his critics as a great appeaser and a staunch supporter of Neville Chamberlain. The Ambassador was reported to have caused Roosevelt discouragement and irritation; the President is even said to have remarked: "Who would have thought that the English could take into camp a red-headed Irishman?"[23] Kennedy nevertheless was a source of influence and pressure on the President, often corresponding with him personally without bothering with regular channels of communications within the State Department.[24] Ambassador Kennedy was also one of the best known Catholic laymen in the United States. He was a close friend of James Farley and a power on the Democratic National Committee. Kennedy's influence, therefore, on American Spanish policy during the whole era of appeasement cannot be overestimated. Ambassador Bullitt was a close personal friend of Roosevelt who often reported the progress of the Spanish War directly to the President through the medium of personal letters.[25] Bullitt, as one Washington observer has stated, believed that the "Reds" in Spain were a curse.[26] Another writer has accused Bullitt of being an appeaser who was sympathetic to fascist policies.[27] It is not within the scope of this work to pass judgment on these two men, but in fairness to Ambassador Bullitt the writer has found little evidence that he favored either side in the Spanish struggle. It is true, however, that both Bullitt and Kennedy were active supporters of the London Non-intervention Committee and strongly advised the State Department to maintain the American policy of strict neutrality.

The American Ambassador to Spain during the Spanish War was Claude G. Bowers. Bowers, likewise, was a personal friend of Roosevelt and was appointed by the President shortly after his first inauguration. Bowers was a liberal, and, although he carried out the American policy of absolute neutrality, there was little doubt of his personal feelings about the Spanish crisis. The German Ambassador to Spain once remarked that Bowers "continues to distinguish himself with his sympathy for the Reds. His reports are said to contain all the propaganda reports regarding conditions in Nationalist Spain and to be responsible for the reports in the American press, some of which are often hair-raising."[28] Secretary Hull has stated that Bowers "felt that the United States should make its policies conform with the vital interests of the liberal forces prosecuting one side of the war." He also indicated that many of Bowers' reports had to be read with some reservation since he was so "strongly inclined" toward the Loyalist Government.[29] Bowers corresponded directly with Roosevelt and often painted vivid descriptions of hostilities in Spain intermixed with pleas for the President to assist civilian refugees caught in the throes of war.[30] Bowers was also concerned with a possible revision of

American policy toward Spain. He hoped that he could personally convince the President that Hull and the State Department should be overruled, thus permitting the shipment of arms to the legally-recognized Spanish Government. Despite his eloquent and even desperate pleas, American policy remained unchanged.[31] Several weeks before the United States recognized the Nationalist Government in April 1939, Ambassador Bowers was withdrawn from his post and returned to the United States.

It was against such a backdrop that the war broke out in Spain. American policy was established quite early and remained unchanged throughout the course of the conflict. Americans were largely indifferent, but this did not prevent the arousing of widespread feeling and positive action by certain groups within the United States. Some saw the conflict as a fight between democracy and fascism; others viewed it as a struggle against communism, while many persons were primarily concerned with the religious issues involved. Whoever one's doctrinal champion happened to be, he could find him engaged against desperate odds in Spain.

NOTES

1. Toynbee, *Survey, 1937*, II, 210-17.   For additional material, see the *Times* (London), August 24, 1937; and Gil Enrique, "Repercussions of the Spanish Crisis in Latin America," *Foreign Affairs* (New York), XV (April, 1937), 547-53.

2. *Congressional Record*, 75 Cong., 1 Sess., LXXXI (January 6, 1937), 94.

3. See also Walter Millis, "Where Dangers Lie," *The Annals of the American Academy of Political and Social Science* (Philadelphia), CXCII (July, 1937), 24-30; and Phillips Bradley, "Storm Warnings of Conflict," *ibid.*, 15-23.

4. *Public Opinion Quarterly* (Princeton, N. J.), III (October, 1939), 599.

5. *New York Times*, January 11, 1938.

6. George Gallup and Claude Robinson, "American Institute of Public Opinion Surveys, 1935-1938," *Public Opinion Quarterly, II* (July, 1938), 381; "Surveys, 1938-1939," *ibid.*, III (October, 1939), 595-96. Well-balanced discussions of the American domestic scene during the 1930's can be found in Dixon Wecter, *The Age of the Great Depression* (New York, 1948) and Robert E. Sherwood, *Roosevelt and Hopkins* (New York, 1948).

7. William L. Langer and S. Everett Gleason, *The Challenge to Isolation, 1937-1940* (New York, 1952), p. 13. This book contains perhaps the best analysis of American attitudes toward foreign affairs during the 1930's. Almost precisely the same arguments were retailed in British Government circles as an argument for British neutrality in the Spanish conflict. See Toynbee, *Survey, 1937*, II, 151-77.

8. A discussion of this legislation can be found in Allen W. Dulles and Hamilton Fish Armstrong, "Legislating Peace," *Foreign Affairs*, XVII (October, 1938), 1-12. See also Raymond Leslie Buell, "The Neutrality Act of 1937," *Foreign Policy Reports*, XIII (October 1, 1937), 166-80.

9. For a behind-the-scenes picture of Administration policy and the subsequent repeal of the arms embargo, see Henry Morgenthau, Jr., "Morgenthau Diaries, IV: The Story Behind Lend-Lease," *Colliers* (New York), CXX (October 18, 1947), 16-17.

10. Langer and Gleason, *Challenge to Isolation*, p. 16.

11. United States Department of State, *Press Releases*, August 15, 1936. Hereafter cited as *Press Releases*.

12. Langer and Gleason report that in their extensive research they were able to find few records of cabinet meetings, even if they were of importance. Roosevelt objected to notes being taken at the meetings; therefore, reliable reports are rarities. Langer and Gleason, *Challenge to Isolation*, p. 4. The writer's experience working in the Roosevelt Papers confirms this.

13. Langer and Gleason, *Challenge to Isolation*, p. 7. This conflict is vividly described in "The Morgenthau Diaries, III: How F. D. R. Fought the Axis," *Colliers*, CXX (October 11, 1947), 11. Also, "The Morgenthau Diaries, IV: The Story Behind Lend-Lease," *ibid.* (October 18, 1947), 16-17.

14. Cordell Hull, *The Memoirs of Cordell Hull*, 2 vols. (New York, 1948), I, 207-08.

15. *Ibid.*, I, 209.

16. The other two being Henry A. Wallace, Secretary of Agriculture, and of course, Morgenthau.

17. Hull, *Memoirs*, I, 209.

18. For example, see Chapter XLIV, "Franklin D. Roosevelt and New Deal Diplomacy," in Thomas A. Bailey, *A Diplomatic History of the American People* (New York, 1946), pp. 732-54.

19. Langer and Gleason, *Challenge to Isolation*, p. 8. When Ambassador Bowers arrived in Washington upon his return from Spain in March 1939, he telephoned Roosevelt and proposed that he call at the White House and report that night. The President refused, however, stating that it would be best if the Ambassador saw Secretary Hull first. Claude G. Bowers, *My Mission to Spain* (New York, 1954), p. 414.

20. See Chapter VIII, p. 183.

21. Hull, *Memoirs*, II, 1227, 1229.

22. Sumner Welles, *The Time for Decision* (New York, 1944), p. 57. The "administrative duel" between Hull and Welles continued into the summer of 1943. In August the President decided that the situation within the State Department could not continue and he asked for Welles' resignation.

23. Morgenthau, "Morgenthau Diaries, IV," *Colliers*, CXX (October 18, 1947), 16.

24. Hull, *Memoirs*, I, 200.

25. For example, see Bullitt to Roosevelt, April 12, 1937 (Franklin Delano Roosevelt Official Files, No. 1124), Roosevelt Library, Hyde Park, New York. Hereafter cited as FDR Official Files.

26. Marquis W. Childs, *I Write from Washington* (New York, 1942), p. 148.

27. Hugh Jones Parry, "The Spanish Civil War" (Ph.D. dissertation, University of Southern California, 1948), pp. 371-72. Another writer who takes the State Department to task for its appeasement policies is Robert Bendiner, *The Riddle of the State Department* (New York, 1943), pp. 1-6, pp. 59-62. See also Louis Fischer, *Men and Politics* (New York, 1941), pp. 303, 470.

28. Department of State, *Germany and the Spanish Civil War, 1936-1939. Documents on German Foreign Policy, 1918-1945* (Washington, 1950), No. 573, "Memorandum by the Ambassador to Spain," pp. 645-46. Hereafter cited as *Documents on German Foreign Policy.*

29. Hull, *Memoirs*, I, 485.

30. Bowers to Roosevelt, December 6, 1938 (FDR Official Files, No. 422A).

31. Dr. Herman Kahn, Director of the Roosevelt Library in Hyde Park, told the writer that a number of personal letters from Bowers to Roosevelt were not yet open for examination. These letters are said to contain Bowers' personal views as to the situation in Spain and a request for reconsideration of American policy.

Chapter Three

The Moral Embargo

The world was startled but not surprised when the long smoldering political conflict in Spain flared into civil war and was soon moving along as destructively as the recent slaughter of Haile Selassie's legions in Ethiopia. The State Department for some time had been receiving dispatches from Ambassador Bowers indicating that the conditions of unrest and tension in Spain could not long be endured without open warfare. On July 14, 1936, Bowers cabled from San Sebastian that

> sensational developments during the past 48 hours have tended to aggravate the serious political situation already existing as the result of continued social and political unrest, and that unless the Government acts energetically to enforce respect for law and order its position may become untenable. . . . Repeated rumors have been circulating for some time. . . regarding the possibility of a military *coup d'état* engineered by Right extremists and the tone of the statements issued by the proletarian organizations . . . clearly shows the fear of such an attempt.[1]

Three days later, on July 17, General Francisco Franco, who had flown from the Canary Islands to take command of the Army in the Spanish zone of Morocco, led Moorish troops into Cadiz and the revolt became a reality.

Although the United States was far removed both politically and geographically from the scene of the conflict, this Government was not left unaffected. The first concern of the State Department was not one of political policy but one of protection of the lives and property of American citizens who might be in danger.[2] Ambassador Bowers reported on July 19 that as far as he could ascertain no American interests had suffered. He added, however, that the political situation in Spain was not at all certain and that complications might arise which would affect American rights and interests.[3] To assure maximum protection for Americans endangered by the fighting in and around Madrid, Eric C. Wendelin, a Third Secretary in charge of the Madrid Embassy, informed all known Americans in the city that the Embassy was open to them and offered its protection. This invitation was accepted by approximately 150 persons.[4] The State Department strongly urged all Americans to evacuate Spain, and within a week the Navy had ordered the U. S. S. *Quincy* and the U. S. S. *Oklahoma* to Spanish waters to remove American nationals. With a note of warning Secretary Hull cabled Wendelin that this Government was lending its every effort in the protection of our citizens and to afford them means of evacuation from Spain, but "it cannot be assured that conditions will remain in such a state that American vessels may at any time enter Spanish ports for the purpose of evacuating Americans."[5]

Ambassador Bowers, Wendelin, and other members of the Embassy staff worked untiringly in an effort to evacuate safely Americans from Spain. The Ambassador spent ten days aboard the U. S. S. *Cayuga* evacuating Americans along the northern coast of Spain.[6] Arrangements were made for special guarded trains and truck convoys to transport additional groups from Madrid and other inland cities to the seaboard where they could be removed by ship.[7] Daily reports were sent to the State Department as to the progress that had been made. Guards were hired to protect the Embassy proper and stores of provisions were collected to prevent a possible food shortage. All of these precautions, however, did not protect Americans from the dangers of the war. Shooting affrays were common outside the Embassy in Madrid and occasional shells fell near-by. In Barcelona, Consul Lynn W. Franklin cabled the Secretary of State asking for thirty gas masks.[8] Hull replied that the United States had urged its citizens to leave Spain and had authorized the closing of the Consulate at Barcelona. Therefore, "any decision to supply gas masks would necessarily be interpreted as a reversal of our policy of urging Americans who can possibly do so to leave Spain."[9]

In September, while the battle was raging at the very gates of Madrid, the State Department seriously considered closing the American Embassy in the Spanish capital. Secretary Hull cabled Wendelin on September 22 that he feared for the safety of the Embassy staff and asked that immediate consideration be given to the closing of the Embassy.[10] Several days later Acting Secretary of State R. Walton Moore instructed Wendelin that he "should withdraw from Madrid at once unless some imperative duty compels you to remain."[11] These instructions, however, did not meet with the approval of Wendelin or Ambassador Bowers. Wendelin replied that he felt the closing of the Embassy at that time was premature. He argued that the military situation for the Madrid Government was not yet considered sufficiently grave; withdrawal while British and French Embassies remained would be a blow to the Spanish Government and would associate the United States with Germany and Italy who had already withdrawn; and withdrawal would prevent Americans in Madrid from receiving favored treatment and having their property protected.[12]

For the time being, at least, the Embassy was allowed to remain open and efforts were continued to evacuate those Americans who would leave. Secretary Hull, seeing that some American citizens would be financially unable to care for themselves, wrote President Roosevelt asking if there was any possibility of using federal funds for this purpose. "It did not seem to us possible," Hull concluded, "to abandon such Americans to the perils of civil war merely because of their financial disabilities."[13] Roosevelt agreed and instructed that the necessary funds were to be provided.[14] Thus many Americans who had remained in Spain for this reason were afforded an opportunity to leave.

Within a month the situation was even more serious in Madrid. Food supplies were running low and there was increased danger from bombs and shells. On November 20, Acting Secretary of State Moore cabled Ambassador Bowers that immediate consideration should be given to the closing of the American Embassy.[15] Bowers replied from his temporary quarters in St.-Jean-de-Luz, France, that he must "acquiesce in whatever decision you may make but I do feel strongly that the closing of the Embassy and the withdrawal of the consulate in Barcelona in the immediate wake of the action of Germany and Italy can have most disagreeable repercussions."[16] Wendelin also replied that he preferred to stay as

long as possible.[17] Nevertheless, the State Department ruled otherwise and on November 23 President Roosevelt was notified that
in view of the dangerous military situation Wendelin and his staff
had been ordered to evacuate Madrid for Valencia. The State
Department declared that it had been made "clear to the Spanish
authorities that in making this decision we have been actuated
wholly by concern for the safety of our nationals and have not
been influenced in any way whatsoever by political considerations."[18] This attitude was reaffirmed several days later during
the course of a conversation between Acting Secretary of State
Moore and Spanish Ambassador Don Fernando de los Ríos.[19]

These orders were immediately carried out although Wendelin
cabled that "every American member of the staff is entirely willing
to continue on duty in Madrid."[20] By November 26 the State
Department was informed that the Embassy in Madrid had been
closed and left on a caretaker status. Approximately sixty-five
Americans, both staff members and persons seeking refuge, were
safely removed to Valencia by trucks and busses provided by the
Spanish Government. Temporary diplomatic quarters were then
established in that city.[21] Remaining Americans in Madrid and in
other danger points throughout Spain were informed that all
reasonable efforts had been made to secure their safety and those
who remained did so "at their own risk and responsibility."[22] Although ample warning had been given of the dangers involved,
there were many Americans who, because of jobs, business interests,
or sentimental attachment to Spain, refused to leave.[23]

In addition to these efforts to protect American lives, the
State Department notified the Spanish Government that it would
be held responsible for the protection of American property and
for indemnification for any delinquency in this respect.[24] American
investments in Spain were estimated at approximately seventy million dollars, comprised primarily of public utilities and automotive
plants.[25] Many reports were circulating in the American press that
much of this property had been seized, but Wendelin cabled on
July 29 that these statements were as yet unfounded. He added
that the only seizure of American property amounted to several
private automobiles.[26] A few days later, however, he cabled that
the Ford and General Motors plants at Barcelona had been seized
by the Spanish Government.[27]

Acting on specific instructions from the State Department, Wendelin vigorously protested to the Spanish Government the seizure of American properties. In reply a formal note was received from the Spanish Foreign Office which stated that

> the Government of the Republic holds as an unalterable principle not to take possession of any property, movable or immovable, belonging to Spanish citizens or foreigners, except naturally in cases of *force majeure*, and especially when it is a question of the safety of the state, or public interests so require. In such cases it will pay the value after a just and equitable appraisal and if possible — and this is the chief desire of the Government — in agreement with the interested parties or their legal representatives.[28]

American consular officials in territory controlled by the Insurgents addressed similar demands to the Nationalist authorities. In general, the reply was the same as that received from the Madrid Government.[29] Very little American property was actually destroyed during the course of the Spanish Civil War. Much of it, however, was expropriated by officials on both sides. Also, large amounts of currency and exchange belonging to Americans were frozen within Spain. At the conclusion of the war, various claims were filed against the Franco Government, but as yet all have not been satisfactorily settled.[30]

At home the State Department sought to formulate a policy regarding the attitude of the United States toward the Spanish War. On July 23 Secretary Hull radioed the President, who was cruising off the New England coast, that

> the reports which we are receiving indicate that the situation is, if anything, becoming worse and it seems like a fifty-fifty chance as to which side may come out on top, and, furthermore, with an equal chance that a completely chaotic condition may arise in Spain which may continue for some time. One of the most serious factors in this situation lies in the fact that the [Spanish] Government has distributed large quantities of arms and ammunition into the hands of irresponsible members of left-wing political organizations.[31]

An early indication of Hull's attitude came several days later during the course of a conversation between the Secretary of State and the Spanish Ambassador. Ambassador Don Luis Calderón[32] called at the State Department to discuss the protection of American lives and property in Spain. Hull replied that he appreciated the Ambassador's visit and he expressed regret at Spain's difficulties, but he was very careful not to intimate the slightest bias in favor of either of the two conflicting groups in the civil war.[33]

It soon became evident that the international aspects of the Spanish War had become more serious, and it was necessary that the United States make some public declaration of policy. Dispatches reaching the State Department clearly indicated that many of the European nations were vitally interested in the outcome of the Spanish struggle. During the early days of the war Ambassador Bowers reported that the situation in Spain had caused strained relations between Italy and Germany on one side and France on the other. He stated that France had already sent twenty planes to the Spanish Government while Germany had sent fourteen planes to the Insurgents. Bowers saw this "important perhaps as indicating a threat to European peace."[34] Likewise, the Soviet Union took an early interest in the Spanish strife. The American Chargé in Russia reported that the

> Soviet press and leaders are beginning more openly to show their sympathy for the Spanish Government as the latter's position becomes more precarious. Mass demonstrations of solidarity with the Spanish people were held in the cities and towns of the Soviet Union yesterday. The Moscow *Pravda* of this morning states that 120,000 demonstrators gathered in the Red Square and that 100,000 took part in the Leningrad demonstration. . . . Funds for the 'assistance of the fighters' are being collected in factories and institutions; meetings of employees are voting from one-half to one per cent of their aggregate monthly salaries to the cause.[35]

The French and British, fearing that foreign intervention in Spain would lead to an international crisis, very early took the lead in an effort to contain the war within Spanish boundaries. Although the French, under Premier Léon Blum, were sympathetic to the Spanish Government, British Prime Minister Stanley Baldwin was able to convince Blum that the threat to peace could be averted only if the major powers would agree to a policy of strict neutrality and nonintervention. The French Government then took the initiative and proposed that the major powers of Europe join in an agreement to remain completely aloof in the Spanish War.[36]

These nonintervention efforts undoubtedly had a strong influence on the formulation of American policy. In his *Memoirs*, Hull noted that within three weeks after the outbreak of the rebellion the State Department was well aware "that the British and French Governments believed that a European agreement strictly to abstain from intervening in Spanish affairs was the best means to prevent the spread of the conflict." Also, he declared "that the initiative in dealing with the Spanish problem lay with the European nations."[37] Hull later remarked that once American policy had been made "clear and public," it could not be changed "without grave embarrassment to the European nations, particularly Britain and France, to whom it was welcome as being in conformity with their own policy of nonintervention."[38] Certainly this would indicate that the policy of the United States was influenced by, and in accord with, the policies of Britain and France.[39]

On August 5 Secretary Hull held a conference of the leading officials in the State Department to consider a public declaration of policy.[40] After considerable discussion a statement was drafted which pointed out the article of the convention signed at Montevideo: "No state has the right to intervene in the internal or external affairs of another."[41] No public pronouncement, however, was issued at that time, although the substance of this discussion was given to the press and received wide publicity throughout the country. Two days later, on August 7, a clear statement of American policy was made by Acting Secretary of State William Phillips in a circular telegram to the diplomatic and consular officers of the United States in Spain. He stated that since

all of our officers have fully appreciated the necessity for maintaining a completely impartial attitude with regard to the disturbances in Spain, and that [since] such an attitude has been maintained at all times by them, it may be well to have a summing up of what this Government's position thus far has been and will continue to be.

It is clear that our Neutrality Law with respect to embargo of arms, ammunition, and implements of war has no application in the present situation, since that applies only in the event of war *between or among nations.* On the other hand, in conformity with its well-established policy of non-interference with internal affairs in other countries, either in the time of peace or in the event of civil strife, this Government will, of course, scrupulously refrain from any interference whatsoever in the unfortunate Spanish situation. We believe that American citizens, both at home and abroad, are patriotically observing this well-recognized policy.[42]

Thus the American policy of nonintervention was reaffirmed so as to leave little doubt as to the attitude of this Government. In commenting on this policy several years after the Spanish War was concluded, the State Department declared that "the attitude of this Government toward the conflict was based squarely on the consistent policy of the United States of promoting peace and at the same time avoiding involvement in war situations."[43] In defense of this policy, Secretary Hull pointed out that a pledge of nonintervention in the affairs of other nations had been included in the Democratic platforms of 1932 and 1936. He also stated that nonintervention was approved as the foundation of the Good Neighbor Policy at the Montevideo Pan-American Conference in 1933. In an address to this Conference, Hull declared that "I feel safe in undertaking to say that under our support of the general principle of nonintervention as has been suggested, no government need fear any intervention on the part of the United States under the Roosevelt Administration." The assumption that this statement was limited to the Latin-American countries was not accepted by Mr. Hull; it was his belief that this policy applied not only to the Western hemisphere, but to other parts of the world as well.[44]

In making public this declaration of American policy toward the Spanish conflict, the United States invoked a moral embargo against the exportation of war materials to either side in Spain. Legally, this Government did not have the right to prohibit the export of arms to countries engaged in civil war, since the Neutrality Act authorized the President to impose an arms embargo only in the event of war "between or among nations." Clearly then, the American policy toward Spain was a policy of moral suasion which was entirely dependent on the cooperation of private interests. An opportunity to reassert this policy came on August

10, when the Glenn L. Martin Company made an inquiry as to the State Department's attitude concerning the prospective sale of eight bombing planes to the Spanish Government. After consultation with President Roosevelt and Cordell Hull, Acting Secretary Phillips replied that this Government had a well-established policy of noninterference with the internal affairs of other countries. Americans, both home and abroad, he continued, were patriotically observing the State Department's request that there be no interference in the Spanish conflict; consequently, "in view of the above, it seems reasonable to assume that the sale of aeroplanes, about which you inquire, would not follow the spirit of this Government's policy."[45] Other firms which made similar inquiries received the same reply as had been sent to the Martin Company.[46]

This American policy of complete neutrality and nonintervention was reaffirmed in several important foreign policy addresses during the late summer and fall of 1936. At Chautauqua, New York, on August 14 President Roosevelt described the scenes of horror he had witnessed during the First World War and pleaded for peaceful relations among nations so that this ordeal would not be repeated. We must remember, he stated, that so long as war exists on earth there will be some danger that even the nation which most ardently desires peace may be drawn into the conflict. Speaking of neutrality, the President said that if a general war should break out on the continent, "let us not blink at the fact that we would find in this country thousands of Americans who, seeking immediate riches — fools' gold — would attempt to break down or evade neutrality." Then, obviously referring to the Spanish situation, he pointed out that no neutrality legislation could be provided to cover every contingency. He added, however, that "with that wise and experienced man who is our Secretary of State, I have thought and worked long and hard on the problem of keeping the United States at peace," but "all the wisdom of America is not to be found in the White House or in the Department of State; we need the mediation, the prayer and the positive support of the people of America who go along with us in seeking peace."[47]

On September 15 Secretary Hull delivered an address before the Good Neighbor League of New York City. Hull's speech closely followed the theme expressed earlier by the President at Chautauqua. American policy, he stated, was "peace, commerce, and honest friendship with all nations, entangling alliances with none;

settlement of disputes by peaceful means, and renunciation of war as an instrument of national policy." Hull continued his speech by relating the importance of foreign trade in the economic life of this country, but he added:

> In trade exchange baleful elements enter, particularly the trade in arms, ammunition, and implements of war. . . . this trade is mainly incidental to the preparation for war . . . it may be an element in stimulating or provoking war. . . . As in the present Spanish situation we assert our influence to the utmost to prevent arms shipped from this country from thwarting national or international efforts to maintain peace or end conflict. . . . We are always ready to discourage to the utmost traffic in arms when required in the interests of peace. . . . Legislation recently passed provides some of the main essentials in a wise anticipatory policy. I have in mind the Resolutions of Congress of 1935 and 1936 which in addition to providing for the licensing of all import and export of arms, prohibit their shipment to belligerent nations. These same resolutions prohibit the flotation of loans and establishment of credits in our markets by belligerent countries.[48]

In this address Secretary Hull reaffirmed the American policy of nonintervention and stated precisely that this country would not allow itself to be projected into the Spanish conflict and thus endanger the peace of the American people. These same ideas were reiterated by Assistant Secretary Sumner Welles several weeks later speaking before the Foreign Policy Association in New York City.[49]

While the President and other officials were assuring Americans that they would not become embroiled in the affairs of Europe, much tension and indignation were created by newspaper headlines reporting the bombing of the American destroyer U. S. S. *Kane* by an unidentified plane in Spanish waters.[50] The *Kane*, enroute from Gibraltar to Bilbao to evacuate American nationals, was attacked approximately forty miles off the Spanish coast but escaped without suffering damage. This attack on "American national honor" was the first incident since the outbreak of the war to evoke a public protest.[51] President Roosevelt, who was touring the Middle West at the time, was apparently aroused by the criticism as he directed Hull to bring the incident to the

immediate attention of the Spanish Government and, with no intention of recognition, to General Franco. The President requested
the State Department to ascertain if either side was responsible
and to insist upon definite assurance that appropriate instructions
would be issued to prevent repetition of another such incident.[52]

The State Department, refusing to exaggerate the seriousness
of the attack, cabled the American Embassy in Madrid and Consul
Charles A. Bay at Seville to bring the matter to the attention of
the Spanish Government and of Franco.[53] Hull stated that the
attack on the Kane was assumed to be a case of mistaken identity
and requested that instructions be issued to prevent any recurrence.
Six days after the attack the Madrid Government, expressing its
regret, replied that it definitely did not possess any planes of the
type described and declared furthermore that no Loyalist planes
were in the area at the time of the incident.[54] On September 12
Franco, on behalf of the Nationalist Government, expressed regret
over the attack but denied any knowledge of the incident. He
added, however, that the possibility of error by the Nationalist
aerial forces could not be overlooked.[55]

This attack strengthened the belief of many pacifists that
American ships did not belong in Spanish waters and that Americans in Spain should either evacuate or remain at their own risk.
The Christian Science Monitor, in reporting the attack on the Kane,
demanded that all American warships be withdrawn from Spanish
waters. The editors declared that "we want no such slogans as
'Remember the Maine,'" and emphasized that the best way to
remain out of a general European conflict was to keep American
ships away from troubled waters. The Monitor felt that American
participation in the Spanish conflict should end when the State
Department warned all United States citizens to leave that country.[56]

American shipping throughout the course of the war suffered
far less than the shipping of large European states but did not
remain untouched. In addition to the attack upon the Kane, the
destroyer Erie, and the merchant ships Exmouth, Wisconsin, and
Nantucket Chief were fired upon by Insurgent aircraft.[57] Protests
were lodged by the State Department in the case of the Exmouth
and Erie but not the last two. The Wisconsin was bombed twice
while running war supplies to the Madrid Government from France,
and the Nantucket Chief, a tramp steamer, was captured by the

Rebels while carrying a cargo of petroleum products from Russia to the Loyalists at Barcelona. After representations were made informally to Franco for its immediate release, the Nationalists complied as soon as the captured cargo had been discharged.[58]

Other than the attack upon the *Kane*, there were no serious incidents to mar relations between the United States and either of the protagonists in Spain. The State Department held to the traditional American policy that because a state of belligerency was not recognized, neither party had a right to interfere with American shipping on the high seas. During the early months of the war, the Spanish Government attempted to blockade Rebel ports and informed the United States that it would not be possible for American merchant vessels or the merchantmen of other nations to enter these ports.[59] In reply, Secretary Hull instructed Wendelin to notify the Loyalists that the United States "cannot admit the legality of any action on the part of the Spanish Government in declaring such ports closed unless the Government declares and maintains an effective blockade of such ports. In taking this position my Government is guided by a long line of precedents in international law with which the Spanish Government is doubtless familiar."[60]

On numerous occasions during the course of the Spanish civil strife the United States was invited to serve as mediator to end the conflict. The war was only a month old when Ambassador Bowers cabled the State Department that the Argentine Ambassador, who was dean of the diplomatic corps at St.-Jean-de-Luz, had called a meeting to consider the possibility of mediation. Bowers was of the opinion that the proposal was premature and he suggested that the Secretary of State instruct him not to attend the meeting.[61] Acting Secretary of State Phillips promptly replied with a positive restatement of American policy. Bowers was told that "while the American Government deplores the terrible strife in Spain and devoutly wishes for peace at the earliest possible moment, our policy, as already announced, is to 'scrupulously refrain from any interference whatsoever in the unfortunate Spanish situation.' In these circumstances, you should not attend this proposed meeting."[62]

Several days later the State Department received a proposal from Uruguay suggesting that the American republics join in an effort to mediate the Spanish conflict. The Uruguayan Minister of Foreign Relations, Dr. José Espalter, passionately stated that "In the face of the civil war which bleeds the Spanish fatherland, the nations of the American continent, discovered and civilized by its genius, cannot remain impassive spectators." Therefore, "I have the honor to consult your Excellency [Secretary Hull] with reference to a cordial mediation to be offered to Spain by the American countries which, to this end, might act jointly either in Washington within the Pan American Union, or in any other American capital which might be chosen."[63] On August 20 Acting Secretary Phillips replied that this Government expressed deep feeling for the Spanish people and earnestly hoped the civil strife would soon cease. He stated that the United States supported the general principles of mediation, but the Department did not believe that the prospect of such mediation was such as to warrant the United States to depart from its policy of noninterference in the internal affairs of other countries.[64]

In late November, Ambassador Bullitt reported from Paris that he had been asked by the French Minister of Foreign Affairs, Yvon Delbos, if there was any possibility that the United States would join England and France in a joint *démarche* demanding that the "Governments of Germany, Italy and the Soviet Union . . . make a gentlemen's agreement on their honor immediately to stop all supplies of men and munitions to the conflicting parties in Spain and to join England and France in an immediate proposal to Franco and the Madrid Government that they should accept mediation at once."[65] Bullitt replied unofficially that it was his opinion that "the President could not join in any such joint *démarche* at the present time, . . . that his purpose now was to produce a solidarity for peace between the nations of the Western Hemisphere, [and] that it might be most prejudicial if he should at this moment involve himself in rearranging the affairs of the continent of Europe."[66] Acting Secretary Moore approved of Bullitt's restrained response to the inquiries by the French Foreign Minister. Moore stated that "these matters should be allowed to remain in abeyance until the President has returned to Washington."[67]

After the President had returned to Washington in early December, a conference of high officials decided that no action would be taken by this Government with regard to the proposed mediation. It was agreed, however, that the United States would issue a public statement giving moral support to the plan.[68] On December 10 Acting Secretary Moore released the following statement to the press:

> It is announced by the Governments of Great Britain and France that they have invited the Governments of Germany, Italy, Russia and Portugal to join them in a mediation offer to end the Spanish Civil War. It is the very earnest hope of our Government that the six nations mentioned may find a peaceful method of accomplishing the great purpose in view. *This expression represents no deviation from our well-known policy of non-interference in the affairs of other countries.* It simply voices as I am certain, the deep distress of the American people that Spain should be involved in a bitter conflict marked by heavy loss of life and indescribable suffering. The conflict affords fresh and inescapable evidence that in these days the perils of war are not confined to the actual combatants, bad as that is, but extend to the entire population within reach of the deadly instruments now employed — to helpless men, women and children — and that no limit can be set to its devastating effects. Human intellect, which has shown its capacity to dreadfully increase beyond what was once dreamed possible, the horrors and wreckage of war, should surely be able to devise expedients to bring about cessation of the present struggle. . . .[69]

Moore cabled the text of this statement to Bullitt informing him that the President and Secretary Hull were "fully informed concerning this matter and they are in full accord with this statement."[70]

Several months later Ambassador Bullitt reported to the State Department a conversation with French Foreign Minister Delbos. Monsieur Delbos suggested that the only hope for a successful mediation in Spain would be if President Roosevelt and the Pope appealed simultaneously for a cessation of hostilities coupled with a proposal of mediation. Bullitt stated in his report that the time was opportune if the President wanted to make such a move.[71] Although it was doubtful that Hull ever considered urging the President to take such a course of action, Ambassador Bowers was requested to give his views on the subject. Bowers replied that such a step would be a serious mistake since the Pope certainly could not be considered a neutral in the conflict. The Ambassador also believed that neither side would make the slightest concession so mediation would be impossible.[72] In a personal letter to the President, Bowers reiterated this stand. He declared that Roosevelt should not try to reconcile a foreign controversy; that the position of the United States had been one of "neutrality . . . rigid and honest"; and that our country should not be precipitated "in the very heart of the bitterest of domestic quarrels."[73] Thus once again did the United States decline to depart from its well-established policy of neutrality and nonintervention in the Spanish strife, even refusing to associate itself with peaceful proposals to end the conflict.[74]

Meanwhile, the war continued to rage in Spain. Both sides prepared for a long and bloody conflict which was destined to last for almost three years. Various nations of Europe projected themselves into the struggle by providing arms and supplies to one or the other of the protagonists in Spain. Naval observers aboard the U. S. S. *Quincy* reported on August 11, 1936, that the German destroyer *Leopard* arrived in the Rebel port of Palma and anchored in the bay. Early the next morning the German cargo ship *Schleswig* arrived and unloaded large quantities of arms and munitions, including the latest modern anti-aircraft machine guns.[75] Likewise, Consul Charles Bay at Seville kept the State Department well informed as to the shipping activities in that large Insurgent port. On August 12 he reported that "10 new Savoia tri-motor bombing aeroplanes with about 20 Italian pilots, 18 Junker tri-motor bombers mostly new with about 30 German pilots" recently arrived.[76] Subsequent reports were very similar, with practically all of them describing the arrival of vast quantities of war material from the Axis powers and Portugal.[77]

Nor was foreign intervention confined to the aid received by General Franco. Only a few days after the outbreak of the revolt Ambassador Bullitt reported the shipment of twelve warplanes from France to the Spanish Government.[78] The International Brigade, comprised of fighters from practically every nation in the world, were instrumental in the defense of Madrid during the early months of the war. Consul Mahlon Perkins reported from Barcelona the arrival of large supplies of munitions and thousands of foreign volunteers to aid the Madrid Government.[79] From his vantage point at St.-Jean-de-Luz, Ambassador Bowers commented that without foreign aid Franco would have been speedily defeated.

"They have in their army," he said, "thousands of the mercenaries of the Foreign Legion from Africa, thousands of the Moors, and as early as August and September they had hundreds of Italian and German Army officers as aviators and tank operators. . . . Five thousand German soldiers, 'not volunteers,' but soldiers have disembarked at Cadiz." But he also stated that augmenting the Government forces were many "actual volunteers whose Governments have nothing whatever to do with their presence here . . . the highest estimate I have heard is 3,000."[80]

Fearing that such activities would increase the likelihood of a general European war, the French Government, supported by the British, pressed negotiations looking toward a general European agreement against intervention in the Spanish War. By early September twenty-seven countries, including all of the Great Powers of Europe, had accepted the French Government's nonintervention proposals, and before the end of the month an International Nonintervention Committee held its first meeting in London. By the end of the year, at the insistence of Great Britain and France, the Committee had agreed upon a system of international control which in theory would have prohibited the flow of foreign volunteers and munitions to Spain. As demonstrated by the subsequent course of events, however, complete nonintervention failed, and by the end of 1937 maintenance of such a policy, even in name only, was in a precarious position.[81]

Although the United States did not desire to be a party to a formal agreement, the State Department followed the European example in attempting to impose a policy of strict nonintervention in the Spanish situation.[82] Only a few days after the outbreak of the war the question arose concerning the refueling of Spanish war vessels in Tangier Bay by the American owned Vacuum Oil Company. The Consul General at Tangier advised the company that it should "inform ships that the company, as an American concern, would prefer to make no deliveries until they knew . . . that the constituted international authority of the zone do not consider such deliveries to violate the statutory neutrality . . . or until the American Legation in Tangier has received instructions in the matter from its Government."[83] The State Department emphatically approved this suggestion to the Vacuum Company. Secretary Hull cabled that "While this Government has not accepted the Statute of Tangier and its provisions are not, therefore, applicable to American nationals, nevertheless the Department, in the interests of international cooperation for the avoidance of complications, would not be disposed to support American nationals in Tangier in any effort to furnish supplies to either side to the present conflict, contrary to the policy adopted by the constituted authorities of the Tangier Zone."[84]

The exercise of moral suasion upon Americans not to export supplies to either side in Spain became a well-established policy. Not only were American firms discouraged from selling directly to either side in Spain, but the State Department Board of Munition Control refused to issue export licenses for implements of war which might be shipped to a third country and then transshipped to Spain. The Mexican Ambassador called at the State Department on September 14 to inform Secretary Hull that President Cárdenas of Mexico wished to inquire "whether the Government of the United States would permit the purchase by Mexico and the shipment to the Spanish Government of munitions and arms from the United States."[85] Secretary Hull replied that this Government had adopted a definite position regarding the shipment of arms and munitions to Spain, and "we have no intention of departing from it."[86]

The Mexican Government agreed to respect the American position and President Cárdenas promised to prohibit the transshipment of American war materials to Spain. Nevertheless, on many occasions American officials were compelled to deal directly with the Mexican President to prevent American supplies from reaching Spain through Mexico. In December 1936 the American Chargé in Mexico (Pierre Boal) advised the State Department that the Mexican Government was preparing certificates of accidental destruction for several American planes brought in under tourist permits so that they might be shipped to Spain.[87] Acting Secretary Moore replied that the United States would appreciate any action taken by the Mexican Government in the enforcement of American laws respecting international traffic in arms. He concluded that "you [Boal] might remind the Mexican authorities of the importance they have always attached to the strict enforcement of our own laws in respect to arms leaving this country for Mexico."[88] The Chargé in Mexico City called on President Cárdenas and explained the problem. The President replied that "he would be glad to cooperate with the Department in the matter and would at once take steps to prevent any airplanes or other war material of American origin from being sent to Spain."[89] Despite this announcement by the Mexican President, the problem persisted throughout the course of the Spanish War and was a constant source of embarrassment to the United States.[90]

In keeping with the policy of neutrality and nonintervention, American diplomatic and consular officials in Spain attempted to maintain a neutral course. During the early weeks of the war, Wendelin cabled from Madrid that the "necessity for maintaining a completely impartial attitude with regard to the disturbances in Spain is fully appreciated by the Embassy and Consulate. We have urged this necessity upon Americans here and the fact that no Americans have been killed or injured seems to warrant belief that they are observing an impartial attitude."[91] Ambassador Bowers was personally very much in sympathy with the Spanish Government but his official actions were carefully impartial. Bowers made long periodic reports to the State Department in which he attempted to analyze the situation in Spain. He vividly described the flagrant violations of the nonintervention agreement, but was never so much in sympathy with the Madrid Government that he could overlook Communist influence and activities. In reviewing American policy Bowers concluded that: "We have thus far retained the respect and confidence of the Government, and we have done absolutely nothing to justify the slightest complaint from the rebels. We have done so by attending strictly to our own business."[92] In July 1937 Bowers stated in his report on the first year of the war that "Our own position during the entire year has been all that could be desired. We have strictly observed our policy of neutrality. We almost alone at this moment can approach either side on official business with the certainty that they will do all within their power to serve us."[93]

Thus, with the Spanish War only a few months old, many fundamental characteristics of American policy had been involved. These included neutrality and nonintervention, protection and evacuation of nationals, conservation of property rights, refusal to recognize belligerency or countenance interference with American shipping on the high seas, and discouragement and prohibition of the export of munitions to either of the protagonists in a civil war. The policy of the United States was in full accord with the nonintervention efforts of the European powers and was continued without variance until the Spanish War ended in March

1939. This Government believed that a complete "hands-off" policy was the best insurance against possible entanglement in the internal affairs of Europe. Secretary Hull later remarked that "Our policy had nothing to do with our views on the right or the wrong in the Spanish Civil War," and that it was not the intention of the United States "to judge between the two sides."[94] Until the end of December 1936 the State Department's policy of moral suasion had been effective in preventing the export of implements of war to either side in Spain. On December 28, however, Robert Cuse, an arms exporter, applied to the Department for licenses to export aircraft materials in the amount of $2,777,000 to the Spanish Government.[95] Since civil war was not embraced in the existing Neutrality Act, Secretary Hull possessed no legal grounds for refusing the request and the Department had no alternative but to grant the licenses. Obviously the Administration had to take some steps to prevent the recurrence of such action if a neutrality policy was to be maintained. President Roosevelt conferred with Congressional leaders and it was decided that the new Congress would be asked to remedy the situation by imposing an arms embargo against Spain.

NOTES

1. Bowers to Hull, July 14, 1936 (State Department File No. 852.00/2296: telegram). State Department File No. hereafter cited as SD File No. Ambassador Bowers was at San Sebastian, on the northern coast of Spain, where the Spanish Government had been accustomed to set up a summer capital. After the outbreak of the rebellion the diplomatic corps moved to the near-by French resort of St.-Jean-de-Luz. Bowers was never able to return to Madrid. In early 1938 Secretary Hull considered opening the American Embassy in Barcelona, which was then serving as the capital city of the Spanish Government. Ambassador Bowers protested, however, on the grounds that the Embassy was functioning properly in St.-Jean-de-Luz and that the change would make no real contribution to the Government of Spain while creating hostility on the other side. Hull agreed and nothing further was said on the subject until the Spanish strife had ended. Bowers to Hull, February 21, 1938 (SD File No. 124.52/225: tel.). Also see Hull to Bowers February 23, 1938 (SD File No. 124.52/425: tel.).

2. On January 1, 1936, there were 1,582 American citizens in Spain. *Press Releases,* July 25, 1936.

3. Bowers to Hull, July 19, 1936 (SD File No. 852.00/2175: tel.).

4. *Press Releases,* July 25, 1936. At the request of the countries concerned, American facilities were also extended to the nationals of Belgium, Philippines, Austria, Chile, Cuba, Finland, Panama, Sweden, and Turkey.

5. Hull to Wendelin, August 1, 1936 (SD File No. 352.1115/346: tel.).

6. Hull to Corcoran (Consul at Vigo), July 27, 1936 (SD File No. 352.1115/136: tel.).

7. Wendelin to Hull, August 1, 1936 (SD File No. 852.00/2348: tel.).

8. Franklin to Hull, August 23, 1936 (SD File No. 352.1115/999: tel.).

9. Hull to Franklin, August 25, 1936 (SD File No. 352.1116/1017: tel.).

10. Hull to Wendelin, September 22, 1936 (SD File No. 124.52/116a: tel.).

11. Moore to Wendelin, September 24, 1936 (SD File No. 124.52/116b: tel.).

12. Wendelin to Hull, September 25, 1936 (SD File No. 124.52/116c: tel.).

13. Hull to Roosevelt, September 26, 1936 (FDR Official Files No. 422C).

14. Roosevelt to Hopkins, September 30, 1936 (FDR Official Files, No. 422C: memo.).

15. Moore to Bowers, November 20, 1936 (SD File No. 124.52/135a: tel.).

16. Bowers to Moore, November 21, 1936 (SD File No. 124.52/135b: tel.). Germany and Italy had closed their diplomatic missions in Loyalist territory and had recognized the Franco Government as the *de jure* Government of Spain.

17. Wendelin to Moore, November 22, 1936 (SD File No. 124.52/135c: tel.).

18. Moore to Roosevelt, November 23, 1936 (SD File No. 124.52/142a).

19. James C. Dunn, November 25, 1936 (SD File No. 852.00/3928: memo.).

20. Wendelin to Moore, November 24, 1936 (SD File No. 124.52/142b: tel.).

21. Wendelin to Moore, November 26, 1936 (SD File No. 852.00/3890: tel.).

22. *Press Releases*, November 21, 28, 1936.

23. On January 9, 1937, Wendelin reported to Hull that 34 American nationals remained at the Embassy in Madrid, which was then under the care of a custodian. Wendelin to Hull, January 9, 1937 (SD File No. 124.52/168: tel.). Acting Secretary of State Moore replied that all Americans should be urged to leave and if necessary the Embassy premises should be closed. Moore to Wendelin, January 10, 1937 (SD File No. 124.52/168: tel.).

24. Hull to Wendelin, August 3, 1936 (SD File No. 352.1115/5: tel.).

25. Norman J. Padelford, *International Law and Diplomacy in the Spanish Civil Strife* (New York, 1939), p. 170.

26. Wendelin to Hull, July 29, 1936 (SD File No. 352.1115/201: tel.).

27. Wendelin to Hull, August 5, 1936 (SD File No. 852.00/2430: tel.).

28. *Ibid.*, August 23, 1936 (SD File No. 352.1115/45: tel.).

29. Padelford, *International Law and Diplomacy in the Spanish Civil Strife*, p. 170.

30. In a recent letter to the author Bowers stated that actual confiscation of American property did not occur although on both sides the American Telephone and Telegraph Company was forced to place its services to the uses of the fighting forces. The former American Ambassador to Spain related an incident that occurred while he was on an evacuation trip in Bilbao.

Upon hearing a report that the Spanish Government was about to confiscate the Firestone plant, refuse the officers permission to leave, and demand the secret formula, Bowers called upon the Governor to ascertain whether such actions were contemplated. When informed of the object of the visit the Governor looked amazed and replied: "No we are not going into business and we do not want the plant, and we do not ask for the secret formula because we are not in business. All we want is that the plant make tires for us for payment in gold, and this is what any government on the face of the globe would do." Bowers to author, February 15, 1954.

31. Hull, *Memoirs*, I, 475.

32. The career diplomat serving as Spanish Ambassador to the United States prior to Calderón was Juan de Cárdenas whom Marquis Childs described as "unadulterated *ancien régime*, with a professional weariness, a professional disdain for anything that breathed and moved and uttered sounds of life." Childs, *I Write from Washington*, pp. 134-135. Prior to the outbreak of the rebellion in Spain, Cárdenas was replaced by Don Luis Calderón. Throughout the Spanish War, Cárdenas lived at the Ritz Carlton Hotel in New York City where he served as Franco's unofficial Ambassador and propagandist in the United States. Calderón served as Spanish Ambassador until September 1936 when he was replaced by Don Fernando de los Ríos, a former distinguished professor at the University of Madrid. Señor de los Ríos served at this post until his Government ceased to exist.

33. Cordell Hull, July 27, 1936 (SD File No. 852.00/2300: memo.).

34. Bowers to Hull, July 30, 1936 (SD File No. 852.00/2325: tel.).

35. Loy W. Henderson (Chargé in the Soviet Union) to Hull, August 4, 1936 (SD File No. 852.00/2395: tel.).

36. For an account of the interests and motives of the European powers, see Toynbee, *Survey, 1937*, II, 126-221; also Vera Micheles Dean, "European Diplomacy in the Spanish Crisis," *Foreign Policy Reports*, XII (December 1, 1936), 222-32. A discussion of British attitudes can be found in John R. Hubbard, "British Public Opinion and the Spanish Civil War, 1936-1939" (Ph.D. dissertation, University of Texas, 1950).

37. Hull, *Memoirs*, I, 477.

38. *Ibid.*, 479.

39. Bowers to author, February 15, 1954.

40. Present were Under Secretary William Phillips, Assistant Secretaries R. Walton Moore and Sumner Welles, and Legal Advisor Green H. Hackworth.

41. Hull, *Memoirs*, I, 477. Reference was to the Pan-American Conference which met at Montevideo, Uruguay, in December 1933.

42. William Phillips (Acting Secretary of State) to all Consularies in Spain, August 7, 1936 (SD File No. 852.00/2510a: tel.). This statement was not made public until August 11, 1936.

43. United States Department of State, *Peace and War: United States Foreign Policy 1931-1941* (Washington, 1943), p. 36.

44. Hull, *Memoirs*, I, 477-78.

45. William Phillips (Acting Secretary of State) to the Glenn L. Martin Company, August 10, 1936 (SD File No. 711.00111/5). During the month of July, prior to the outbreak of the rebellion, the United States shipped

airplane engines valued at $19,554 to the Spanish Government. *Press Releases*, August 22, 1936.

46.   The *New York Times* reported that one broker had refused an advance commission of $450,000 when informed it might embarrass his Government. Twenty other companies also declined orders. *New York Times,* December 29, 1936.

47.   Text of the address can be found in the *New York Times*, August 15, 1936.

48.   Cordell Hull, *Our Foreign Relations and Our Foreign Policy*, SD Publication No. 925 (Washington, 1936), pp. 3-12.

49.   Sumner Welles, *Our Foreign Policy and Peace*, SD Publication No. 946 (Washington, 1936). There is some doubt if this speech reflected Welles' personal view toward Spain, although this was the attitude of the State Department. Welles later wrote that the Spanish Government, as the legally constituted and recognized Government of Spain, should have been permitted to purchase arms in this country. Welles, *Time for Decision*, pp. 57-61.

50.   *New York Times*, August 30, 1936.

51.   Public reaction to this incident is described in O. W. Riegal, "Press, Radio, and the Spanish Civil War," *Public Opinion Quarterly*, I (January, 1937), 135-36.

52.   *Press Releases*, August 29, September 5, 1936.

53.   Hull to Wendelin, August 31, 1936 (SD File No. 852.00/1624a: tel.). Hull to Bay, August 31, 1936 (SD File No. 852.00/1624b: tel.). Seville was the headquarters for the Insurgent forces of General Franco. At the request of the State Department, American consular officials in Insurgent territory frequently made unofficial representations to the Nationalist Government.

54.   *Press Releases*, September 5, 1936.

55.   *Ibid.*, September 12, 1936.

56.   Editorials in the *Christian Science Monitor*, September 2, 19, 1936. It is interesting to note that later the *Monitor* became one of the strongest advocates to lift the arms embargo against Spain. The editors felt that the Spanish Government was the legally elected, democratic Government of Spain and should be assisted in its fight. *Ibid.*, January 27, 28, 1939. The Navy Department ordered all American warships out of Spanish waters on September 10, 1936.

57.   *New York Times*, July 24, August 30, December 19, 1936.

58.   *Press Releases*, January 22, February 5, 12, 1938; *New York Times,* January 22, June 20, 1938.

59.   *Press Releases*, August 29, 1936. The Spanish note was dated August 20.

60.   Hull to Wendelin, August 25, 1936 (SD File No. 852.00/2742: tel.).

61.   Bowers to Hull, August 17, 1936 (SD File No. 852.00/2629: tel.).

62.   Phillips to Bowers, August 17, 1936 (SD File No. 852.00/2938: tel.).

63.   J. Richling (Uruguayan Minister) to Hull, August 17, 1936 (SD File No. 852.00/2741a: tel.).

64. Phillips to Richling, August 20, 1936 (SD File No. 852.00/2741b: tel.). On August 27, 1937, the Uruguayan Government again asked the United States to aid in a mediation move to end the war in Spain. The State Department for a second time politely declined. *Press Releases*, September 4, 1937.

65. Bullitt to Moore, November 28, 1936 (SD File No. 852.00/3922: tel.).

66. *Ibid.*

67. Moore to Bullitt, November 30, 1936 (SD File No. 800.51W89 France/1058: tel.). The President was in Buenos Aires attending the Inter-American Conference for the Maintenance of Peace.

68. James C. Dunn, December 9, 1936 (SD File No. 852.00/4144: memo.).

69. *New York Times,* December 11, 1936. Italics mine.

70. Moore to Bullitt, December 10, 1936 (SD File No. 852.00/4062a: tel.).

71. Bullitt to Hull, July 30, 1937 (SD File No. 852.00/6122: tel.).

72. Bowers to Hull, August 11, 1937 (SD File No. 852.00/6216½).

73. Bowers to Roosevelt, August 11, 1937 (FDR Official Files, 422C). This letter was sent by the President to Hull. The Secretary of State returned the letter with the notation, "I agree. C. H."

74. In October 1937 the Cuban Government proposed that all American countries join in representations to both factions in Spain during which the contending forces might discuss, before an international commission, terms for ending the war. Once again the United States refused to associate itself in any such proposal. Welles to Wright (Ambassador in Cuba), October 30, 1937 (SD File No. 852.00/6760). A similar proposal by the Mexican Government was also declined. Roosevelt to Welles, July 3, 1937 (SD File No. 852.00/5906½). As described in Chapter VIII, Roosevelt in late 1938 suggested a reversal of policy and was agreeable to the United States assuming the lead in securing an armistice in Spain. Such plans did not materialize however.

75. Dispatch from the U.S.S. *Quincy* to Naval Communications. Sent to the Department of State for information, August 14, 1936 (SD File No. 852.00/2589).

76. Bay to Hull, August 12, 1936 (SD File No. 852.00/2574: tel.).

77. For examples, see Bay to Hull, November 18, 1936 (SD File No. 852.00/3796: tel.); November 29, 1936 (SD File No. 852.00/3918: tel.); December 30, 1936 (SD File No. 852.00/4235: tel.). Portugal likewise served as a port of entry for war materials bound for Franco. The American Minister in Lisbon reported that "from the beginning of the Spanish revolution there have been clear indications that the Portuguese Government has regarded the success of the revolutionary movement as a matter of almost life and death and that it had indicated in many ways a definitely benevolent attitude to the principles represented by the revolutionary cause." Robert G. Caldwell (Minister in Portugal) to Hull, August 3, 1936 (SD File No. 852.00/2660: tel.).

78. Bullitt to Hull, July 30, 1939 (SD File No. 852.00/2325: tel.).

79. Franklin to Hull, December 2, 1936 (SD File No. 852.00/3960: tel.); also, *ibid.*, December 31, 1936 (SD File No. 852.00/4248: tel.).

80. Bowers to Acting Secretary Moore, December 10, 1936 (SD File No. 852.00/4179: tel.).

81. Detailed accounts of the activities of the Nonintervention Committee may be found in Toynbee, *Survey, 1937*, II, 222-376; Padelford, *International Law and Diplomacy in the Spanish Civil Strife*, pp. 53-120; Francis O. Wilcox, "Localization of the Spanish War," *American Political Science Review* (Menasha, Wis.) XXXII (April, 1938), 237-60. For British policy and the nonintervention system see Hubbard, "British Public Opinion and the Spanish Civil War, 1936-1939," 62-211. In reviewing the activities of the Nonintervention Committee former Ambassador Bowers commented that the "Non-Intervention Committee was the most cynically, disgracefully dishonest group that I know in history. It was completely under the thumb of Hitler and Chamberlain." Bowers to author, February 15, 1954. Foreign intervention in Spain will be more fully treated in Chapter IV.

82. There were press reports that the United States would be invited to become a member of the Nonintervention Committe. On August 7, however, the French Chargé d'Affaires (Jules Henry) called at the State Department and informed Acting Secretary of State Phillips that such reports were false. In explaining the American position, Phillips replied that the United States was in sympathy with French efforts to keep the Spanish War from spreading, but that this country preferred to inaugurate its own nonintervention system without collaboration with the countries of Europe. William Phillips, August 11, 1936 (SD File No. 852.00/2692: memo.).

83. Maxwell Blake (Consul General at Tangier) to Hull, July 21, 1936 (SD File No. 852.00/2190a: tel.).

84. Hull to Blake, July 22, 1936 (SD File No. 852.00/2190b: tel.).

85. Edward L. Reed (Chief of the Division of Mexican Affairs) September 14, 1936 (SD File No. 852.24/108: memo.).

86. *Ibid.*, September 15, 1936 (SD File No. 852.24/109).

87. Boal to Moore, December 30, 1936 (SD File No. 711.00111/1: tel.).

88. Moore to Boal, December 31, 1936 (SD File No. 711.00111/5: tel.).

89. Boal to Moore, December 31, 1936 (SD File No. 711.00111/6: tel.).

90. For examples see correspondence between Hull and the American Ambassador to Mexico dated January 8, 1937 (SD File No. 711.00111/17); March 30, 1937 (SD File No. 852.24/349); March 31, 1937 (SD File No. 852.24/351); April 11, 1937 (SD File No. 852.24/370); and April 15, 1937 (SD File No. 852.24/379). A personal plea was made by the Mexican Ambassador to President Roosevelt in an effort to persuade the United States to sanction the transshipment of American arms to Spain via Mexico, but the President only reiterated the American position which had already been made clear by the State Department. Hull to Josephus Daniels (American Ambassador to Mexico), April 26, 1937 (SD File No. 852.24/379a: tel.).

91. Wendelin to Hull, August 8, 1936 (SD File No. 852.00/2489: tel.).

92. Bowers to Phillips, December 10, 1936 (SD File No. 852.00/4179: tel.). For other of Bowers' reports, see *ibid.*, November 9, 1936 (SD File No. 852.00/3728: tel.); also, *ibid.*, November 20, 1936 (SD File No. 852.00/3937: tel.).

93. Bowers to Hull, July 20, 1937 (SD File No. 852.00/6132).

94. Hull, *Memoirs*, I, 483.

95. *Press Releases*, December 28, 1936.

Chapter Four

Legislating Neutrality

Within six months after the outbreak of the Spanish Civil War it had clearly assumed a threefold character: there was a military conflict between contesting Spanish factions; there was a violent social struggle between advocates of revolutionary change and those of reaction; and there was the international complication of Spain as a pawn in the European struggle for power. Power politics and clashing policies led to open German and Italian aid for the Insurgents and Soviet aid for the Loyalists. Thus, foreign interference and intervention served to increase the bitterness of a domestic struggle and threatened to turn the Spanish conflagration into an international war.

In Europe twenty-seven nations had accepted a French proposal to form an international committee to supervise the application of the nonintervention accord. In actual practice, however, the Nonintervention League had thus far failed to accomplish its objectives and the international aspects of the Spanish conflict became increasingly evident.[1] Had the United States permitted arms and munitions to be shipped to Spain, the purpose of the nonintervention agreement, at least as envisioned by Great Britain and France, would have been defeated. The President, however, was powerless to prevent such shipments because the Neutrality Act of February 1936 authorized him to impose an arms embargo only in the event of war "between or among nations."[2] In lieu of any legal right to prohibit shipment of war implements to Spain, the State Department had publicized its policy of moral suasion in an effort to prevent the American people from using the Spanish War as a means of personal profit.

It was not until the conflict had been in progress for over five months that any American citizen defied this policy. On December 28, 1936, the Department of State found itself obliged to grant licenses for the export to the port of Bilbao of a shipment of airplane engines valued at $2,777,000.[3] Under the law the Department had no alternative than "reluctantly" to issue the licenses and publicly to express regret that one citizen had "insisted upon his legal rights in the face of this government's noninvolvement policy, and with full understanding thereof."[4] While the Madrid Government was naturally pleased with the news of these licenses, President Roosevelt, at a press conference the following day, denounced the action of the American exporter as unpatriotic, though legal.[5]

This incident occurred at a time when France and Great Britain were attempting to implement and strengthen the program of nonintervention. The British Foreign Office, according to one dispatch, queried the American Ambassador in London concerning the rumored export of American planes to Spain and indicated anxiety lest such action undermine the efforts of the Nonintervention Committee.[6] Ambassador Bowers cabled the State Department that the granting of the licenses was causing much comment. The British Ambassador, he said, declared that the announcement came at a most critical moment of negotiations with Berlin and that it did much damage since the Germans cited American action in justification of Hitler's policy of intervention in Spain.[7] Acting Secretary Moore notified the European embassies that the licenses had been granted because the existing Neutrality Act did not apply to civil strife. Under no circumstances, he continued, should the incident be regarded by any foreign government as a change in American policy. Moore also stated that the State Department regretted the "unfortunate non-compliance by an American citizen with this Government's strict nonintervention policy . . . . [but] the right to a license could not be denied."[8]

The Spanish Ambassador called on Acting Secretary Moore and expressed regret that the United States should look with displeasure on the Cuse shipments. Ambassador de los Ríos stated that "he considered our policy of nonintervention extremely unfortunate as he felt that the democratic countries should support the Spanish Government in its struggle against fascism." Moore explained that the American policy of nonintervention "was based upon our desire and determination that this country not become involved in a situation in Europe which might lead to war, and that no doubt steps would be taken to grant legislative authority to this Government to prevent shipments of arms and implements of war to both sides in the Spanish struggle."[9]

The State Department was very concerned that one citizen in the assertion of his legal rights could draw the United States closer to European complications which the Congress had tried to avoid. In an attempt to remedy the situation President Roosevelt announced on December 28 that he had given his approval to amend the Neutrality Act to cover Spain as soon as Congress convened in January.[10] Several days later the President conferred with Acting Secretary Moore, Senator Key Pittman (D-Nevada), Chairman of the Senate Foreign Relations Committee, and Representative Sam McReynolds (D-Tennessee), Chairman of the House Committee on Foreign Affairs, concerning revision of the neutrality law. At that conference it was agreed that Pittman and McReynolds would introduce resolutions to ban shipments of arms, ammunition, and implements of war to Spain. Pittman was of the opinion that the Spanish situation should be considered along with general neutrality legislation. Moore, however, realizing how much time would be consumed in such a debate, finally prevailed upon the Senator to deal with the matter as an emergency measure which would apply solely to existing conditions in Spain.[11]

From the State Department's point of view time was essential as the licensed munitions were being loaded in New York, and if they were to be stopped within the jurisdiction of this country, quick legislative action must be taken. On January 6 the President delivered his annual message to Congress, in which he requested that the Neutrality Act be amended "to cover specific points raised by the unfortunate civil strife in Spain."[12] The way was cleared for immediate action in both houses, apparently in the hope that not only could the law be amended before the Cuse shipments left New York, but also that prompt action would revoke nineteen licenses which the State Department had been obliged to issue on January 5 to a San Francisco arms broker covering the export of $4,607,000 in aircraft, rifles, machine guns, and cartridges to the Spanish Government.[13]

Originally, the President had favored a grant of discretionary authority to extend embargoes in the event of civil wars generally, but it was feared that opponents of such a measure would delay action on the matter. To expedite legislative action Senator Pittman asked the unanimous consent of the Senate for consideration, without prior reference to committee, of a resolution (S. J. Res. 3) specifically imposing an embargo on the shipment of munitions to Spain.[14] The preamble of the resolution stated that certain governments had recognized the Insurgents and that the Loyalists were receiving aid from the nationals of other countries; mention was also made of the nonintervention agreement among the European powers. This preamble was withdrawn, however, following criticism by Senator Arthur Vandenberg (R-Michigan) that it contained equivocal statements.[15]

In the discussion on the resolution Senator Gerald Nye (R-North Dakota) made it clear that he did not support either of the opposing sides in Spain, but added that he hoped the resolution was not going to be passed "in the name of neutrality, for, strictly speaking, neutrality it is not." Nye pointed out that the embargo placed a greater hardship on the Republican Government than on the Insurgents and suggested that if the United States wanted to undertake a strict neutrality policy, it should avoid singling out one country as Spain and should draft "an embargo policy that would apply automatically to every country when trouble like that in Spain may come anywhere upon the earth."[16] Senator Pittman answered the arguments of Nye by declaring that the Spanish embargo was neutrality because there is no "discretion" between either side in Spain. Besides, the Senator added, "I do not have the ability to formulate language which would define when such a state of civil war existed as we wanted to guard against."[17] Apparently the argument advanced by Pittman was convincing, because the Senate passed the arms embargo resolution without a dissenting vote on the same day that it was introduced.[18]

The resolution aroused considerably more discussion in the House. Some Congressmen were dismayed that the existing neutrality law had failed but were undecided whether it would be wise to pass an embargo directed against one state. Perhaps the most outspoken critic of the measure was Representative Maury Maverick (D-Texas), who posed several disconcerting questions to administrative leaders. Maverick cited the importance of the

Spanish Civil War and objected to unanimous consideration of the resolution without adequate time for debate. He pointed out that an embargo would be a reversal of long-standing American policy and added:

> I do not say that this resolution is wrong, but it refers to Spain alone. Last year I stated that the resolution on neutrality we enacted then was no good, and times have shown this to be true. I now say that this one is not either. If we are going to have neutrality, let us have it for the whole world; and if we do not have it for the whole world, let us not have it at all.
>
> We wanted neutrality the last time and we did not get it. This is not neutrality, it is against neutrality. We are taking a stand against a democratic government, the parliamentary Government of Spain; and we are not indulging in neutrality, because this is the opposite. I am in favor of neither side in any foreign country. But we must face the facts. I think we should have some time to discuss the matter and not just 20 minutes. We talk for hours, days, and weeks on matters which are unimportant, and we rush through matters of such grave importance as this.
>
> . . . I think this legislation is hasty and ill-advised. . . . It just covers Spain. Why should we not apply it equally to all countries? The revolution in Spain has been going on for 7 months. It has always been the practice of our Government to send munitions to the legal government, irrespective of its merits. If we are to send munitions at all send them to every nation — to Hitler or Mussolini if they have a revolution. It has always been the policy of this Nation to maintain the status quo of the recognized parliamentary government or of the de facto, or even the Fascist government. Why, then, should we pick out Spain and suddenly say that we will pass this bit of emergency legislation? . . . If we exclude Spain, let us exclude also Germany, Soviet Russia, Japan — all nations on earth, except possibly nations on our own Continent, which is another question.[19]

Other Congressmen agreed with the views expressed by Maverick. Representative Hamilton Fish (R-New York) stated that the Republican minority did not desire to "delay, obstruct, or hamper the majority in the passage of this bill," but asserted that since the resolution was a complete change of United States policy there should be adequate debate.[20] Representative Thomas Amlie (Progressive-Wisconsin) supported Maverick's stand that passage of the resolution constituted an unneutral act. He stated that the proposed measure was "an unfriendly act toward a government that is friendly to the United States."[21]

Representative McReynolds answered the critics of the resolution by declaring that an emergency existed and requested immediate action by the House.[22] He asked for unanimous consent to consider the resolution without debate, but the motion failed because of an objection by Representative John Bernard (Farmer-Laborite-Minnesota). The House then adjourned for fifteen minutes and upon reconvening received a message that the Senate had passed the Spanish embargo by vote of 81 to 0. Although this helped weaken House resistance considerably, McReynolds was forced to agree to a one-hour debate during which he argued that a full-dress debate on neutrality could come later when Congress considered a new neutrality law. He also pointed out that the resolution had the personal approval of President Roosevelt and Secretary Hull and then added: "I want to save this country from becoming involved in European wars, and I shall not be a party to the carnage and crucifixion that is going on in Spain."[23] As a point of order McReynolds objected to amendments applying the embargo to all countries instead of Spain alone.[24] Assisting the chairman in defending the measure during the short time allowed for debate were several other members of the House Committee on Foreign Affairs. Representative Luther Johnson (D-Texas) spoke of the necessity for immediate action and declared that the only persons who should oppose the measure were the munitions dealers;[25] while Representative Frank Kloeb (D-Ohio) stated that passage of the resolution was mandatory to meet an "immediate crisis."[26] Sam Rayburn (D-Texas) also lent his powerful support in favor of the Spanish embargo by maintaining that it was an emergency measure deserving prompt consideration.[27]

Despite the opposing arguments the House adopted the resolution on the same day that the President had requested it by a vote of 406 to 1.[28] The sole negative vote was cast by Representative Bernard who explained his vote by declaring that "Fascism is engaging in the open rape of Spain," and that the present legislation was "sham" neutrality because its object was to "choke off democratic Spain from its legitimate international rights at a time while it is being assailed by the Fascist hordes of Europe."[29] A somewhat similar view was expressed by Representative Burdick, who, in an extension of his remarks in the *Congressional Record*, defended the duly elected Government of Spain and regretted that the arms embargo was directed against it. He stated that it was impossible to vote against the bill for that would have indicated that he favored supplying arms to Spain; yet when voting for the bill he felt that he was giving aid and comfort to an enemy seeking to destroy the legal Government of Spain. He charged that many Congressmen voted for the resolution not knowing whether it was presented in good faith or was intended to take sides in the Spanish conflict.[30] There was also a bloc of thirty Congressmen who declared that they had voted for the Spanish embargo only with misgiving. They believed that "if an embargo is enforced against the Spanish Government, but not against other nations shipping to the Spanish Rebels, the United States is placed in the position of actually or constructively acting as cobelligerents with the forces attempting to overthrow the Spanish Government."[31]

The joint resolution of January 8, 1937, made it "unlawful to export arms, ammunition, or implements of war from any place in the United States, or possessions of the United States, to Spain or to any other foreign country for transshipment to Spain or for use of either of the opposing forces in Spain."[32] It also canceled previous licenses issued for that purpose. Although the resolution was passed by both houses of Congress on January 6, 1937, a legal technicality delayed the President's signature until January 8. On the previous day, however, the *Mar Contábrico*, carrying only a part of the cargo of planes and equipment sold by Cuse to the Spanish Government, had sailed hastily from New York harbor.[33]

The embargo resolution of January 8 was warmly received by General Franco, who declared: "President Roosevelt behaved in the manner of a true gentleman. His neutrality legislation, stopping export of war materials to either side — the quick manner in which it was passed and carried into effect — is a gesture we Nationalists shall never forget."[34] The Germans were also pleased. The semiofficial *Diplomatische Korrespondenz* saw the resolution as a furtherance of peace and stated: "Germany is loud in her praise of the United States embargo on arms shipments to Spain. The American attitude is compared favorably with that of all other nations, and regret is expressed only that the present definition of neutrality was not adopted twenty years ago."[35]

In contrast, the resolution met with intense opposition from certain groups in the United States. The editors of the *Nation* expressed the opinion that

> to take action now in denying supplies to the Spanish government in its hour of need would be a deliberately unfriendly act. . . . The United States would be taking sides in the Spanish conflict, and taking the side of the militarists, Hitler and Mussolini, against the government chosen by the Spanish people.[36]

A similar view was expressed by the editors of the *New Republic*, who stated that the American policy of neutrality left much to be desired and that the embargo on arms to Spain was a "violation of precedent and an unneutral gesture."[37]

Both the Communists and Socialists bitterly assailed the strict neutrality policy of the Administration. Earl Browder told 20,000 Communists gathered in New York City that the embargo was a "hostile act" toward a legally constituted, duly recognized government engaged in a fight against fascism.[38] Roy E. Burt, National Executive Secretary of the Socialist party in the United States, called the ban on arms to Spain a "pro-Fascist step" which was not neutrality but a form of direct aid to the Fascists. He declared that "this neutrality legislation coming now on the heel of British and French hypocrisy merely puts the United States in the camp of these false upholders of peace and democracy," and he concluded: "We will continue to exert every effort to aid the workers of Spain, confident that the solidarity of the workers of the world will be the only path for defeating Franco and insuring a working class victory in Spain."[39] Other representatives of the Socialist party expressed a similar view. Norman Thomas wrote President Roosevelt to request that the United States not impose an arms embargo against the Spanish Government as the Loyalists were fighting against fascism. He declared that

> in the long run it is not peace for the world, or even for America, which will be served by applying to the Spanish rebellion a general principle which should be asserted more

rigorously than is yet the case in congressional legislation concerning neutrality in international war. We plead for recognition of the possibly disastrous effects of your action in disarming the Spanish Government in the face of well-armed and ruthless rebel armies.[40]

At the request of the President, Assistant Secretary of State Moore drafted a suggested reply which was later sent to Thomas with Roosevelt's signature.[41] The President emphatically stated:

The Department of State, with my entire approval, soon after the beginning of the Civil War in Spain, took a definite stand on the subject of the export of arms to that country — a stand which was in entire conformity with our well-established policy of non-intervention and with the spirit of the recent neutrality act.

. . . it [is] clear that the civil conflict in Spain involves so many non-Spanish elements and has such wide international implications that a policy of attempting to discriminate between the parties would be dangerous in the extreme. Not only would we, by permitting unchecked the flow of arms to one party in the conflict, be involving ourselves directly in that European strife from which our people desire so deeply to remain aloof, but we would be deliberately encouraging those nations which would be glad of this pretext to continue their assistance to one side or the other in Spain and aggravating those disagreements among the European nations which are a constant menace to the peace of the world.[42]

From another quarter certain spokesmen for business interests appeared to question the advisability of an embargo if the commercial transactions of private firms were affected. The editors of the *Wall Street Journal* declared that the extension of the Neutrality Act to include Spain was desirable insofar as it prevented involvement in a general war, but asked whether this country was prepared to go so far as to ban shipments on a "cash and carry" basis to nations engaged in war, revolt or otherwise. They added that strict isolation might not be advisable if exports were to be prohibited.[43] The editors of the *Commercial and Financial Chronicle* also denounced the embargo as foreign intervention and charged that the State Department had violated diplomatic propriety by publicly arraigning a private shipment of arms to enable a friendly government to cope with a formidable rebellion. "If the commercial operations of private firms are to be denounced," they concluded, "for no better reason than that they do not accord with some policy which the administration hopes may be established later, we have exchanged government by law for government by executive opinion."[44]

The *New York Times* called the resolution a Congressional attempt to legislate foreign policy which might involve the country in war. The editors of the *Times* maintained that the Government must prepare for such emergencies, but that the President should have the authority to use discretion in the matter of applying embargoes.[45] A similar view was expressed in the *San Francisco Chronicle* by Chester Rowell, who feared that the exporting of munitions to Spain might lead to involvement in Europe. He was concerned, however, that Congress would enact a measure intended to keep the country out of war but which might have the opposite effect. Like the editors of the *New York Times*, Rowell believed that the President's hands should not be tied and that he should have the authority to take the steps necessary to maintain peace. He foresaw little or no opposition to the arms embargo and declared: "We have no avowed Communists and few conscious Fascists there [Congress] to try to get us into the Spanish War on one side or the other."[46] The editors of the *Louisville Courier-Journal* agreed that the President should have a free hand in determining the manner in which embargoes should be applied. They believed that arms embargoes alone were not effective and that an embargo on all supplies might become necessary for complete neutrality, but in any event such a policy should be determined by the President.[47]

Other papers were outspoken in their endorsement of the Spanish embargo. The editors of the *New Orleans States* congratulated Congress on its action. "Some Congressmen opposed the resolution," they asserted, "on the ground that, under international precedent, we enjoy the right to sell to an organized government in a civil conflict. But the European nations no longer show any regard for international law and why should this nation? Congress has done well to take its firm stand and say to Europe that we want no part in any new selfish struggle over there."[48] The editors of the *Christian Century* strongly approved of the embargo resolution, describing it as "an emphatic representation of the minds of the American people." The *Christian Century* was definitely isolationist at that time and pleaded for the United States to remain aloof from any European crisis.[49] Many Catholics and the Catholic press generally favored the embargo. The Catholic weekly, *America,* declared that the embargo would prevent the United States from becoming embroiled in the Spanish catastrophy.[50] Monsignor Frank A. Thill asserted that "our President has been highly and rightly commended for his true Americanism in insisting that we observe rigorous neutrality and keep out of all danger calculated to draw us into a European conflict."[51]

After the Spanish embargo had been imposed Congress promptly turned its attention to the revision and extension of the existing neutrality law which would expire on May 1, 1937. The legislation regarding the Spanish conflict had been a separate emergency act, and it was necessary that Congress decide what permanent neutrality measures would continue in effect. At that time neutrality by legislation was at the height of its popularity, and although there were some dissenters,[52] they were definitely in the minority as most Congressmen favored some type of mandatory measure to assure American nonintervention in the affairs of other nations. That there would be some kind of neutrality legislation was inevitable, but there was a long argument over the method to be employed.

As the new Congress convened in January 1937 some twenty bills were introduced, all designed to legislate peace for the United States. Both the Senate Committee on Foreign Relations and the House Committee on Foreign Affairs began hearings on the new legislation. During these hearings representatives of the Socialist party, the American League Against War and Fascism, the North American Committee to Aid Spanish Democracy, and the American Friends of Spanish Democracy protested against the arms embargo invoked against Spain, as well as provisions in the proposed legislation which would give the President authority to control the solicitation of war contributions. Herman F. Reissig, Executive Secretary of the North American Committee to Aid Spanish Democracy, told the Congressmen that the joint embargo resolution adopted in January ". . . is an affront to the recognized and friendly government of Spain. . . . It seems to be impossible to ask the people of a democracy like the United States, if they really believe in democracy, to be neutral as between a democratic government and a Fascist government." He concluded by saying that "sooner or later, we must decide whether we favor democracy or fascism. The only way permanently to establish peace is to remove the major cause of war, of which the greatest is fascism."[53] Similar statements were made by Roy E. Burt, Executive Secretary of the Socialist party, and Gardner Jackson, Chairman of the American Friends of Spanish Democracy.[54]

By the end of February the neutrality bills were reported back to both houses of Congress and debate began on the subject. The principal argument concerned the matter of Presidential discretion as to whether the so-called "cash and carry" formula should be applied. The House version of the bill stated that the President should have discretion as to what action should be taken in the event of war, either civil or among nations.[55] The Senate favored the clause which made it mandatory that the provisions of "cash and carry" go into effect as soon as the President issued a proclamation that certain countries were at war.[56] The final version of the bill as enacted into law provided that it would be applicable upon a finding by the President that there existed a state of war between two foreign states, or a state of civil strife in a foreign state. After the President had issued a proclamation to this effect, the law stated that it was mandatory that the trade in arms, the sale of securities of belligerents, and travel by Americans on belligerent vessels be prohibited; however, under the "cash and carry" provisions of the measure, the President was given the discretionary right to impose further restrictions on the carrying of goods other than arms. In addition the resolution made the collection of charitable funds for belligerents or factions in a civil war subject to the approval and regulation of the President.[57]

In regard to Spain the permanent Neutrality Act contained two principal provisions: the discretionary embargo power of the President in the event of civil strife; and the prohibition against solicitation of war contributions except under such rules and regulations as the President may prescribe. On the same day that the President signed the new neutrality law he issued a proclamation declaring that a state of civil strife existed in Spain "under such conditions that the export of implements of war would threaten and endanger the peace of the United States."[58] Thus the arms embargo that was imposed against Spain on January 8, 1937, was continued.[59]

The State Department issued regulations on May 5 governing the soliciting and receiving of contributions for use in Spain. This portion of the Neutrality Act had aroused considerable debate in Congress. Chairman McReynolds of the House Committee on Foreign Affairs defended this provision on the grounds that "we must keep our people as neutral as possible," but added that the bill would not prohibit solicitations of funds by the Red Cross or other organizations "not a party to the Government."[60] Representative Johnson (D-Texas) referred to funds already collected in the United States on behalf of one faction in Spain and declared: "We want our people to be neutral, and having meetings and raising money for factions at war is not neutrality."[61] Senator Pittman told opponents of this provision in the Senate that it was merely to prevent fraudulent solicitation and that no legitimate group would be bothered. "The whole policy of our legislation with regard to Spain," he added, "is to keep out of the fight over there and to show no preference for either side."[62] Such arguments, however, did not silence those who opposed the regulation of contributions. Representative Gerald Boileau (Progressive-Wisconsin) declared: "I do not believe that in the name of neutrality we should forget those finer instincts of humanity and close our eyes to the suffering of men, women, and children who are in need of medical aid."[63] Senator Nye likewise strongly opposed any phraseology in the Neutrality Act which would prohibit medical aid to Spain.[64] Nevertheless, in spite of such strong criticism, the House defeated by a vote of 87 to 16 an amendment which would have lessened governmental restrictions on humanitarian assistance to foreign agencies.[65]

Twenty-six organizations complied with the regulations as stipulated by the State Department and it was believed that the law did increase the possibility that the funds would be used for *bona fide* relief purposes. In many instances the Department refused to permit an organization to solicit funds until assurances were received to this effect.[66] The publicity given the monthly statements tended to keep down administrative expenses and insure that the funds were to be used for which they were collected.[67] The Department was very lenient and in no case did it refuse to register an applicant, but such organizations as the Society for Technical Aid to Spanish Democracy did not register and were presumed to have suspended activities.

Although the United States possessed legislation which prohibited the shipment of arms to either Spanish faction, other nations continued to supply their Spanish partisans despite commitment to the nonintervention agreement. The action of Germany and Italy was a case in point. On March 4, 1937, Ambassador William E. Dodd quoted German Minister of Foreign Affairs Konstantin von Neurath as stating that "we shall never allow the present government of Spain to win the civil war. It is Communism and we shall never allow that in any European state."[68] Mussolini, anxious to extend his power and influence in the Mediterranean, likewise declared that Italian forces would remain in Spain until a final Franco victory was assured.[69] This intervention in Spain by the Fascists was an "open secret," and in the spring and summer of 1937 sentiment developed in the United States to extend the arms embargo to Germany, Italy and possibly Portugal. It was the bombing of Guernica by the Franco forces, employing German and Italian planes, so vividly described in the American press, which served to increase this feeling.[70] The editors of the *Nation*, for example, argued that there was not a civil war in Spain, but an invasion of Spanish territory by Italian and German troops; therefore the arms embargo should apply to Germany and Italy as well as Spain.[71]

This demand was supported by a number of Congressmen, several antifascist organizations, and a large portion of the American press. As early as February 19, 1937, Representative Bernard introduced a joint resolution to extend the existing neutrality law to Germany and Italy.[72] In support of his resolution he declared:

These countries have invaded the territory of Spain and are now actively engaged in a war against the democratically elected government of that country with which the government of the United States continues to maintain friendly relations. . . . I think that we should support the people of Spain against the Fascist armies who are now conducting a murderous war against the Spanish people, which spares neither women nor children. The least we can do to make up for the embargo against the Spanish Government is to impose equal restrictions against the Fascist governments who are engaging in an act of unwarranted aggression. Passage of this resolution will, I feel, reflect the sentiments of the great many of the American people whose sentiments are quite properly with the struggle of the Spanish people for democracy and against fascism.[73]

Representative John Coffee added that "this joint resolution seeks to remove the unfortunate stigma attached to the passing of the recent Neutrality Act placing an embargo on shipment of munitions to Spain by applying the 1935 Neutrality Act against those belligerents seeking to overthrow other democracies."[74] This proposal was referred to the House Committee on Foreign Affairs and was promptly shelved. It did, however, focus attention on the part Germany and Italy were taking in securing a fascist victory in Spain.[75]

Within the next few months efforts were continued by certain members of Congress to extend the arms embargo to Germany and Italy. In June 1937 a delegation of twenty-one Congressmen presented a formal statement to Secretary Hull which declared:

Further delay in including Italy and Germany within the embargo now enforced against the legitimate government of Spain is tantamount to a declaration that the United States Government, despite all official statements to the contrary, has sided with the traitor General Francisco Franco and his allies, the Fascist invaders of Spanish soil.

After Almería the American people certainly cannot accept the reply made by you on a former occasion — namely, that German and Italian participation in the Spanish war has not been established by evidence. To the plain people of this country evidence of German and Italian aggression now appears overwhelming. We have also found the evidence more than sufficient to warrant prompt action.[76]

Hull received the Congressmen in his office at the State Department and after hearing the statement replied that "this is not our war. We must be cautious. We must be quiet."[77] Even as late as May 11, 1937, the Secretary of State was apparently not convinced that the reports of German and Italian participation in the Spanish Civil War were actually true. Hull had received a letter from Congressman Jerry O'Connell calling his attention to the situation in Spain, and demanding that Germany and Italy be subjected to the arms embargo as set forth in American neutrality laws. The Secretary replied that it would be impossible

for the United States to take such a step as "there is no evidence"
to support the claim that units of the German and Italian military
forces are in Spain.[78]

Evidently Hull had his personal reasons for making such a
statement. Dispatches from practically every American Ambassador in Europe had for many months kept the State Department
fully informed as to foreign intervention in Spain. For example,
Ambassador Bowers wrote the Secretary of State on March 16,
1937, that

> . . . the disclosures of the past weeks have reduced to utter
> mockery the pretension that the war in Spain is anything other
> than a foreign war of the Fascist Powers against the Govern-
> ment of Spain. There are now thousands of the regular Italian
> army on the Guadalajara front and under the command of
> Italian Generals, who are the real directing command. With
> the Italian army are a much smaller number of German soldiers.
> These, from all accounts, have taken precedence even over the
> Moors, on whom Franco has formerly depended for his hardest
> fighting.[79]

In another report dated February 23, 1937, Lieutenant Colonel
Horace H. Fuller, American Military Attaché in France, stated
that he had learned from the German Military Attaché that there
were between thirty and fifty thousand Italians with Franco and
thirty thousand Germans.[80] It is difficult to believe that Hull was
uninformed of these reports.

Nor was sentiment to extend the embargo confined to members of the House. In commenting on the bombardment by the
German navy of the Spanish city of Almería, Senator William E.
Borah (R-Idaho) declared that apparently an act of war had been
committed and that "we should apply our Neutrality Law to all
participants."[81] In March 1937 Senator Nye submitted a resolution (S. Res. 100) stating

> that the Secretary of State is hereby requested, if not incom-
> patible with the public interest, to advise the Senate through
> its Committee on Foreign Relations whether the existing Neu-
> trality Laws of the United States are sufficient to provide an
> embargo against nations whose armed forces are engaged in
> active warfare in a nation where a state of civil war exists,

which state of civil war has caused our Government to declare embargoes against exportation of arms, ammunition, and implements of war to that nation.[82]

The Nye resolution was widely acclaimed in the liberal press throughout the country. The editors of the *Washington Post* cited evidence of alleged proof that active foreign troops were in Spain, and declared that it is not optional but mandatory that the Neutrality Law be extended to the Axis nations.[83] The editors of the *Pittsburg Press* stated that

Offhand, we would say that Italy is certainly fighting somebody in Spain, for she has an estimated 80,000 troops there, plus several hundred airplanes and tanks. Even the Italian Foreign Office cannot maintain that the soldiers are there simply for maneuvers or that they are innocent bystanders. . . . In traditional diplomatic fashion, the Department could sidestep Senator Nye's question. But we hope that it won't. This is too serious a crisis to play blind man's bluff.[84]

Similar expressions were found in the editorial columns of the *Philadelphia Record* and the *New Republic*.[85]

On the other hand Senator Pittman expressed his opposition to the Nye resolution and requested that it be referred to the Committee on Foreign Relations. In justifying this move Pittman maintained that the resolution was not in proper form since it asked the Secretary of State to render a legal opinion which by law he cannot do. In further argument against the measure Pittman declared that "as to whether or not any armed forces, under the definition of 'armed forces' generally recognized in military matters, are engaged in war in Spain, I have no evidence," and concluded:

The situation is as well in hand as the great governments in the world who are in the area of this threatened world war can have it in hand. They have authorized committees to try these questions. . . . In that circumstance why should we attempt to drag our Government into the fire of this serious and dangerous question which threatens universal war? . . . I think this matter should not be stirred up in this country when there is nothing that we can accomplish by stirring it up except to arouse hatred.[86]

Thus on a motion by the Senator from Nevada it was agreed that the resolution be referred to the Committee on Foreign Relations. There it was shelved and failed to reach the floor of the Senate for final consideration.[87]

As a result of the strong agitation to extend the embargo to Germany and Italy, a conference was held by high State Department officers to consider this new development. The decision was reached that there was no existing state of war between nations and that the presence of foreign "volunteers" in Spain did not create a state of war. Secretary Hull maintained that it would be illogical for the United States to find that a state of war existed between Spain on the one hand and Germany and Italy on the other when the Spanish Government itself had not taken that position. He believed that the Nye resolution was an effort to influence the United States into taking sides in the conflict, and that the proposed embargo would be ineffective since Germany and Italy were importing a relatively insignificant quantity of war materials from this country. It was agreed, therefore, not to attempt an embargo against the Axis powers as such action might also seriously endanger the nonintervention efforts of Great Britain and France.[88]

Despite the State Department's expressed disapproval of extending the embargo, on June 29 the President sent the following note to Hull:

> For many reasons I think that if Mussolini or the Italian Government or Hitler or the German Government have made any official admissions or statements that their Government armed forces are actually taking part in the fighting in Spain on the side of Franco, or are engaging in the Spanish War, then in such case we shall have to act under the Neutrality Act. I am thinking about precedents and the future. It has been our contention that war exists if the government armed forces of any nation upon the territory of another nation are engaged in fighting.

The President requested that the Department cable the American Ambassadors in Rome and London to determine their opinion on the matter. "According to some newspapers," he commented, "Mussolini has personally directed participation by the regular Italian armed forces — and Hitler has also made the same kind of statement."[89] Roosevelt was not totally dependent on the press for this information, since Ambassadors Bowers and Bullitt kept him fully informed by means of personal letters. On April 12, 1937, Bullitt wrote the President that Franco's army was composed of 60,000 Italians, 15,000 Moroccans, and only 15,000 to 20,000 Spaniards, while the Spanish Government forces were almost all Spaniards with the exception of 6,000 to 10,000 foreigners. Bullitt added that withdrawal of volunteers would not hurt the Government but would cost Franco three fourths of his army.[90] The President was also possibly influenced in taking this step by an old Harvard schoolmate, José Camprubí, who was at the time editor of *La Prensa*, a Spanish language newspaper in New York. Camprubí wrote several letters to Roosevelt and visited the White House in an effort to convince the President that the United States should take some action to stop foreign intervention in Spain.[91]

In deference to the President's wishes, Secretary Hull sent cables to the American Ambassadors in London and Rome asking for their views and comments on this proposed step. Hull explained that considerable pressure had been brought to bear upon the President by members of Congress, private individuals, and organizations and societies for placing an embargo upon the shipment of arms to Germany and Italy on the grounds that a state of war existed between those countries and Spain. The Secretary declared that because of recent overt acts by Germany and Italy it may become necessary at any moment to give serious consideration to the relationship of Germany and Italy to the Spanish conflict.[92] Ambassador Robert W. Bingham replied that the British felt that any departure from the spirit of neutrality legislation would be regarded by Europe as a "gratuitous interference in continental affairs." Furthermore, he continued, any application of the arms embargo to Germany and Italy might logically have to be extended to other countries as well.[93] Ambassador William Phillips cabled that the Italians were of the opinion that France and Russia had given assistance to the Madrid Government, and since Italy formally recognized the Franco Government, the Italians were justified in giving aid to the Insurgents. He added that the Italian Government would resent any embargo directed solely against it unless similar action was taken in regard to all countries believed to have rendered aid to the Loyalists. Phillips warned that if the President declared a state of war existed between Italy and Spain, other countries might do likewise, which would increase the possibility that the war would spread beyond Spanish frontiers.[94] When these facts and comments were placed before the President, he agreed that American policy should remain unchanged and that an arms embargo would not be applied against Germany and Italy unless a general war broke out in Europe.[95]

There was renewed agitation to extend the embargo to Germany and Italy in the fall of 1937. The publication of the *Spanish White Book*, with photostatic copies of captured Italian documents indicating that complete units of the Italian army were serving in Spain, and the publication of Italian casualty lists suggested that the State Department had sufficient evidence that Italy had committed acts of war against the Spanish Government.[96] The National Lawyers Guild urged the State Department to extend the embargo to Germany and Italy,[97] and Norman Thomas wrote a personal letter to the President asking that such action be taken.[98] Roosevelt was still concerned about the matter, since he sent the letter to Hull along with the query, "What do you think I can reply to this?"[99] The Secretary drafted a reply which, said Hull, "purposely refrained from discussing issues involved, since publicity will undoubtedly be given to your reply and new developments . . . in Spain . . . may occur to change the picture overnight."[100] In the reply sent to Thomas, Roosevelt stated that he was "continuing to give [his] closest attention to all developments with regard to the situation in Spain which may affect the application of the Neutrality Act to Italy or to any other country." He also pointed out that Italy had exported only $169,260.18 in such products during the first seven months of 1937 and there was no evidence that these materials were going to Spain.[101] Thomas replied that he appreciated the President's letter but aside from the cash volume of shipments "there is the question of principle and of the even-handed application of neutrality which has to be considered."[102]

It is possible that President Roosevelt declined to extend the arms embargo because he did not wish to pronounce moral judgment on the activities of the Axis powers in Spain. There was the further consideration that by going beyond the judgment of the Nonintervention Committee, the President would have assumed for the United States single-handed responsibility for localizing the Spanish War.[103] In any event it was probable that most Americans were more disturbed by the danger that the United States might become involved in European affairs than by acts of alleged injustice committed against the Republican Government of Spain.

NOTES

1. Of course it could be argued that the Nonintervention Committee did eventually accomplish its objective as the war was kept from spreading beyond Spanish frontiers. Nevertheless, the Committee was unable to keep a steady flow of Italian and German arms from reaching Franco, and, to a lesser extent, Soviet and French arms from reaching the Loyalists.

2. Department of State, *Peace and War,* pp. 313-14.

3. The applicant for the licenses was Robert Cuse, a naturalized Latvian and a representative of the Vimalert Company of Jersey City, New Jersey, which had been acting as an agent for the Spanish Government.

4. *Press Releases,* December 30, 1936. Since the enactment of the Neutrality Law, no export of arms, ammunition, or implements of war was lawful without a license from the Board of Munitions Control, whose authority was vested in the State Department. Airplanes for military use were included in the category of controlled exports.

5. *New York Times,* December 30, 1936. A spokesman for the aircraft industry (L. W. Rogers, President of the Aeronautical Chamber of Commerce) declared: "American aircraft manufacturers are cooperating with the government 100 per cent in seeing that their products are not exported abroad contrary to the spirit of neutrality expressed by the present law and the policy of administration . . . [but] American manufacturers have no way of controlling resale of their products on the part of private owners." *Ibid.*

6. *Ibid.,* December 29, 1936.

7. Bowers to Moore, December 31, 1936 (SD File No. 711.00111/52/15: tel.).

8. Moore to Bullitt, December 29, 1936 (SD File No. 711.00111/10: tel.).

9. James C. Dunn, December 31, 1936 (SD File No. 711.00111/52/38: memo.).

10. *New York Times,* December 29, 1936.

11. Moore to Roosevelt, January 5, 1937 (FDR Official Files, R. Walton Moore File). See also Franklin D. Roosevelt, January 5, 1937 (FDR Official Files, No. 1561: memo.).

12. *Congressional Record,* 75 Cong., 1 Sess., LXXXI (January 6, 1937), 84.

13. *Press Releases,* February 6, 1937. These licenses were later revoked on January 8, 1937, in accordance with the joint resolution of Congress passed on that date.

14. The text of the resolution was as follows: "Resolved: That during the existence of the state of civil strife now obtaining in Spain it shall, from and after the approval of this resolution, be unlawful to export arms, ammunition, or implements of war from any place in the United States, or possessions of the United States, to Spain or to any other foreign country for transshipment to Spain or for use of either of the opposing forces in Spain.

"Arms, ammunition, or implements of war, the exportation of which is prohibited by this resolution, are those enumerated in the President's proclamation No. 2163, of April 10, 1936.

"Licenses hithertofore issued under existing law for the exportation of arms, ammunition, or implements of war to Spain, shall, as to all future exportations thereunder, ipso facto, be deemed to be cancelled.

"Whoever in violation of any of the provisions of this resolution shall export, or attempt to export, or cause to be exported, either directly or indirectly, arms, ammunition, or implements of war from the United States or any of its possessions, shall be fined not more than $10,000 or imprisoned not more than 5 years, or both. When in the judgment of the President the conditions described in this resolution shall have ceased to exist he shall proclaim such fact, and the provisions thereupon cease to apply." *Congressional Record,* 75 Cong., 1 Sess., LXXXI (January 6, 1937), 90.

15. *Ibid.,* 76.

16. *Ibid.,* 77-79. Senator Nye later became one of the strongest advocates to repeal the Spanish arms embargo.

17. *Ibid.,* 78.

18. *Ibid.,* 80.

19. *Ibid.,* 86-87.

20. *Ibid.,* 93-94.

21. *Ibid.,* 93. For similar points of view see remarks by Representatives John Bernard (Farmer-Laborite, Minnesota), Harold Knutson (R-Minnesota), Usher Burdick (R-North Dakota), Thomas O'Malley (D-Wisconsin), and Harry Sauthoff (Progressive-Wisconsin). *Ibid.,* 86-99, A13-14.

22. McReynolds was referring to the loading of the Cuse shipment in New York which was being expedited so that the Spanish vessel, *Mar Cantábrico,* could clear the three-mile limit before Congress could take action.

23. *Congressional Record,* 75 Cong., 1 Sess., LXXXI (January 6, 1937), 92.

24. *Ibid.,* 96-97. Under the rules of the House amendments can be objected to on the ground that they are not germane to the bill. Therefore, there was no possible chance to make amendments to a limited and narrow neutrality resolution if the objection is made and sustained by the Chair, as happened in this case.

25. *Ibid.,* 90-91.

26. *Ibid.,* 93.

27. *Ibid.,* 89.

28. *Ibid.,* 99.

29. *Ibid.,* (January 22, 1937), A65-66.

30. *Ibid.,* (January 6, 1937), A13-14.

31. *Ibid.* (February 2, 1937), A130.

32. *Ibid.* (January 6, 1937), 90.

33. At the request of two American fliers claiming back pay of $1,200 owed them by the Spanish Government, the Coast Guard served a writ granted by a federal judge on the Captain of the *Mar Cantábrico* after the vessel had cleared Sandy Hook in Long Island Sound. The writ, however, applied only to personal property assigned to War Minister Indalecio Prieto. None was found and the vessel was allowed to proceed on course. A Coast

Guard cutter and plane remained with the *Mar Cantábrico* until the three-mile limit was passed in the event a message was received that the arms embargo against Spain had been signed into law by the President. After the vessel left the United States it proceeded to Vera Cruz, Mexico, where it took on additional supplies. The drama came to an ironic close when, despite camouflage as a British ship, the vessel was captured by Franco's forces in the Bay of Biscay. *New York Times,* March 10, 1937. Senator Nye charged that Garcia and Diaz, owners of a steamship firm in New York, were part of an espionage system serving General Franco, and that the *Mar Cantábrico* was apprehended because it was spied upon by agents reporting to Garcia and Diaz. The Senator declared that such activities threatened and violated American neutrality. *Congressional Record,* 75 Cong., 1 Sess., LXXXI (May 10, 1937), 4269-72.

34. *New York American,* February 1, 1937.

35. *New York Times,* January 8, 1937.

36. *Nation* (New York), CXLIV (January 9, 1937), 33-34.

37. *New Republic* (New York), XCI (July 14, 1937), 261.

38. *New York Times,* January 21, 1937.

39. *Socialist Call,* January 16, 1937.

40. Norman Thomas to President Roosevelt, December 29, 1936 (FDR Official Files, No. 422C).

41. Franklin D. Roosevelt, January 4, 1937 (FDR Official Files, No. 422C: memo.). Moore to Roosevelt, January 7, 1937 (FDR Official Files No. 422C).

42. Roosevelt to Thomas, December (?January) 25, 1937 (FDR Official Files, No. 422C).

43. *Wall Street Journal,* January 2, February 5, 1937.

44. *Commercial and Financial Chronicle* (New York), CXLIV (January 14, 1937), 14-15.

45. *New York Times,* December 30, 1936.

46. Chester Rowell, *San Francisco Chronicle,* January 2, 5, 13, 1937.

47. *Louisville Courier-Journal,* January 21, 24, 1937.

48. *New Orleans States,* January 7, 1937.

49. *Christian Century* (Chicago), XLIV (January 20, 1937), 70. This attitude toward the embargo was not maintained throughout the course of the war. Later the editors took issue with the Catholics over the Spanish conflict and strongly suggested that the democratic Government of Spain be permitted to purchase arms in this country to defend itself against fascism.

50. *America* (New York), LVI (January 9, 1937), 314.

51. *Tidings* (Los Angeles), the official organ of the Archdiocese of Los Angeles, January 22, 1937.

52. Representative Charles Eaton (R-New Jersey) decried the "universal belief that you can enact a law to govern everything and settle everything" and stated that he was skeptical of "neutrality by legislation." *Congressional Record,* 75 Cong., 1 Sess., LXXXI (March 12, 1937), 2171-72; Senator Joseph Robinson (D-Arkansas) declared that laws passed by Congress cannot accomplish everything because there is no law which will prevent war. *Ibid.* (April 29, 1937), 3946.

53. U. S. Congress, House, *Hearings Before the Committee on Foreign Affairs: American Neutrality Policy, 1937*, H. J. Res. 147, 75 Cong., 1 Sess. (Washington, 1937), 143-46.

54. *Ibid.*, 131-32, 150-51.

55. The House Committee on Foreign Affairs majority report favored giving the President discretionary power to levy embargoes, while the minority report felt that this discretionary power might lead to war. *Ibid.*, 164-77.

56. *Congressional Record*, 75 Cong., 1 Sess., LXXXI (April 29, 1937), 3940-45; 3974-75.

57. The text of the Neutrality Act of 1937 can be found in State Department, *Peace and War*, pp. 355-67. The measure was passed by a vote of 63 to 6 in the Senate and 377 to 12 in the House. For an analysis of the Act see Buell, "The Neutrality Act of 1937," pp. 166-80; and Dulles and Armstrong, "Legislating Peace," pp. 1-12.

58. *Press Releases*, May 1, 1937.

59. A controversial point, however, was whether the President's proclamation of May 1, 1937, superseded the joint resolution of January 8, 1937, which imposed the Spanish embargo. Advocates of repealing the embargo argued that it did, and thus the President, by revoking his May 1 proclamation could alter American Spanish policy so as to allow the Loyalists to purchase arms in this country. Those who desired retention of the embargo claimed that even if the President revoked his proclamation of May 1, the arms embargo would still remain in effect because of the joint resolution passed in January.

60. *Congressional Record*, 75 Cong., 1 Sess., LXXXI (March 12, 1937), 2157. Later, McReynolds declared: "No war occurs in Europe but what some of the foreign population groups in the United States immediately begin to take sides. We want to stop, as much as possible, the anger and rivalry which would thus occur among our own citizens, who should think more of the United States of America than they seem to think of the countries whence they came." *Ibid.* (April 29, 1937), 3973. It would seem, however, that the Congressman overlooked the fact that most individuals sympathetic to one of the opposing sides in Spain were native-born Americans.

61. *Ibid.* (March 18, 1937), 2401.

62. *Ibid.* (April 29, 1937), 3953.

63. *Ibid.* (March 16, 1937), 2294.

64. *Ibid.* (April 29, 1937), 3953. See also remarks by Representative John Coffee (D-Washington), *ibid.* (March 16, 1937), 2295-2302; and Representative Henry Teigan (Farmer-Labor-Minnesota), *ibid.* (March 16, 1937), 2301-02.

65. *Ibid.* (March 18, 1937), 2401. To placate his critics, however, Chairman McReynolds introduced, and the House adopted, an amendment which stated: "Nothing in subsection (a) shall be construed to prohibit the solicitation or collection of funds to be used for medical aid and assistance or for food and clothing to relieve human suffering when made by a person or persons or organizations when not acting for or on behalf of such government or political factions wherein civil strife exists." *Ibid.* (March 18, 1937), 2399.

66. By the end of the war in March 1939 the records of the State Department showed that twenty-six organizations had collected over two million

dollars, most of which was expended in a humanitarian effort to aid the Spanish Government. *Press Releases,* April 1, 1939.

67. One witness told the House Un-American Activities Committee that little money raised by the North American Committee to Aid Spanish Democracy actually reached Spain, but was used to buy luxuries for the political commissars. *New York Times,* November 30, 1939.

68. William E. Dodd, Jr., and Martha Dodd (eds), *Ambassador Dodd's Diary* (New York, 1941), p. 389.

69. *New York Times,* February 5, 1939. For a thorough account of Axis intervention in Spain, see Hubbard, "British Public Opinion and the Spanish Civil War," pp. 78-99.

70. G. L. Steer, Spanish correspondent for the *New York Times,* wrote: "I have seen and measured the enormous bomb holes at Guernica, which, since I passed through the town the day before, I can testify were not there then." *New York Times,* April 28, 1937. The bombing of Guernica is more fully treated in Chapter VI.

71. *Nation,* CXLIV (January 23, 1937), 88.

72. *Congressional Record,* 75 Cong., 1 Sess., LXXXI (February 19, 1937), 1452.

73. *New York Times,* February 20, 1937.

74. *Ibid.*

75. A similar resolution (H. J. Res. 390) was introduced by Representative Jerry O'Connell on June 1, 1937. It too died in committee. *Congressional Record,* 75 Cong., 1 Sess., LXXXI (June 1, 1937), 5236.

76. *New York Times,* June 3, 1937. On May 29 the German battleship *Deutschland,* in the Insurgent port of Iviza, was bombed by Loyalist planes. Twenty-three men were reported killed and eighty-three wounded. Two days later the German navy bombarded the Loyalist city of Almeriá in retaliation, with heavy loss of life and property.

77. *Ibid.*

78. *Congressional Record,* 75 Cong., 1 Sess., LXXXI (May 11, 1937), A1131-32. See also Hull to O'Connell, May 7, 1937 (SD File No. 852.48 Relief/4).

79. Bowers to Hull, March 16, 1937 (SD File No. 852.00/5051). In a letter to the author Bowers wrote that he was "amazed" that as late as 1937 Hull said that there was no evidence to support the claim that units of the German and Italian armies were in Spain. "He knew better," said Bowers, because "I had informed him minutely and even the press was reporting their activity and presence." Bowers to author, February 15, 1954.

80. Horace H. Fuller, February 23, 1937 (SD File No. 852.00/4989: Rept.).

81. *New York Times,* May 31, 1937.

82. *Congressional Record,* 75 Cong., 1 Sess., LXXXI (March 25, 1937), 2737.

83. *Ibid.* (April 9, 1937), 3317.

84. *Ibid.,* 3318-19.

85. *Ibid.,* 3317; *New Republic,* XCI (July 14, 1937), 261.

86. *Congressional Record,* 75 Cong., 1 Sess., LXXXI (April 9, 1937), 3319.

87. In support of the Committee's judgment in deferring action on the Nye resolution, Pittman announced that "it might endanger our peace." He then added: "The President has authority to decide if a state of war exists and if the Neutrality Act should be invoked. The European nonintervention nations are seeking to keep the war localized in Spain, and so far they have succeeded. There is nothing that we can do to aid them, and any attempted action on our part might disrupt their efforts and endanger our own pact." *New York Times,* June 3, 1937.

88. Hull, *Memoirs,* I, 510-11. Another related problem giving the State Department concern was the demonstrations before the Italian and German embassies protesting intervention in Spain by Italy and Germany. Secretary Hull wrote Senator Pittman that if the United States did not extend protection to foreign representatives here, American interests would suffer abroad in retaliation. He also told the Senator that the picketing of embassies was so embarrassing that some foreign representatives had found it necessary to move their families from Washington. Consequently, Pittman introduced a resolution making it unlawful for pickets to approach within five hundred feet of any embassy or legation in order to "intimidate, coerce, or bring into public odium any foreign government, party, or organization, or any officer or officers thereof, or to bring into public disrepute, political, social, or economic acts, views, or purposes of any foreign government, party, or organization." Although Senators Arthur Vandenberg and Robert M. LaFollette, Jr., opposed the bill on the grounds that it violated freedom of speech, the Senate adopted the Pittman proposal. The House, however, failed to act before adjournment. *Congressional Record,* 75 Cong., 1 Sess., LXXXI (August 10, 1937), 8586-93.

89. Hull, *Memoirs,* I, 511.

90. Bullitt to Roosevelt, April 12, 1937 (FDR Official Files, No. 1124).

91. Camprubí to Roosevelt, January 30, 1937 (FDR Official Files No. 422C).

92. Hull to Bingham, June 30, 1937 (SD File No. 852.00/5839: tel.). Hull to Phillips, June 30, 1937 (SD File No. 852.00/5885: tel.).

93. Bingham to Hull, July 6, 1937 (SD File No. 852.00/5931: tel.).

94. Phillips to Hull, July 1, 1937 (SD File No. 852.00/5890: tel.). In August 1936 Under Secretary of State William Phillips was sent to Rome as the American Ambassador.

95. Hull, *Memoirs,* I, 513.

96. Spanish Foreign Office, *The Italian Invasion of Spain* (Washington, 1937).

97. *New York Times,* October 27, November 26, 1937.

98. Thomas to Roosevelt, August 26, 1937 (FDR Official Files, No. 422C).

99. Cordell Hull, August 29, 1937, *ibid.,* memo.

100. Hull to Roosevelt, September 4, 1937, *ibid.*

101. Roosevelt to Thomas, September 6, 1937, *ibid.*

102. Thomas to Roosevelt, September 16, 1937, *ibid.*

103. This point is stressed in Raymond Leslie Buell, "U. S. Neutrality in Spanish Conflict," *Foreign Policy Reports,* XIII (November 15, 1937), 215.

Chapter Five

The Evasion of Neutrality

Neutrality legislation to the contrary, numberless individuals in the United States held that the issues involved in the Spanish Civil War were so fundamental to the maintenance of their concept of democratic principles that no true believer in those ideals could be a dispassionate observer of the Spanish scene. This body of opinion held that the conflict, reduced to its simplest terms, was essentially a defense of democracy against a wanton attack by dictatorship; furthermore, many of those who shared this view were quite prepared to underwrite their conviction by direct action in the Spanish arena.

Aware of the existence of such opinion, the State Department took additional steps to decrease American involvement in the Spanish War. It was announced on January 11, 1937, that in an effort to discourage Americans from traveling in Spain all passports were to be marked "not valid in Spain."[1] Additional regulations were imposed several months later when the Department ordered that anyone desiring to travel abroad had to make an affidavit that he would not travel in Spain.[2] This action, however, did not prevent American citizens from traveling to Spain and taking an active part in the Spanish Civil War. Consul General Mahlon Perkins in Barcelona cabled the State Department in early January 1937 that seventy-six American volunteers had passed through that city enroute to active service with the Loyalist army. Consul Perkins stated that so far as he knew these were the first Americans to arrive in Spain except for a few scattered individuals. He quoted several volunteers as declaring that "they had come to fight for their principles."[3] In reply, the Department

101

issued a statement making it clear that under existing legislation it was illegal for an American citizen to enter the military service of a foreign state.[4] It was also pointed out that if an American thus enlisting takes an oath of allegiance to a foreign government, he is deemed to have expatriated himself and cannot expect the services of the American Government. "The enlistment of American citizens in either of the opposing forces in Spain," the statement concluded, "is unpatriotically inconsistent with the American Government's policy of the most scrupulous non-intervention in the Spanish internal affairs."[5]

The legislation prohibiting the enlistment of volunteers in the services of a foreign government contained many loopholes and had never been rigidly enforced. One reason for this lack of enforcement was that it must have been established that a person was recruited by the enlisting government within the territorial limits of the United States or its possessions before enlistment becomes illegal. The agents for a foreign government, however, could easily avoid making a contact in this country by paying the passage of a person and delaying employment until arrival on foreign soil.[6] Although the United States refused to allow its citizens to travel in Spain, many volunteers obtained passports to France, and once there this Government and evidently the French Government as well could not prevent them from receiving Spanish passports and joining Spanish forces.[7] Moreover, in foreign wars which have aroused strong feelings in the United States, it has always been difficult to obtain jury convictions in cases involving violation of neutrality laws. Because of these various reasons the Federal Bureau of Investigation did not start prosecutions during the Spanish Civil War, although numerous investigations were made concerning recruiting activities.[8]

It was not until the struggle had shown indications of becoming a prolonged one that Americans went to Spain in considerable numbers. Aside from a few individuals, the first organized group arrived on January 5, 1937, and within a few weeks sufficient numbers had arrived to form a battalion of their own — the Abraham Lincoln Battalion. Although the majority had little previous training they first went into action in the middle of February. While the Lincoln Battalion was still in the front lines, additional volunteers arrived to form a second battalion — the George Washington.[9] When the XV International Brigade entered

the Brunete offensive on July 6, both American battalions participated and were reported to have given a good account of themselves.[10] During this offensive, losses were heavy and the two
American battalions were merged into one — the Lincoln-Washington Battalion, which participated in every engagement fought by
the XV Brigade. The participation of American volunteers was not
limited to these battalions, for a large number fought in the Canadian Mackenzie Battalion and in a small anti-tank unit known as
the John Brown Company. Americans were also prominent in the
transportation corps and medical detachments.[11] Whether the Insurgents lacked sufficient recruiting agencies in this country, or
whether their cause did not appeal to American volunteers is not
apparent, but evidence was lacking which would indicate that
Americans fought on the side of the Spanish Rebels.[12]

There are varying estimates as to the number of Americans
who served and died in the Spanish conflict. The Veterans of the
Abraham Lincoln Brigade asserted that of the 3,000 Americans who
served with the Lincoln Battalion in Spain, some 1,200 survived
that "first battle against international fascism."[13] Edwin Rolfe
estimated that there were 18,000 men in the International Brigades,
2,800 of them Americans, and that approximately 1,000 of these
Americans survived the "democratic crusade against fascism."[14]

The American Consul at Valencia, Thomas D. Davis, reported
to Secretary Hull in March 1937 that approximately 1,700 American
citizens were enlisted in the Government forces in Spain. Davis
stated that fatal casualties among American volunteers had been
exceedingly heavy, some estimates placing total casualties in the
Lincoln Battalion as high as seventy-five per cent. He claimed that
the Americans were invariably used as shock troops with insuf-
ficient preliminary training and inexperienced and inefficient officers.[15] Several months later the Vice Consul, Milton K. Wells,
reported that the original estimate was perhaps excessive. He
believed that the concensus would place the number nearer 1,000.[16]
In July 1937, however, Consul Wells informed the State Department that if certain reports he had received were correct, the
total of those American volunteers arriving since the outbreak of
the Civil War was "close to 2,000." Many of these were engaged
in transport units, he stated, but at least 1,100 had gone into front
line action.[17]

In spite of heavy casualities and desertions the estimates of Americans serving in Spain continued high. From another source came the report of Walter C. Thurston, Counselor of the Embassy. Thurston cabled Secretary Hull that approximately 110 American doctors, nurses, and relief workers were operating in Spain under the auspices of the Medical Bureau of the North American Committee to Aid Spanish Democracy. He advised that the Military Attaché, Colonel Stephen O. Fuqua, had estimated that 2,000 American volunteers were serving with the Spanish Government forces of whom 900 were in active combat service, 300 in hospitals or rest areas, 300 in training centers, and 500 in non-combatant activities with motor and hospital units. Thurston added that recent military operations had reduced the number of American combat troops to approximately 450 and had increased the number of those in hospitals. His total estimate of Americans serving with the Loyalists as of April 16, 1938, was "1,600 or 1,700."[18] A short time later another estimate was received from the Military Attaché in Barcelona who placed the number at 1,250, of whom 300 were in hospitals. He stated that the total killed and missing in action was 500.[19] As the war neared its conclusion in November 1938 Counselor Thurston reported that official figures furnished by the Spanish Government showed 1,103 American volunteers in Spain.[20] By December, however, all Americans had been evacuated.[21] In that month Spanish Premier Negrín announced before the League of Nations that every foreign volunteer fighting for the Republic had been withdrawn from the front lines and repatriated to his homeland. This action was taken in the hope that German and Italian soldiers fighting for the opposition would be forced to leave, but such was not the case, at least not until Franco's victory was assured.

The motives influencing these Americans to endanger their lives fighting for the Spanish Republican Government were many and varied. Men who fought in the International Brigade generally maintained that they went to Spain to take part in the democratic crusade against international fascism, or, as stated by the Veterans of the Abraham Lincoln Brigade, because they felt that the cause of Spain was "the cause of all progressive mankind."[22] Rolfe asserted that Americans fought in Spain because of "their profound anti-fascist convictions";[23] and Frank Tinker, a Loyalist fighter pilot, declared that he was not recruited, but fought for the Madrid Government because of Axis intervention in Spain and the ruthless aerial attacks on Spanish cities.[24] Another American fighting in Spain dramatically described his feelings concerning the Spanish conflict: "I picked out my man — a Heinkel and went in after him with the machine guns going. . . . A minute later he was falling in flames. As the Heinkel plunged downward, I saw neither plane nor pilot falling. I saw fascism itself crashing to earth."[25]

Undoubtedly, some participated in the Spanish Civil War for motives which were not ideological. Two American flyers, Bert Acosta and Gordon Berry, instituted legal proceedings against the Spanish steamship, *Mar Cantábrico*, in an effort to collect $1,200 back pay due them by the Spanish Government; while Harold E. Dahl, a former U. S. Army pilot, declared that he was engaged at $1,500 a month to serve as an aviation instructor. Acosta and Berry, after fighting in Spain for two months against the Insurgent forces of General Franco, returned to the United States in January 1937. Legal efforts to collect the full amount of the back pay allegedly owed them by the Spanish Government were futile.[26] Dahl, a twenty-eight-year-old flyer from Champaign, Illinois, traveled to Spain in December 1936 with a fake Mexican passport under the assumed name of Hernandez Diaz. Later, he was captured and imprisoned after parachuting from his disabled plane over Rebel territory. Dahl was quickly arraigned for trial and charged with "rebellion" against the Nationalist Government. He protested his innocence on the grounds that he had been engaged by the Spanish Government to act as a flying instructor, but he was forced into combat at "pistol point." At the court martial, however, Dahl was convicted and sentenced to death.

The plight of the condemned aviator received wide publicity in the United States and many Americans made personal appeals to General Franco in his behalf. Dahl's very attractive wife, who was living on the French Riviera at the time, sent her portrait to the Generalissimo and pleaded for her husband's life.[27] Colonel Charles W. Kerwood, who had campaigned with Franco in Morocco in 1925 and 1926, also requested that Dahl be reprieved. The Colonel wired the Nationalist leader that "eleven years ago we were fighting side by side in North Africa and today on behalf of the Advertising Club of New York I trespass upon our friendship in asking that you save the life of a brother airman, Harold E. Dahl."[28]

The American Consul at Vigo, Harold Graves, kept the Department fully informed as to the progress of the Dahl case. Upon learning of Dahl's death sentence, Secretary Hull instructed Consul Charles Bay at Seville to call upon General Queipo de Llano[29] and request that he inform Franco that it is "our understanding that the execution of prisoners of war is not sanctioned by any rules of civilized warfare."[30] Through these intercessions, General Franco commuted the death sentence to life imprisonment and later placed the name of Dahl on a list of prisoners to be exchanged.[31]

There is also evidence to indicate that numerous Americans went to Spain as a result of publicity campaigns and recruiting activities by certain political groups in this country. The Socialist party, through its organ, the *Socialist Call*, attempted to recruit a Eugene V. Debs Brigade which was organized to "aid the Spanish masses." The *Call* declared that

this is our small fighting contribution to our class comrades across the sea. We are moved to do this not only out of loyalty to those who are fighting our battle in another land, but also because we are confident that worker's aid to the workers of Spain will hasten the day when Europe and then the world will see a worker's victory, a Socialist Commonwealth, wherein all men may live together in true peace.[32]

The *Call* solicited funds to send the volunteers to Spain, carried full-page advertisements for recruiting purposes, and encouraged enlistments by printing banner headlines such as "200 Join Brigade for Spain in Week."[33] The *Nation* also published a full-page advertisement of the "Friends of the Debs Column" pleading for funds to send American volunteers to Spain.[34] Although vigorous recruiting activities were conducted, the "Debs Column" did not succeed in sending men to Spain in any great numbers, and after the Neutrality Act of May 1, 1937, was enacted, all open efforts to send American volunteers to Spain ceased.

Testimony before the Dies Committee in 1938 indicated that the Communists had also been active in recruiting volunteers for the Spanish Loyalists in the United States. Two witnesses, Abraham Sobel and A. L. Halpern, described themselves as "escaped" American volunteers and stated that ninety per cent of the Americans preferred to return home but were prevented from doing so by the Communists.[35] Another witness testified that he had been recruited by a high ranking Communist leader in Houston, Texas.[36] Still others testified that "the international brigades in Spain were formed at the suggestion of the Soviet Government and that they incorporated all elements of the Russian system, including 'Communist Cells', political commissars and espionage." These witnesses claimed that Earl Browder and Robert Minor, both leading American Communists, were active in recruiting on behalf of the Loyalists.[37] This evidence was turned over to Attorney General Robert H. Jackson by Congressman Martin Dies (D-Texas) with the demand that he conduct an inquiry into "Red recruiting" in the United States. No action was taken by the FBI until March 1940, when raids were conducted in Detroit and seventeen persons were arrested and accused of having aided Loyalist recruitment in the United States.[38] Those arrested, however, were ordered released by the Attorney General who stated that "no public injury seems to have been suffered from the fact that individual Spanish sympathizers, who had become so heated over the foreign conflict as to want to fight, left this country to do so."[39] Jackson was bitterly assailed by Congressman Dies for dismissing the indictments, while Father Joseph F. Thorning asserted that the Attorney General's statement "misrepresented the character of recruiting carried on in the United States by the Third International. . . . It is one thing for individual . . . citizens to volunteer for services in foreign wars. It is an altogether different proposition for an acknowledged arm of an alien power systematically to recruit American boys to carry out the ruthless, selfish policy of the despot of the Kremlin."[40]

These alleged recruiting activities did not go unnoticed by certain members of Congress. In January 1937 Representative Samuel Dickstein (D-New York) told the House that offenders against the spirit of American democracy were "all those misguided individuals who see fit to send Americans to fight for some foreign ideology," and he introduced a bill which would authorize the President to prohibit any American citizen from engaging in any foreign war, under penalty of a $10,000 fine and five years imprisonment.[41] Representative Alfred Phillips, Jr. (D-Connecticut) likewise denounced Americans fighting in Spain, declaring that individuals calling themselves American citizens were responsible for some of that destruction, death, and carnage [in Spain]. . . . I think the majority of the Members of this House, as well as the majority of the American people, agree that we should take away citizenship from those who are willing to sell themselves as murderers for any cause anywhere at any time.

To remedy this situation Phillips offered a resolution that would deprive such offenders of "all rights and privileges of citizenship."[42]

Members of the Senate also had their attention called to the activities of the Abraham Lincoln Brigade. Senator Robert Reynolds (D-North Carolina) introduced a resolution asking the Attorney General, Secretary of State, and Secretary of Labor for any information they possessed "with respect to activities in the United States of persons (including diplomatic and consular representatives of foreign states) who have recently been engaged or are now active in enlisting persons residing in the United States for service in the armed forces of any foreign state or of any faction in any foreign state where civil strife exists." The Senator was of the opinion that Americans should "keep their mouth out of affairs in Asia and Spain and every other country of the world."[43] No legislative action was taken, however, on any of these proposals. Thus, the circumstances of the war in Spain would seem to have rendered the rules against foreign recruiting on American soil a complete anomaly.

Mindful of the many protests against Americans volunteering for service abroad, the Department of State made every effort to keep citizens of this country out of Spain. Not only were American passports invalidated for Spanish travel, but American officials in Spain were instructed not to extend protection or assistance to Americans illegally serving in the armed forces of either of the protagonists.[44] Secretary Hull was also very concerned about alleged recruiting activities in the United States. Consul Perkins of Barcelona sent to the Department a picture published in the local press depicting the recruiting of volunteers in the United States for the Spanish Government forces, the caption of which was translated as follows: "In spite of the decree forbidding it, and doubtless because Mr. Roosevelt is inclined in favor of the combatants of the Republic, there is functioning in New York a recruiting office of true volunteers to round out the Popular army in Spain."[45] Consul Davis reported from Valencia the case of one volunteer who divulged the method of recruiting in the United States. This soldier asserted that the Communist party had units in certain American colleges and universities, and that these and other Communist organizations had been very active in getting volunteers for the Spanish Army. He stated that the Communist party was careful to do nothing officially, but operated through agents who pretended to be acting entirely upon their own responsibility as individuals. He described a well-organized "underground railway" leading from Chicago and New York, from which volunteers were handled almost as if under military command to Le Havre, Paris, Barcelona, Valencia, and Albacete. Albacete was pointed out as the final concentration point for foreign volunteers. Here they were formally enlisted, issued uniforms, given a brief training and sent to the front.[46]

In June 1937 John P. Hurley, the Consul General at Marseille, reported to Secretary Hull his observations concerning those Americans who chose to "disregard the appeal of the Government and the people of the United States that they remain neutral." It would appear, stated Hurley, that among the American citizens who entered the conflict, some could be classified as recruiting agents, whose purpose was to lead others to the scene of the hostilities and then perhaps vanish; others came because of their inability to find employment but were probably not overly enthusiastic under existing conditions; others were inspired by motives ideological; and many could be found whose predicament could be traced to an "unscrupulous exploitation of their spirit of romance and adventure." He concluded by stating that such volunteers as he had questioned had shown no disposition to reveal persons and agencies within the United States responsible for their recruitment.[47]

Secretary Hull was particularly concerned over an article by *New York Times* correspondent W. P. Carney who quoted Harold Dahl as stating that he and four other Americans "were engaged by the Secretary of the Spanish Embassy in Washington who produced contracts for them to sign and provided transportation to Spain."[48] Consul Graves at Vigo was instructed to get a signed statement from Dahl "setting forth all the circumstances incident to the enlistment of himself and his companions and the issuance to them of Spanish passports by representatives of the Spanish Government in this country."[49] In an interview with Graves, however, Dahl denied that either he or any other American pilot had any dealings either directly or indirectly with the Spanish Embassy in Washington and that the only part played by the Spanish Consul General in New York was the payment of allotments to wives of American citizens flying for the Spanish Government.[50]

Exactly what persons or agencies in the United States originally contacting Dahl and other American flyers has not been definitely established. In an earlier statement the Spanish Ambassador informed Secretary Hull that the Spanish Consulate General in New York had received many letters from American citizens offering their services to the Loyalists. He stated, however, that all offers had been declined. Those American aviators fighting in Spain, he added, were not recruited but dealt directly with the Spanish Government, signing at Valencia.[51]

Such efforts by Secretary Hull and the State Department did not prevent those Americans desiring to fight for the Loyalists from traveling to Spain and participating in the conflict. Many saw dramatized in the Spanish crisis the fight against international fascism. Others were soldiers of fortune and adventurers; some were Communists recruited in the United States. Whatever their motivation may have been, many fought and died in Spain. As volunteers, they joined an army of mixed nationality publicized as the International Brigade; yet they were too few to alter the outcome of this epic struggle.[52]

NOTES

1. *New York Times,* January 12, 1937.

2. *Press Releases,* March 6, 1937.

3. Perkins to Hull, January 8, 1937 (SD File No. 852.2221/190: tel.). Louis Fischer claims to have been the first American to enlist in the International Brigade, having volunteered his services to the Spanish Government in September 1936. His period of service (in the Quartermaster Corps) was brief, however, as he was ousted in December 1936 by an old enemy, André Marty, French Communist Deputy and Chief Commissar of the Brigade. Fischer, *Men and Politics,* pp. 386, 401.

4. Section 5282 of the Revised Statutes of the United States declares: "Every person who, within the territory or jurisdiction of the United States, enlists or enters himself, or hires or retains another person to enlist or enter himself, or to go beyond the limits or jurisdiction of the United States with intent to be enlisted or entered in the service of any foreign prince, state,

colony, district, or people, as a soldier, or as a marine or seaman, on board any vessel of war, letter of marque, or privateer, shall be deemed guilty of high misdemeanor, and shall be fined not more than $1,000, and imprisoned not more than 3 years." Title 18, section 22, United States Code.

5. Moore to Perkins, January 13, 1937 (SD File No. 852.00/4327: tel.).

6. For example see the cases cited in the *New York Times*, January 5, 1937.

7. The French Government arrested a large number of Americans attempting to cross the border into Spain. The French claimed the American "volunteers" were violating French laws and the nonintervention agreement. Numerous dispatches to the State Department reported these arrests and subsequent convictions carrying prison sentences of from twenty to forty days. Secretary Hull expressed full approval of this action taken by the French Government. He instructed American authorities to "make it clear to all . . . concerned that these persons were proceeding to Spain in violation of this Government's stipulation." Hurley to Hull, March 29, 1937 (SD File No. 852.2221/311: tel.). Hull to Hurley, March 30, 1937 (852.2221/311: tel.). See also *New York Times*, April 10, 14, 16; May 9, 13, 22, 1937.

8. The legal aspects of this problem are treated in Padelford, *International Law and Diplomacy in the Spanish Civil Strife*, pp. 184-87. Another authority points out that when men wish to volunteer ways may be found of getting them to their destination without technically infringing the law. Under such circumstances the State Department is powerless to act. Richard W. Van Alstyne, *American Diplomacy in Action* (Stanford University, 1944), pp. 633-34.

9. Originally known as the Thomas J. Mooney Battalion; the name was changed in July 1937. Milton K. Wells (Vice Consul at Valencia) to Hull, July 15, 1937 (SD File No. 852.2221/493).

10. *Ibid.*

11. *Volunteer for Liberty* (Madrid), II (November 7, 1938), 9. This publication was the official organ of the English-speaking battalions of the International Brigade which fought for the Republic during the Spanish Civil War. It was written for and by those men. The first issue was published in Madrid on May 24, 1937, and its sixty-third and last in Barcelona on November 7, 1938. The purposes of this weekly paper were many. It carried editorials, foreign and domestic news, interviews, photographs, maps, cartoons, jokes, and war correspondence. It was also an instrument of propaganda and morale builder for the men in the International Brigade. Ralph Bates, a British novelist, was the first editor; Edwin Rolfe, an American poet, the second; and John Tisa, an American worker, was the last. Files of the paper are very rare; there are, however, complete sets in the Los Angeles Public Library and the New York Public Library.

The State Department placed Americans serving in Spain into three categories: (a) nurses, doctors, and relief workers who entered Spain with valid passports; (b) wounded American volunteers who were under the orders of the Spanish military authorities; (c) American volunteers in active service. Hull to Thurston (Counselor of the Embassy in Spain), April 1, 1938 (SD File No. 852.2221/769: tel.).

12. A study of State Department files did not reveal a single reference to Americans serving in the armies of Generalissimo Franco.

13. *Volunteer for Liberty* (Bound File, Introduction), p. 2.

14. Edwin Rolfe, *The Lincoln Battalion* (New York, 1939), p. 15.

15. Davis to Hull, March 15, 1937 (SD File No. 852.00/5118).

16. Wells to Hull, May 26, 1937 (SD File No. 852.2221/435½).

17. Wells to Hull, July 15, 1937 (SD File No. 852.2221/493).

18. Thurston to Hull, April 16, 1938 (SD File No. 852.2221/806: tel.).

19. Thurston to Hull, June 23, 1938 (SD File No. 852.2221/967: tel.).

20. Thurston to Hull, November 22, 1938 (SD File No. 852.2221/1302: tel.).

21. Thurston to Hull, December 2, 1938 (SD File No. 852.2221/1323: tel.). Edwin C. Wilson (Chargé in France) to Hull, December 6, 1938 (SD File No. 852.2221/1384).

22. *Volunteer for Liberty* (Bound File, Introduction), p. 2.

23. Rolfe, *Lincoln Battalion*, p. 15.

24. Frank Glasgow Tinker, *Some Still Live* (New York, 1938), p. 1.

25. *Ben Leider: American Hero: Spanish War Pamphlets* (New York), II (n.d.), 12. This pamphlet was obviously a propaganda device to raise funds. When Leider was lated killed, Heywood Broun, Chairman of the Ben Leider Memorial Fund, wrote: "Freedom and Democracy— these things Ben Leider loved above all things. And what better memorial to Ben than a fund for the battle of Democracy? He gave his life for that cause, what will you give?" *Ibid.*

26. *New York Times,* January 1, 7, 1937. Spanish Consul General Luis Careaga declared that "all the clauses have been fulfilled with them [Acosta and Berry], as per arrangements contained in said clauses and, therefore, absolutely no moneys are due to the said aviators." *Ibid.,* January 17, 1937.

27. *New York Times,* October 7, 1937.

28. *Ibid.,* October 10, 1937.

29. A member of Franco's staff.

30. Hull to Bay, September 1, 1937 (SD File No. 852.2221/39: tel.).

31. Bay to Hull, September 14, 1937 (SD File No. 852.2221/61: tel.). See also, Graves to Hull, October 8, 1937 (SD File No. 852.2221/72: tel.). Dahl was never exchanged. He was finally released in February 1940 and returned to the United States. On several other occasions the State Department unofficially intervened with the Franco Government on behalf of American citizens captured and sentenced to long prison terms or death. In particular see the cases of Mr. and Mrs. Antonio Fernandez Villa described in the following dispatches: Bay to Hull, August 17, 1937 (SD File No. 352.1121/72: tel.); Hull to Bay, August 20, 1937 (SD File No. 352.1121/74: tel.); Hull to Bowers, November 24, 1937 (SD File No. 352.1121/117: tel.). These two American citizens were not finally liberated until October 1940, and then only after repeated pleas by the State Department.

32. *Socialist Call,* January 2, 1937.

33. *Ibid.*

34. The advertisement was not included in the bound files of the *Nation* but is referred to in CXLIV (January 30, 1937), 113-14. The editors announced, however, that because of the stand taken by the State Department

they had decided, on advice of their lawyers, to discontinue publishing the advertisement. Nevertheless, the editors declared that the "*Nation* hopes that the United States law will not be applied against American volunteers to Spain as it has been so loosely interpreted in the past. We have ourselves used foreign volunteers. If we stop our volunteers from Spain it will only help fascism." *Ibid.*

35. *New York Times*, August 19, 1938. Friends of the Abraham Lincoln Brigade assailed these two men for their testimony before the Dies Committee. A joint statement by Captain Carl Bradley, Executive Secretary of the Abraham Lincoln Brigade, and Lieutenant Frank O'Flaherty denied such allegations and declared: "Whom are we to believe, two persons, deserters and turncoats, or 300 veterans of the Lincoln Brigade who returned only because of their wounds, and any one of them would readily return to the fray again in the interest of the cause which they know to be the cause of democracy and the American people." *Ibid.*, August 21, 1938.

36. *Ibid.*, April 21, 1939.

37. *Ibid.*, April 13, 1940.

38. *Ibid.*, March 2, April 3, 1940.

39. *Ibid.*, April 11, 19, 1940.

40. *Ibid.*, April 19, 1940. Father Thorning, Professor of Sociology and History at Mount St. Mary's College, Emmitsburg, Maryland, was one of the outstanding crusaders for the Franco cause in the United States. During the course of the conflict he made lengthy tours throughout North and South America rallying sympathy and support for the Nationalists. His efforts did not go unrecognized by Franco for later he was personally awarded the Grand Cross of Isabella the Catholic, one of the highest honors that can be conferred upon a non-Spaniard. *Ibid.*, January 24, 1946.

41. *Congressional Record*, 75 Cong., 1 Sess., LXXXI (January 12, 1937), 197; (April 26, 1937), 3821.

42. *Ibid.* (January 27, 1937), 501. Phillips periodically reminded his colleagues of the Americans who were fighting in Spain. On August 3, 1937, he cited the case of Harold Dahl, former U. S. Army pilot who was reportedly hired by the Spanish Embassy in Washington to fight for the Spanish Government. *Ibid.* (August 3, 1937), 8156.

43. *Ibid.*, 75 Cong., 3 Sess., LXXXIII (January 8, 1938), 217.

44. Hull to Perkins (Consul General at Barcelona), February 1, 1937 (SD File No. 852.2221/190: tel.).

45. Perkins to Hull, February 4, 1937 (SD File No. 852.00/4772).

46. Davis to Hull, March 15, 1937 (SD File No. 852.00/5118).

47. Hurley to Hull, June 22, 1937 (SD File No. 852.2221/468).

48. *New York Times*, July 23, 1937.

49. Hull to Graves, July 23, 1937 (SD File No. 852.2221/5: tel.).

50. Graves to Hull, July 27, 1937 (SD File No. 852.2221/10: tel.).

51. Fernando de los Ríos, January 26, 1937 (SD File No. 852.2221/198: memo.).

52. There are many Americans who still cherish the memory of their wartime experiences in Spain by holding membership in a group called "The Veterans of the Abraham Lincoln Brigade." This organization, which has

been placed on the subversive list by the Department of Justice, maintains headquarters at 23 West 26th Street in New York. In a letter to the author Moe Fishman, the Executive Secretary, explained that the "troubles experienced by these Americans who fought for democracy in Spain continues unabated in these troublesome times — yet despite it we have been able to make a few contributions to the continuing fight against our government's pro-Franco policy." (Fishman to author, January 17, 1955.) In a subsequent letter Fishman complained that "the number of our supporters has dwindled with the severity of the government attack against us." (*Ibid.*, May 17, 1955.)

In defense of their position the Veterans of the Abraham Lincoln Brigade have raised their voices in the following statement:

> There are not many veterans of the Abraham Lincoln Brigade — the majority are dead. Almost two thousand have fallen on the battlefields of two wars against fascism. Their bodies are part of the hills and groves of Spain — the beaches and jungles of the Pacific — the hedgerows of Normandy and the sands of North Africa — and many went down at sea.
>
> Those who died and we who survive were volunteers — acting under no compulsion except clear understanding — spurred only by the demands of conscience — asking nothing except the right to defend freedom from reaction — world peace from the on-slaught of war — the right to be actually and physically in the front lines against fascism.
>
> Our organization, the Veterans of the Abraham Lincoln Brigade, springs from the very heart of America. It came into existence only to give expression to the anti-fascist feelings of America. It is the living symbol of the hatred and detestation most Americans feel for that last survivor of the Axis, Francisco Franco, the butcher of the Spanish people. . . .
>
> The essential character of the Veterans of the Abraham Lincoln Brigade is best expressed by the phrase. . . 'premature anti-fascists.' And it is true that first and last we are anti-fascists. To be called premature, was to acknowledge our early readiness to volunteer our lives to stop fascism when so many in high places were making deals with fascism and slandering those who stood against it. Our taking up arms against Franco in 1936, '37, and '38 was a vital factor in creating that climate of anti-fascism in America which was so important for the mobilization of the powerful national effort which defended our country in World War II.
>
> Yes — when the demanding need of the time was to cut through the net of hypocritical words — when the hour came for men and women to bar fascism with their bodies — the Abraham Lincoln Brigade was born. And when the World War we tried to prevent engulfed our land — when the fascism we attempted to halt in Spain attacked our nation — veterans of the Abraham Lincoln Brigade again gave leadership by example on the battle-

fields of World War II. (Veterans of the Abraham Lincoln
Brigade, *Is it Subversive to be Anti-Franco?* [New York, n.d.],
pp. 3-15).

The Veterans of the Abraham Lincoln Brigade held their fifth national
convention in New York City in 1946. National Commander Milton Wolff,
who served as a major in the Spanish War and was the last commander of
the battalion, told the assembled delegates that the objectives of the organization were as follows:

(1) To keep alive the principles for which the Lincoln Brigade
    fought in Spain and to this end to educate and activize
    the membership in the social and political life of the
    country. To continue and promote fraternal relations among
    the members.

(2) To assist in the medical and occupational rehabilitation of
    its members.

(3) To continue the campaign to free all American and Inter-
    national prisoners in Franco Spain and to aid them in every
    way possible while they are in prison.

(4) To help rally the American people to exert their influence
    on the Franco Government to grant real amnesty to all Re-
    publicans in Spain and to aid the Spanish and International
    Brigade refugees.

(5) To cooperate with all organizations and groups interested
    in promoting peace, democracy and civil liberties.

(6) To maintain fraternal relations with organizations of veter-
    ans of the Spanish Republican Army in other countries.
    (Veterans of the Abraham Lincoln Brigade, Inc., *Press
    Releases, Speeches, Congratulatory Messages, etc., Concern-
    ing First Post War National Convention September 21-22,
    1946,* Bound Documents, David McKelvey White Collection,
    New York Public Library. The files of the VALB have been
    deposited in the New York Public Library cataloged under
    the David McKelvey White Collection. This material in-
    cludes fifteen bundles of pamphlets, each bundle containing
    from ten to twenty-five items; files of the *Volunteer for
    Liberty;* several volumes of pamphlets in Spanish; and six
    volumes of miscellaneous material, including press releases,
    speeches, resolutions, and letters. David McKelvey White
    was National Chairman of the Friends of the Abraham
    Lincoln Brigade. This organization collected funds for the
    care and repatriation of wounded Americans who had fought
    for the Spanish Government in Spain).

Also present at the convention was General Waltern of Poland, the former
divisional commander. Official minutes of the meeting disclosed that a medal
was awarded to Paul Robeson, an honorary member of the Brigade, who was
described as "an example to all of us as a true anti-fascist." Estimates as to
the number of delegates attending the convention were lacking, although one

delegate reported that the membership in New York was "nearly 1,000." (*Ibid.*)

Apparently the convention of 1946 was the last national assembly to be held. On December 4, 1947, the Department of Justice listed the Veterans of the Abraham Lincoln Brigade as an organization of questioned loyalty to the United States. In more recent action the Subversive Activities Control Board holding hearings under the McCarran Act rendered a decision which branded the VALB as a "communist front" organization. Despite the severity of these attacks the veterans have continued to voice their protests against United States loans to Franco Spain in exchange for military bases on the Iberian Peninsula.

Chapter Six

The Great Debate

The Spanish War aroused the interest and feeling of certain Americans to a greater intensity than Japan's conquest of Manchuria or Mussolini's invasion of Ethiopia. Democracy, nonintervention, and humanitarianism have long been recognized American principles, and when the democratic government in any country is threatened there are elements of the American public that are very outspoken in the matter. On the Spanish issue many Americans were influenced by certain ideological considerations resulting from the alleged struggle between fascism and communism. Behind the Loyalists rallied those who were generally united in their hatred of the Fascist governments of Germany and Italy and who felt that the defeat of General Franco would also be a defeat for fascism. Among this group were many who believed in democracy and who were convinced that the Spanish Popular Front Government was fighting in defense of democracy. On the other hand, General Franco quickly gained the support of avowed fascists such as Hitler and Mussolini, anticommunists who were convinced that the Loyalists took their orders from Moscow, and many Catholics who felt the Madrid Government was anticlerical, anti-Catholic, and atheistic.

Even a choice of nomenclature distinguishing the protagonists in Spain was often the subject of violent argument. The two largest news gathering agencies, the United Press and the Associated Press, used the terms "Spanish Government forces" and "Insurgents" in referring to the belligerents, but many papers would alter the dispatches to read "Loyalists" or "Fascists." In the Hearst press or in the Catholic press the Rebels were seldom, if ever, described as fascists, but as "Insurgents," "Nationalists," or the "forces of General Franco." When these papers referred to the Spanish Government, the terms "Reds" or "Communists" were almost always used. Other papers, such as the *New York Times, Christian Science Monitor, Louisville Courier-Journal, New Orleans Times-Picayune* and *Washington Post* commonly referred to the Rebels as "Fascists" and used the term "Loyalist" in describing the Republican Government. This practice was strongly protested by certain Americans who resented the use of these terms. One irate letter to the editor of the *Review of Reviews* bitterly complained: "To the great majority which constitutes the Great Stupidity, 'Loyalist' sounds good, loyalty is supposed to be a virtue. But it has been misapplied to the supposedly republican or democratic part of the Spanish nation, whereas the present government at Madrid and Barcelona is in the hands of bloodthirsty Bolsheviks, who are confiscating all private and church property and who ruthlessly butcher all those opposed to them. . . . To the average citizen 'rebel' has a treasonable, revolutionary sound. Just as misleading is the term 'fascists' applied to the troops who are fighting for law and order."[1] There is little doubt but that these terms evoked a conditioning of thought and feeling which helped to formulate a neutral's attitude toward the issues and people involved in the war.[2]

While the civil war raged in Spain, ideological warfare raged throughout the rest of the world. It was a war of propaganda, with leaflets, rallies, books, and pamphlets as weapons rather than planes, tanks, and guns. The importance of this propaganda was that although neither side could win the war with it, sufficient propaganda might influence a "neutral" country to adopt a position of "benevolent neutrality" favoring one side or the other. The Loyalists contended that they represented the legally elected Government of Spain which had the overwhelming support of the Spanish people. The supporters of the Republic admitted that atrocities had been committed in the chaotic period prior to the revolt, but they absolved the Madrid Government of any responsibility. On the contrary, they claimed the Government acted quickly to restore order and stop the outrages that were being committed throughout the country by the Fascists. The Loyalists also denied the Nationalist charges that the Government was controlled by Communists, and pointed out that in reality the battle was between democracy and fascism. They emphasized that the Cortes of 473 members included only 16 Communists, none of whom were members of the Government, and that the Spanish Republic had never established diplomatic relations with the Soviet Union. These facts bolstered the Loyalist contention that Franco was being aided by other Fascist powers in an attempt to destroy democracy and to establish fascism in Spain. In numerous speeches intended for world-wide consumption President Azaña declared that if Germany and Italy had not poured troops, warplanes, tanks, and guns into Nationalist Spain, and if Loyalist shipping had not been destroyed by Italian submarines, Franco's revolt would have been suppressed within two weeks.[3]

The Nationalist propaganda followed a different pattern of thought. Supporters of General Franco charged that the Loyalists did not represent the majority of the Spanish people, and that the elections in February 1936 were marred by fraud. They claimed that Spain had no effective government before the revolt and that the Madrid Government had been unwilling or unable to keep order. The charge of communism was made against the Republican Government and the Nationalists denied all accusations that they were fascist. Shortly after the outbreak of the rebellion Franco is reported to have told Jay Allen of the *Chicago Tribune*: "This movement is not fascist," and added, "Fascism is ridiculous in Spain, ridiculous."[4] Outstanding Franco apologists in the United States emphasized this point. The Reverend Edward Lodge Curran, in his book, *Franco*, said, "The Nationalist cause is not a fascist cause. . . . Franco himself is not a fascist."[5] Merwin K. Hart, President of the New York State Economic Council, likewise denied that Franco was fascist.[6]

Throughout the course of the Spanish War the United States was subjected to a barrage of propaganda which was designed to influence the course of neutral thought. A number of news services, hitherto unknown and unrecognized, flooded the press with *ex parte* material in the form of daily pamphlets or news releases which supported the political ideology of one or the other contesting factions in Spain. The principal outlet for Nationalist propaganda was the Peninsula News Service, Inc., with offices in New York City, while the primary source of Loyalist propaganda in this country was the Spanish Information Bureau, also of New York City.[7] The Spanish conflict was the first civil war in which both sides had an opportunity to use the radio as a weapon of propaganda. The United States was within range of the transmitters of the rival factions, and both sides filled the air with their respective versions of the issues and events of the war. Very early during the conflict station EAQ, one of the most powerful radio stations in Europe, was seized by the Madrid Government and used to beam official bulletins to all parts of the world in several different languages. The Insurgents had a similar station which was often used by their much publicized commentator, General Queipo de Llano. The General, who was commander of the Southern Rebel Army, sent out almost daily broadcasts describing the glorious Nationalist victories and threatening the enemy with annihilation. The radio war also involved other countries in Europe. The Italians and Germans slanted radio broadcasts to favor the Insurgents, while the Russians and French were generally biased toward the Loyalists. In any event the broadcasts of both sides were familiar to many listeners in the Americas. This made it particularly difficult to ascertain what was really happening in Spain.[8]

The accuracy of reporting the Spanish conflict was a matter of heated controversy in the United States throughout the course of the war. One observer has stated that in his opinion two general principles with respect to public opinion may be drawn from the Spanish strife. First, little reliance could be placed upon international communications in a crisis for a complete and accurate description of the news although they had reached a point of remarkable efficiency. Second, modern efficiency of press and radio had made it increasingly difficult for the maintenance of neutrality in thought.[9] Since this neutrality in thought was obviously lacking in the United States, supporters of each side charged the other with deliberately falsifying the news. Partisans of General Franco lashed out bitterly against the American correspondents in Spain who daily reported the aid that Germany and Italy were pouring into Spain and who wrote eyewitness reports of the bombings of defenseless Spanish towns. Such men as Herbert Matthews, Lawrence Fernsworth, Frank Kluckhohn, Harold Callendar, and G. L. Steer of the *New York Times;* Vincent Sheean, James Minifie, and Leland Stowe of the *New York Herald Tribune;* Ernest Hemingway of the North American Newspaper Alliance; John Whittaker and Richard Mowrer of the *Chicago Daily News;* and Jay Allen of the *Chicago Tribune*[10] were accused of distortion, ignorance, Communist sympathies, and propagation of falsehoods.

Fletcher Pratt, for one, charged that most conservative journals reported the Spanish War from almost as prejudiced a point of view as the *Communist Daily Worker*. The *New York Times* was especially singled out for its "one-sided, partial, prejudiced" reporting. Pratt claimed that the *Times* had been printing propaganda which might well have drawn the United States into a general European war.[11] Edward H. Knoblaugh stated that the Loyalist public information bureau was operated by a group of Russian-trained propagandists;[12] while Father Joseph F. Thorning writing in the *Catholic World* on "Why the Press Failed on Spain," charged that five days out of seven the wires "hum" with "Red" victories and Nationalist defeats. He wondered if the reporters in Spain had been deceived or if American newspapers refused to print their dispatches as they sent them. He further contended that ninety per cent of the correspondents could not read Spanish and had to depend on the daily bulletins issued from military headquarters in Madrid. Thorning stated that what the United States needed was competent reporting not financed by "red-gold."[13]

Similar opinions were expressed by Michael Williams, editor of the Catholic weekly, *Commonweal*. Editorials, in the form of "Open Letters to Leaders of the American Press on Spain," were published in which the editor gave his reasons why the "greater part of the American secular press has failed in its job of gathering and distributing news from the rival camps of Spain." Williams was convinced that it was "demonstrably certain that by far the greater mass of news sent from Spain by the press associations, and particularly by the special correspondents of the daily newspapers, has come from Madrid, from Valencia, from Barcelona, and the Basque country, and is biased toward the Loyalists." He maintained that it was because of this "inability" to present both sides that the editorial writers, magazine writers, lecturers, radio commentators, and "liberal" Protestant clergymen were failing in their efforts to interpret the true meaning and probable effects of the struggle. He charged that the news and interpretations of the Spanish conflict, especially in journals like the *Nation* and *New Republic*, were utterly unfair. Williams also named the Scripps-Howard papers and such New York papers as the *Times, Evening Post, Herald Tribune, Evening Sun,* and *World-Telegram* as "not telling the truth about Spain and not reporting the Spanish news properly."[14]

Apparently some Catholics were of the opinion that the Catholic press was the only accurate and unbiased news source reporting the Spanish Civil War. Reverend James M. Gillis reminded his readers that "when the war in Spain is over the reading public will see that from first to last the Catholic papers alone told the truth about it."[15] A similar opinion was expressed by Father Thorning, who declared that "one of the brightest spots in the Spanish situation has been the success of the Catholic press, led by N. C. W. C. news service, in securing accurate, adequate, and interesting news about both sides in Spain." He continued: "The news as reported in the Catholic press, may not always have been sensational, but it was authentic."[16]

The Catholic press did not depend upon the wires of the United Press or the Associated Press for their news reports from Spain. Rather, such services were provided by the press department of the National Catholic Welfare Conference, which was and possibly still is the largest special interest news service in the United States. This agency provided some 450 Catholic newspapers and magazines daily news service, a news picture service, a feature service of special articles, an editorial information service, a biographical service, and a Washington news letter. During the Spanish Civil War the N. C. W. C. maintained a large staff of correspondents in Spain to report the progress of the conflict.[17] A close examination of these dispatches would seem to indicate that factual reporting was circumscribed for the purpose of promoting Catholic interests. All of the dispatches examined were strongly sympathetic to the Nationalist cause with little effort made whatsoever toward objective reporting.[18] Since the N. C. W. C. news service was controlled by the Catholic hierarchy, and as most Catholic publications relied upon this service for news coverage in Spain, the hierarchy was in position to control the political convictions of many Catholics from a central point.[19]

One particular Spanish correspondent who was the subject of Catholic criticism was Herbert L. Matthews of the *New York Times*. Father Thorning charged that Matthews had "abandoned any pretense of serving as anything more or less than a rabid Red partisan," and, "upon analysis his dispatches are revealed as nine-tenths 'interpretations' of official policy," or " 'human interest' narratives of events behind the Red front." At the same time he added that W. P. Carney, *New York Times* correspondent in Insurgent territory, had shown in his reporting a "high degree of journalistic responsibility and personal courage," while confining himself to "straight news stories."[20] Matthews, however, was not without supporters in the United States. On January 8, 1938, the *New York Times* published a letter from eight prominent editors and journalists which stated their admiration for Matthews and pointed out the unreliability of Carney. The letter concluded; "We shall continue to read Herbert Matthews to discover what is really going on in Spain."[21] Nevertheless, strong criticism of Matthews continued and the Catholic Press Association, meeting at its annual convention in New York City, passed a resolution stating that it had no confidence in Matthews "in view of his alleged unfair reporting in Spain."[22] One editor, Vincent Fitzpatrick of the *Catholic Review,* stated that Matthews was either "inaccurate or unfair" while Carney was "consistently accurate."[23] It is true that Matthews was personally sympathetic to the Spanish Government. Several years after the Spanish Civil War he wrote that "today, whenever in this world I meet a man or woman who fought for Spanish liberty, I meet a kindred soul."[24] This strong personal feeling, however, was not so readily found in Matthews' dispatches as his critics have charged.

Few papers and magazines of the secular press in the United States were sympathetic to General Franco. Perhaps the most notable example of this small group were the newspapers controlled by William Randolph Hearst.[25] These papers habitually branded the Loyalists as "Reds," played down their victories, and built up their defeats. The Hearst press used Spanish-American War methods in writing about "atrocities" in Spain. In an editorial entitled "Red Savages of Spain," the editors of the *Los Angeles Examiner* stated that out of a total of 33,500 priests in Spain, 14,000 had been slain by the "Reds," and in twenty-three dioceses "all" churches had been burned.[26] On another occasion a story appeared in the same paper describing the horrors of "Red tortures" in Spain. Some of the unfortunate victims, related the *Examiner,* were burned in oil with the cries of "Mercy! Mercy!" often heard.[27] In discussing the reporting of the Spanish War in the American press, President Roosevelt wrote to Ambassador Bowers, "You are right about the distortion of the news. . . . Over here the Hearst papers are playing up all kinds of atrocities on the part of what they call the

Communist government in Madrid — nothing about atrocities on the part of the rebels."[28]   This campaign against the Republican Government by the Hearst papers was relentlessly carried on throughout the course of the Spanish War.[29]

American opinion was frequently shocked at the brutality shown by the bombing of civilians in Spain. The provisions of the neutrality law did not prevent widespread expressions of indignation when Insurgent aircraft attacked the Basque city of Guernica, and, according to press reports, killed eight hundred noncombatants.[30]   The editors of the New York Times declared that the "bombing . . . of Guernica . . . has aroused world-wide indignation against the Rebel leadership." Are the foreign and Spanish forces of Franco, they continued, "deliberately flouting world opinion" in bombings which are "reckless and inexcusable massacres?"[31]   Seventy-six prominent American leaders in religion, education, politics, professions, and business were moved to sign a public protest. The signers stated that

> the ancient Basque city of Guernica has been razed to the ground by Fascist Insurgent airplanes. We refuse to condone such atrocities by our silence. We do not attempt to assess the contending causes which now struggle for mastery in Spain, but we do insist that this ruthless aerial warfare upon women and children stands outside the pale of morality and of civilization. We insist that there is no such thing as partisanship when this type of mass murder occurs, or is permitted to occur. We denounce the monstrous crime of Guernica in the name of justice and humanity.[32]

This appeal was sent to five thousand clergymen of all denominations throughout the country with the request that it be read from the pulpit.[33]

A similar statement was issued by ninety-eight American writers who stated that the neutrality policy of the United States should not prevent condemnation by private citizens of "the military faction which with its allies is making war upon the legally and democratically elected republican government of Spain." They condemned the deliberate bombardment of hospitals, playgrounds, and orphan asylums, and the "cowardly and cruel" attacks on Madrid and Guernica.[34]   The editors of the Catholic weekly, Commonweal, acidly observed that a large number must have signed the statement without thinking about "the many thousands of priests and nuns and civilian men, and women, and children, brutally and often horribly slain, and sometimes tortured, by the Anarchists and Communists and criminals, both before the revolt of the Army and after it, but entirely apart from the actual fighting in the Civil War." The Spanish Reds, the *Commonweal* concluded, "are attacking democracy far more so than their opponents."[35]

Senator Borah was not merely content to sign protests condemning the "air terror" at Guernica; he addressed the Senate and described to his colleagues this "example of Fascist strategy." After recalling the recent slaughter of the Ethiopians by Mussolini's legions, Borah said it was the Spanish Civil War, however, where

fascism presents to the world its masterpiece. . . . So long as men and women may be interested in searching out from the pages of history outstanding acts of cruelty and instances of needless destruction of human life they will linger longest and with the greatest horror over the . . . Fascist war in Spain. . . . It remained for the Fascist warfare to select the deadliest weapons which the ingenuity of man has contrived and to show to the world how thorough and effective these weapons are when used for the destruction of women and children. . . . Fascism boasts of courage, of the bravery of its soldiers; boasts how it makes men of its adherents, and tells other peoples that fascism makes heroes of the young. And, as evidence of the fulfillment of its creed, it points to the subjugation of the wholly weak and disarmed Ethiopia, and now doubtless will take pride in the successful slaughter of women and children throughout Spain. No language can describe the scene at Guernica, and Guernica was not a single instance; it was simply a culmination of a long line of unspeakable atrocities.[36]

Also in protest against the Guernica attack, Senator Matthew Neely (D-West Virginia) inserted in the *Record* an editorial from the *Wheeling Intelligencer* entitled, "The Unmasking in Spain." The editors of the *Intelligencer* declared:

It is no longer war in bleeding Spain. It is slaughter; cruel, cold, calculated extermination of men, women, and children. There has been terror on both sides as always in such a conflict, but nowhere in all the shocking records has one read of such fiendish ferocity as that exhibited by the Nazi aviators at Guernica and Durango, with their leaden hailstorms, poison gas and incendiary bombs let loose on the fleeing populace of the peaceful and piously Catholic Basque country.

Dictatorship, as represented by Hitler and Mussolini, and the would-be dictator, Franco, has left a fitting memorial before Bilbao, before which liberty loving and humane people everywhere must stand aghast. . . .

It has been made plain that the important thing to remember is this: That Franco and his foreign troops are invaders seeking to overthrow a government that the Spanish people duly elected at the polls; that regardless of its many mistaken policies, it was a constitutional government.[37]

Many of the supporters of General Franco expressed doubt that such atrocities had ever occurred. Edward H. Knoblaugh charged that the principal damage in Guernica was committed by "Anarchist incendiaries" and "Asturian dynamiters";[38] while Merwin K. Hart said that "aside from isolated cases, if any, I don't believe that the Nationalists have been guilty of atrocities."[39] Father Thorning, at a session of the American Catholic Historical Association, strongly criticized the *New York Times* for its "partisan" editorial condemning Franco for the bombing of Guernica. The Catholic press, he emphasized, was the "only" news source to secure accurate news about both sides in Spain.[40] Another writer admitted that the bombing of women and children by the Rebels was a terrible thing, but, he added, "If France and England were at war the same thing would happen to Paris and London. It is absolutely unavoidable under modern conditions in time of war."[41]

During the early months of 1938 the Insurgents, aided by the recent arrival of heavy bombers from Germany and Italy, unleashed a campaign of open bombings directed primarily against Barcelona and other coastal cities. The heaviest series of attacks occurred between the night of March 16 and the afternoon of March 18. The city of Barcelona was subjected to eighteen air raids, and missiles were dropped on all sections, residential as well as business. At least 1,000 persons were reported killed and twice that number wounded.[42] Supporters of the Loyalists argued that the attacks had a deliberately terroristic purpose – to lower the morale of the civilian population. The Insurgents, however, declared that Barcelona contained over 180 military objectives and that the attacks were directed against those points.

The bombing of Barcelona, like the attack on Guernica, aroused public opinion in this country. Secretary Hull released a statement in which he declared that "this Government holds that no theory of war can justify such conduct as the bombing of civilians during the recent air raids." The Secretary manifested a sense of horror at what had taken place, and expressed the hope that civilian populations would not again be bombed from the air.[43] Two months later, in June, Acting Secretary Welles released the following statement concerning the bombings in Spain:

> The Government of the United States has on numerous occasions expressed the belief that the outbreak of serious hostilities anywhere in the world might in some way affect the interests of this country. . . .

> In Europe there have been going on hostilities, every aspect of which the American people and this Government have deplored. . . . When methods used . . . take form of ruthless bombing of unfortified localities with the resultant slaughter of civilian population and in particular women and children, public opinion in the United States regards such methods barbarous. . . . This Government, while scrupulously adhering to the policy of nonintervention, reiterates this nation's emphatic reprobation of such methods and acts.[44]

The editors of the *Christian Science Monitor* bitterly assailed Franco for the raids on Barcelona and described the attack as a "needless slaughter of defenseless people." It was suggested by the *Monitor* that an appeal from the Catholic clergy could save thousands of lives.[45] Other groups likewise appealed to Catholic influence to stop the indiscriminate civilian bombings in Spain. Sixty-one Protestant Episcopal and Methodist Episcopal bishops signed an open letter asking the Catholic hierarchy to "disavow any tacit approval of these appalling tactics." "We realize," they stated, "that the Catholic hierarchy in this country has for reasons which seem good to it, chosen to defend the Franco cause [and] it is for this reason, knowing that word from you would carry weight and force, that we call upon you to act."[46] Similar voices of protest were expressed by a petition to President Roosevelt asking him "to speak for us, voicing the protest of the American people."⁴⁷ The editors of the *New Orleans Times-Picayune* declared:

> Outrages of this kind have been so frequent as to leave no doubt that they are approved by the insurgent chieftain, Franco, and his foreign allies. The mental and moral qualities of commanders who order such atrocities — and of governments which sanction their continuance in defiant disregard of protests and appeals from humane people the world over — can never be used for pointing-with-pride purposes by truthful historians present and future — nor by their own right-thinking peoples.⁴⁸

The Catholic press and hierarchy were quick to reply to the atrocity charges hurled at General Franco. In commenting on the Barcelona bombing Cardinal O'Connell remarked, "General Franco would not do a thing like that. It must have been a military manoeuvre." The Cardinal criticized the American press and American people for a tendency to favor the Loyalist cause. Nor should Americans be so bitter on the question of fascism, he said; if European countries want this "wall of defense against communism, it is not up to us to say what kind of government they should have."⁴⁹ In a direct reply to the Protestant bishops, Father Thorning, speaking before a meeting of the Knights of Columbus attended by 1,200 Catholics, declared that the Protestants should make a "dignified apology." He stated that General Franco was "the highest type of Christian gentleman and Spanish officer, who is leading his hosts to victory in a triumph that will have its impact on the civilized world." Father Thorning particularly wanted to know why the bishops did not "utter an appeal on behalf of the slaughtered priests and against gangster murders of the religious and of innocent laymen as well as women by the Reds."⁵⁰ Some Catholics also took offense at the statement issued by Secretary Hull concerning the bombing of civilians in Spain. The editors of *Catholic Action* criticized the Secretary for his

> complete silence when, also in Spain, not hundreds but thousands of priests and religious were wantonly murdered. The killings had back of them not even the attempted justification of military exigencies; they were perpetrated on the simple basis of the victims being religious. . . . One would . . . expect from the leading Cabinet officer of our Government some-

what more consistency in the matter of such expression as Mr. Hull has just issued.[51]

Because many persons in the United States felt a deep sympathy and concern for one of the opposing factions in Spain, literally thousands of Americans openly displayed this feeling by joining one of the numerous humanitarian organizations for the purpose of sending funds and relief to the people of that war-torn country. Most of these groups favored the Loyalists but a small minority, mostly led and supported by Catholics, worked on behalf of the Insurgents. The largest organization supporting the Republican Government was the North American Committee to Aid Spanish Democracy, with Bishop Francis J. McConnell, who was a leader of the liberal forces within the Methodist Episcopal Church, as chairman, and Reverend Herman F. Reissig, likewise of the Methodist Episcopal Church, as secretary. This organization represented approximately fifteen groups, including the Medical Bureau to Aid Spanish Democracy, American League against War and Fascism, the American Student Union, the League for Industrial Democracy, and the Socialist and Communist parties. The Committee had about sixty chapters throughout the country which held meetings, distributed literature, and collected food, clothing, and funds.[52] These organizations were most active in the New York area, where many meetings and benefits were held.[53]

One of the affiliated bodies, the American Friends of Spanish Democracy, headed by Bishop Robert L. Paddock, a retired Episcopal bishop, was primarily concerned with issuing protests designed to influence American policy toward Spain. The Medical Bureau to Aid Spanish Democracy, headed by Dr. Walter B. Cannon of the Harvard Medical School, was particularly active and not only raised funds and supplies but sent doctors and nurses to Spain. By July 1937 the Bureau was reported to have collected $118,045 and to have established six hospitals in Spain, with eighteen ambulances and ninety-nine American surgeons, nurses, and ambulance drivers.[54] The American Consul General at Barcelona, Mahlon F. Perkins, sent photographs to the State Department of an ambulance unit which had passed through that city. This unit was described as the "Benjamin Franklin Corps" of the Medical Bureau — American Friends of Spanish Democracy. Perkins commented that "a survey of the facts can leave no reasonable doubt that these expeditions have been sent to Spain, not from purely humanitarian motives, but with the primary purpose of assisting one of the opposing parties to win the war." He suggested that it was doubtful if a single member of these American units would be willing to perform humanitarian services for the Nationalists. The Consul General declared that the alternative in Spain was not between "Right" and "Left" but between "chaos" and "tyranny." He believed that Bishop Paddock and the Friends of Spanish Democracy should devote their energies to fields where they were more "precisely informed."[55]

Both the Communist and Socialist parties, especially in New York, were active in their support of these organizations. Only a few weeks after the outbreak of the war in Spain the New York State District of the Communist party adopted a resolution declaring its support for the Spanish people in their struggle against fascism.[56] Earl Browder was a frequent speaker for the Loyalist cause, asking "all progressives, trade unionists, liberals, and labor to support the Loyalists morally and financially."[57] Many of these organizations aided volunteers to reach Spain or enlisted "technical" assistants for the Spanish Government. The American Society for Technical Aid to Spanish Democracy stated that every American worker going to Spain "would free a Spanish worker to join the military forces of his own country." The Society felt confident that "many electricians, steel workers, truck drivers, miners, bakers, and others are ready to respond to the call to serve in freedom's cause, though behind the firing line."[58]

Other Americans devoted their efforts to the reception, care, and repatriation of wounded and able-bodied American volunteers who had served in Spain. One small group composed of Edgar Mowrer of the *Chicago Daily News,* Ernest Hemingway, and Charles Sweeney took a particular interest in this matter. These men were especially apprehensive lest the Spanish Government collapse and the wounded Americans in hospitals be massacred by Franco's Moorish troops. Efforts were made to obtain sufficient funds from the organizations which sent these volunteers to Spain for the cost of their care and repatriation.[59] Earl Browder, David McKelvey White, National Chairman of the Friends of the Abraham Lincoln Brigade, and Louis Bromfield, Chairman of the Emergency Committee of Americans Wounded in Spain, along with the Medical Bureau, North American Committee to Aid

Spanish Democracy, undertook special drives for such funds. Bernard Baruch, among many, was prevailed upon to contribute $10,000 "to get those boys back home."[60] The American Red Cross also made available to the State Department certain funds for the repatriation of destitute Americans. These funds were contributed, however, on the understanding that they would not be used for repatriating persons who had proceeded to Spain after the outbreak of the conflict for services in the armed forces of that country.[61] Although the State Department refused to allocate any funds to defray the expenses of wounded Americans returning from Spain, American diplomatic officials cooperated fully with private organizations and individuals in making arrangements for the evacuation of these repatriates.

Besides New York City there was also a considerable amount of pro-Loyalist activity in Hollywood, California. Edward Sullivan, special investigator for the Dies Committee, reported that the motion picture industry had donated "large sums" to the North American Committee to Aid Spanish Democracy.[62] The Motion Picture Artists Committee, headed by Dashiell Hammett, was likewise active in support of the Loyalists. At least one public statement was made indicating that the Committee had purchased eighteen automobiles for the Madrid Government.[63] One Hollywood observer has commented that the Spanish Civil War "roused eager partisanship for the anti-Fascist cause. Stars gave benefit parties; screen writers spoke at meetings; [and] directors raised money for ambulances."[64]

The leading organization supporting the cause of General Franco was the American Committee for Spanish Relief, headed by Michael Williams, editor of the *Commonweal*. The Spanish Embassy branded this organization as "pro-Rebel"; however, Ogden H. Hammond, committee treasurer, stated that "although the committee funds were to be distributed in Rebel territory, its work was nonpolitical and money would go to victims regardless of politics."[65] Other Catholics took an active role in obtaining funds for Spanish Catholics. Rev. Thomas E. Molloy, Bishop of the Diocese of Brooklyn, authorized the collection of money to aid "persecuted" Catholics in Spain. Bishop Molloy declared that since the "Reds" in the United States were active in the Spanish fight, American Catholics must aid their religious brothers in Spain.[66]

In addition to the activities previously mentioned, the American Red Cross actively supported efforts to make shipments of supplies for impartial relief in Spain. On September 17, 1938, Secretary Hull stated that the State Department realized the growing human misery and starvation of the people in Spain. Since the American people could not remain indifferent, the Secretary indicated that the American Red Cross would handle for distribution a large quantity of flour to be processed in the United States from surplus wheat to be turned over by the Federal Surplus Commodities Corporation. Hull added that the flour would be sent to Spain for impartial distribution.[67] Three months later the State Department announced that 60,000 barrels of flour had been sent to Spain, but since this was still not a sufficient amount the Federal Surplus Commodities Corporation made available 500,000 additional bushels of wheat which were handled in a similar manner.[68] Secretary Hull instructed the American Ambassador in Brazil, Jefferson Caffery, to bring "discreetly and tactfully" to the attention of Brazilian authorities the possibility of donating a certain amount of surplus coffee to the Spanish refugees.[69] Ambassador Caffery replied a few days later that the Brazilian Government had decided, "solely because we are suggesting it," to donate coffee to the Spanish refugees.[70] The American Red Cross transported the coffee from Brazilian ports and supervised its distribution in Spain in the same manner as the flour shipments from the United States.

Ambassador Bowers frequently pleaded with President Roosevelt to do something for the civilian refugees in Spain.[71] Roosevelt replied that he was "anxious that the United States make just as large a contribution as is possible," and he explained to Bowers the efforts made by the Red Cross and various Government agencies for Spanish relief. "All I can say," the President concluded, "is that what can be done will be done."[72] Later Roosevelt was prevailed upon, possibly by Mrs. Morgenthau or Mrs. Roosevelt, to appoint a committee of prominent Americans to raise funds for humanitarian relief in Spain. Such funds were to be applied through the Red Cross.[73] Mrs. Roosevelt was likewise very active in Spanish relief work, often being subjected to strong criticism for this reason. Her efforts were fully appreciated by the Spanish Government, which on February 13, 1939, presented her with a collection of Goya etchings through Ambassador de los Ríos in commemoration of her humanitarian activities.[74]

To decrease further the danger of involvement in the Spanish Civil War, the State Department announced early in 1937 that Americans desiring to travel abroad must make an affidavit that they did not intend to travel in Spain. "No exceptions have been deemed feasible," Secretary Hull stated, "notwithstanding the eminence and fine character of the organizations under whose auspices a person or persons may go to Spain." The Department pointed out that the American Red Cross was not sending personnel to Spain but was contributing to the International Red Cross which had representatives in both Loyalist and Rebel cities, and intimated that Americans who wished to aid the Spaniards might contribute to that organization.[75] No opposition apparently arose over the sailing of the first unit sent to Spain in January 1937 by the Medical Bureau to Aid Spanish Democracy. Early in March, however, the departure of the second unit was blocked by the new regulation affecting the issuance of passports.

This ruling was vigorously opposed by liberals throughout the country. Representative McReynolds reported that he had received literally thousands of communications expressing sympathy for the Loyalist cause and protesting the decision of the State Department.[76] The editors of the *Nation* declared that the neutrality policy was going beyond any legal authority and complained that the new regulation was probably inspired by a desire not to antagonize the Catholics whose support was desired on the Supreme Court issue.[77] Apparently as a result of pressure from these and similar sources, the Department reversed its original decision and announced that passports would be issued to physicians, nurses, and necessary attendants of *bona fide* medical and relief missions destined from this country to Spain.[78] Thus medical units were permitted to sail and solicitations for funds continued.

Perhaps the most militant crusaders for the Loyalist cause in the United States were members of the Communist and Socialist parties. On October 16, 1936, Stalin is reported to have written the Central Committee of the Communist party in Spain that "the toilers of the Soviet Union only do their duty when they give all their aid within their power to the revolutionary masses of Spain. They realize that the liberation of Spain from the oppression of the fascist reactionaries is not a private affair of the Spaniards. It is the common cause of all advanced and progressive mankind."[79]

Expressing the same sentiment, *Pravda*, central organ of the Communist party in the Soviet Union, stated:

> The working people of the world cannot remain indifferent and keep silent when the fate of the Spanish people is being decided and when the mercenaries of Franco are trying to annihilate the free people of Spain with bayonet, bullets, bombs, and hunger. The brave people of Spain turn their eyes toward the Soviet Union. In our struggle for Socialism the Spanish people find their strength, inspiration and energy.[80]

Appeals were also transmitted from the Comintern to the working classes of the world to rally "millions of forces of the international worker's movement in defense of the Spanish people against fascist barbarians."[81] Georgi Dimitrov, Secretary General of the Communist International, asserted: "To speed up and facilitate the victory of the Spanish people, a greater increase of concrete activities on the part of the international proletariat and all democratic forces is needed. . . . It can be said without exaggeration that there is no loftier duty for the international proletariat and for all honest elements of humanity than increasing assistance to the Spanish people to insure their victory."[82]

The Communists in the United States soon accepted the challenge that Communists throughout the world would lead the fight against Spanish fascism. On August 18, 1936, the New York State District of the Communist party, at a mass meeting in New York City attended by 12,000 persons, pledged sympathy and financial support for the Loyalist Government. A resolution was adopted which declared that the New York State District of the Communist party would support the Spanish people in their struggle against fascism by demonstrations and fund raising campaigns.[83] Two months later Earl Browder, Secretary of the Communist party and Communist candidate for President, delivered an address over the network of the National Broadcasting Company in which he made a strong plea for the Spanish Republican Government, stating that

> I appeal to the working class leaders and parties in the United States, to the trade unions, to Progressives everywhere, to join us in united action to help save Spanish democracy. I appeal to the Socialist Party as well as to the Right-wing Socialist

leaders in New York, Connecticut and elsewhere to work out an independent program of action against the Spanish fascists.[84]

The Socialist party and its leader, Norman Thomas, likewise were sympathetic to the Loyalist cause but during the early days of the Spanish conflict were less outspoken than the Communists. On August 31, 1936, Thomas wrote in the *Socialist Call*:

France and Russia and Great Britain might at the beginning have ended the menace of Spanish fascism and worked for peace by compelling the pro-fascist nations to keep hands off or by supporting a duly recognized government with the means to meet a military attack.[85]

The Executive Council of the Socialist party issued an appeal for financial support to aid the Spanish Government and in a public statement declared, "The least the United States can do is to remain neutral and insist through diplomatic and other peaceful channels that all other countries shall do the same."[86] Later, however, the Socialists joined with Communists and other extreme left-wing groups in shifting from an antiwar to an antifascist policy. Norman Thomas reminded his fellow workers that "to aid Loyalist Spain is not an act of generosity; it is a debt of honor."[87] The American Socialist attitude toward Spain was largely influenced by the internal political scene within that country. The Socialists were quick to resent any possible domination by the Communists. Sam Baron, Spanish correspondent for the *Socialist Call*, at one time reported that the Stalinist Communists were splitting the Loyalist Government. He indicated that the Loyalists would win but "Communist tactics in suppressing working class groups may endanger the possibility of an early victory."[88] In the spring of 1938, when the Socialists in Spain regained much of their power that had previously been lost to the Communists, the American Socialists increased the tempo of their campaign to aid the Loyalists. Whereas the *Socialist Call* on March 12 heralded a "Nation Wide Movement Against War," the theme had changed by April 2 with the headline: "Socialists Show Solidarity with Loyalist Spain." The Socialists actively assisted the North American Committee to Aid Spanish Democracy in fund collecting drives and tried, but failed, to recruit a Eugene V. Debs Column to fight in Spain.

Representatives of organized labor also took early notice of the war in Spain. The Executive Board of New York Local 144 of the Cigar Makers International Union of America announced that it was appealing to all its members to support the United Front in Spain against fascism.[89] Likewise, at the fifty-sixth annual convention of the American Federation of Labor in 1936, there was a strong sentiment favorable to the Loyalist regime. A resolution was introduced by the Cleaners, Dyers, and Pressers Union No. 19989 of Los Angeles which stated that the Fascists in Spain were attempting to overthrow the legally constituted government, attempting to destroy the trade union movement, and that a victory by the Axis-supported Franco would increase and encourage fascism. Therefore be it

> Resolved: That the American Federation of Labor go on record to aid the Spanish Loyalists by exposing the fascist countries whose anti-labor governments are supporting the fascist rebels in Spain, and, that the American Federation of Labor agree to cooperate with those groups and organizations that are rallying public opinion and financial and material help for the Spanish Loyalists.

Although there was a vigorous plea on the floor of the convention favoring the resolution, the delegates adopted a committee's recommendation that the resolution be referred to the Executive Council for further consideration.[90] The proponents of the resolution were never able to muster sufficient strength in subsequent conventions to get it approved.[91] Nevertheless, elements of organized labor assisted in humanitarian campaigns to send supplies to the Loyalists as well as exerting considerable influence on the American Government to alter its Spanish policy.[92]

Although there were many persons in the United States who actively sympathized with one or the other of the protagonists in Spain, the American Institute of Public Opinion reported in 1937 that a majority of the voters were indifferent as to which side triumphed. Dr. Gallup stated that two-thirds of the voters were unconcerned with the war, while slightly more than a fifth backed the Loyalists because of hatred for Mussolini and Hitler, and approximately a tenth favored Franco because of a hatred for Stalin. The Institute pointed out that as far as Spain was concerned, most people commented that to defend a legally constituted government was a better cause than attacking it, although they doubted whether the Spaniards would have a democratic government regardless of the outcome of the war.[93] The *Fortune* Survey, conducted by Elmo Roper, supported these conclusions.[94] The well-known historian, Thomas A. Bailey, concluded that in regard to the Spanish conflict the majority of the American people "had no opinion, they did not know, they did not care, they were confused as to what it was all about." Americans were convinced, he continued, that no true democracy could come from a war with the Communists supporting one side and Fascists supporting the other. The people were "still under the spell of neutrality at any price" and the Roosevelt Administration was responding to the desires of the people.[95]

As the war progressed, however, the Gallup Polls reported less and less impartiality among American voters. Whereas in February 1937, 22 per cent favored the Loyalists, 11 per cent favored Franco, and 67 per cent were neutral;[96] in December 1938, almost two years later, 46 per cent favored the Loyalists, 14 per cent favored Franco, and 40 per cent were neutral.[97] Among those persons who actually expressed a preference for one side the percentage was even higher in support of the Loyalists. In February 1937 in answer to the question, "Which side do you sympathize with in the Spanish Civil War — the Loyalists or Franco?" 65 per cent of the people who expressed a decided preference favored the Loyalists. In February 1938 this figure had risen to 75 per cent and in December 1938 it had climbed one percentage point to 76.[98] This was due in part to increased intervention of the Axis powers in Spain, to the savage bombing of civilians by the Franco forces, and the propaganda drives of pro-Loyalist organizations in this country.

The feeling for one side or the other in the Spanish conflict was purely ideological, however, and does not suggest that Americans wanted the United States to intervene actively in Spain. On the contrary, most people were probably in full accord with the statement of the *Commercial and Financial Chronicle* which declared, "Grievous and fateful as the Civil War in Spain undoubtedly is, it is not an American concern. . . . The experience of 1914-16 should be a warning against allowing propaganda to deflect either the administration or the country at large from a strictly neutral course."[99] Nevertheless, most of the American people and the American press were convinced that the Spanish Government had much the better of the argument in its fight to save Spain from the inroads of fascism.

NOTES

1. *Review of Reviews* (New York), XCV (April, 1937), 82.

2. An excellent discussion of words as symbols of emotional involvement in the cause for one or the other of the Spanish factions can be found in O. W. Riegal, "Press, Radio, and the Spanish Civil War," *Public Opinion Quarterly*, I (January, 1937), 131-36. In this study the present writer's choice of terms is for convenience only.

3. President Azaña, Premier Negrín, Álvarez del Vayo, et al., *Spain's War of Independence* (Washington, 1937), p. 3.

4. Institute of Propaganda Analysis, "Spain: A Case Study," *Propaganda Analysis* (New York), II (July 1, 1939), 1.

5. Edward Lodge Curran, *Franco* (New York, 1937), pp. 14-15.

6. Merwin K. Hart, *America — Look at Spain* (New York, 1939), p. 234.

7. The Peninsula News Service and affiliated agencies in the United States were objects of much criticism. Senator Nye told his colleagues in the Senate that General Franco had a well-perfected espionage system in the United States. This spy ring, Nye charged, included former Spanish Ambassador to the United States, Juan Francisco de Cárdenas, who maintained headquarters at the Ritz Carlton Hotel in New York. The North Dakota Senator stated that such people threatened American neutrality. "They have sought to collect funds for the Franco cause," he said, "and have carried on in a way to indicate that they constitute the clearing house for the Spanish Insurgents in the United States." *Congressional Record*, 75 Cong., 1 Sess., XLXXXI (May 10, 1937), 4269-72. On the other hand, Ambassador de los Ríos was charged by Franco supporters with conducting a propaganda exchange at the Spanish Embassy in Washington. Needless to say both sides denied these accusations. Louis Minsky, "Propaganda Bureaus as 'News Services'," *Public Opinion Quarterly*, II (October, 1938), 677.

8. Lester Ziffren (former manager of the Madrid Bureau, United Press), "The Correspondent in Spain," *Public Opinion Quarterly*, I (July, 1937), 112-16; also see Riegal, "Press, Radio, and the Spanish Civil War," pp. 134-35. The noted news commentator, H. V. Kaltenborn, was in Europe at the outbreak of the Spanish War and through the facilities of the Columbia Broadcasting System he was able to transmit directly from the battlefield describing the conflict to thousands of Americans in the United States. Kaltenborn recalls his experiences in *Kaltenborn Edits the News* (New York, 1937), pp. 11-32.

9. Riegal, "Press, Radio, and the Spanish Civil War," p. 135.

10. With one or two notable exceptions such as W. P. Carney of the *New York Times* and Edward H. Knoblaugh of the Associated Press, American newspaper men in Spain were decidedly sympathetic to the Loyalist cause.

11. Fletcher Pratt, "Propaganda From Spain," *American Mercury* (New York), XLI (July, 1937), 409-22.

12. Edward H. Knoblaugh, "The Loyalist Propaganda Machine," *Catholic World* (New York), CXLVI (January, 1938), 479-81. This is a chapter from Knoblaugh's book *Correspondent in Spain* (New York, 1937).

13. Father Joseph F. Thorning, "Why the Press Failed on Spain," *Catholic World*, CXLVI (December, 1937), 289-91.

14. *Commonweal* (New York), XXVI (May 7, 1937), 33-37; (May 21, 1937), 85-87; (June 4, 1937), 102-06.

15. Rev. James M. Gillis, "The Catholic Press Shows the Way," *Catholic Action of the South*, August 19, 1937. Father Gillis for many years was editor of *Catholic Action*.

16. *New York Times*, December 30, 1937.

17. "The Catholic Press in the Present World Crisis," *Catholic Action* (Washington, D. C.), XXI (February, 1939), 19-21.

18. Typical feature stories were: "Franciscans Civil War Dead Now Pass 130 Mark," *Catholic Action of the South*, December 17, 1936; "Leftists Propaganda Flops," *ibid.*, April 14, 1938; "Pressure Used in Attacks on Neutrality Law," *ibid.*, May 12, 1938; and "Spanish Embassy Branded No. 1 Red Station," *ibid.*, December 8, 1938.

19. In 1935 the *Catholic Press Directory* reported Catholic newspapers and magazines in the United States had a combined circulation of 7,000,000.

20. *New York Times*, December 30, 1937.

21. *Ibid.*, January 8, 1938. Signing the letter were W. W. Norton, Archibald MacLeish, Bruce Bliven, Lynn Carrick, Bennett Cerf, Richard S. Childs, Kyle Crichton, and Freda Kirchwey.

22. *Ibid.*, June 25, 1939.

23. *Ibid.* On September 10, 1939, Carney was awarded a special gold medal by the Knights of Columbus "for distinguished service to journalism in reporting the Spanish Civil War." *Ibid.*, September 11, 1939.

24. Herbert L. Matthews, *The Education of a Correspondent* (New York, 1946), p. 67. Matthews has emerged as a great journalist and is now one of the leading editorial writers for the *New York Times*.

25. Others include *The American Mercury* and, for a short period early in the war, *Time* magazine.

26. *Los Angeles Examiner*, February 10, 1937.

27. *Ibid.*, April 9, 1939.

28. Roosevelt to Bowers, September 16, 1936 (FDR Official Files, Drawer 2).

29. For a scathing condemnation of Hearst and his papers, see Evelyn Seeley, "Hearst Fights the Spanish Republic," *New Republic*, LXXXVIII (September 30, 1936), 217-20.

30. *New York Times*, May 2, 1937. This attack is also described in Bowers to Hull, April 30, 1937 (SD File No. 852.00/5276: tel.).

31. *Ibid.*, May 7, 29, 1937.

32. *Ibid.*, May 10, 1937.

33. Among the signers were Bishop Francis J. McConnell, Rabbi S. S. Wise, Bishop James E. Freeman, Dr. Harry Emerson Fosdick, Dr. Edgar DeWitt Jones, Senators Robert F. Wagner, Arthur Capper, Gerald P. Nye, Elmer Thomas, William E. Borah, Carter Glass, Homer T. Bone, Repre-

sentatives Hamilton Fish and Caroline O'Day and Presidents James Rowland Angell of Yale, Ray Lyman Wilbur of Stanford, and Mary E. Woolley of Mount Holyoke College. Others included Newton D. Baker, Charles A. Beard, Harvey Cushing, William Green, Alfred M. Landon, Henry L. Stimson, Dorothy Thompson, William A. White, Albert Einstein, and Clarence Darrow. *Ibid.* Senator Nye brought this protest to the attention of the Senate and had the full text of the message printed in the *Congressional Record,* 75 Cong., 1 Sess., LXXXI (May 10, 1937), A1225-26.

34. *New York Times,* March 1, 1937. Signers included Louis Adamic, F. P. Adams, Maxwell Anderson, Sherwood Anderson, Carl Becker, Robert Benchley, Van Wyck Brooks, W. E. B. DuBois, Erskine Caldwell, John Dewey, William Faulkner, John Gunther, Dorothy Canfield Fisher, Langston Hughes, Matthew Josephson, Sinclair Lewis, Walter Millis, Christopher Morley, Carl Sandburg, Upton Sinclair, Harold E. Stearns, Ida M. Tarbell, Thorton Wilder, Clifton Fadiman, George Soule, and Robert M. Lovett.

35. *Commonweal,* XXV (March 12, 1937), 537-38.

36. *Congressional Record,* 75 Cong., 1 Sess., LXXXI (May 6, 1937), 4237.

37. *Ibid.* (May 13, 1937), A1172-73.

38. Knoblaugh, *Correspondent in Spain,* pp. 170-85.

39. Hart, *America — Look at Spain,* p. 102.

40. *New York Times,* December 30, 1937.

41. Charles Vezin, letter to the editor, *Review of Reviews,* XCV (April, 1937), 82.

42. *New York Times,* March 27, 1938; *Times* (London), April 7, 1938.

43. *Press Releases,* March 26, 1938.

44. *Ibid.,* June 4, 1938.

45. *Christian Science Monitor,* March 22, 1938.

46. *New York Times,* March 21, 1938.

47. *Ibid.,* February 7, 1938. This petition was signed by 477 persons.

48. *New Orleans Times-Picayune,* May 27, 1938.

49. *New York Times,* March 19, 1938. The editors of *Advance,* official organ of the Congregational Church, remarked that efforts to promote better relations between Protestants and Catholics undergo heavy strain when attitudes like that of the Cardinal are made known. *Advance* (New York), CXXX (April 1, 1938), 156.

50. *New York Times,* March 28, 1938.

51. "Our Common Catholic Interests," *Catholic Action,* XX (April, 1938), 4.

52. Buell, "U. S. Neutrality in the Spanish Conflict," pp. 206-07.

53. See Appendix B.

54. Buell, "U. S. Neutrality in the Spanish Conflict," p. 207.

55. Perkins to Hull, April 20, 1937 (SD File No. 852.00/5392).

56. *New York Times,* August 19, 1936.

57. *Ibid.,* October 24, 1936. See also speeches by Norman Thomas and Earl Browder before 22,000 persons at a mass meeting in New York City. *Ibid.,* July 20, 1937.

58. *New Masses,* January 26, 1937.

59. Edwin C. Wilson (Chargé in France) to Hull, April 6, 1938 (SD File No. 852.2221/785: tel.).

60. Robert D. Murphy (Consul at Paris) to Hull, August 8, 1938 (SD File No. 852.2221/1131).

61. Hull to Wilson, April 9, 1938 (SD File No. 852.2221/785: tel.).

62. *New York Times,* August 15, 1938.

63. *Ibid.* Also see Leo C. Rosten, *Hollywood: The Movie Colony and the Movie Makers* (New York, 1941), pp. 140-43.

64. Margaret Farrand Thorp, *America at the Movies* (New Haven, 1939), p. 149.

65. *New York Times,* May 6, 1937. By the end of September 1937 the Committee reported that it had received $28,514 but that administrative and publicity expenses had amounted to $30,189. Consequently, nothing had been sent to Spain. *Press Releases,* September 29, 1937. Later, however, some supplies were sent to Spain.

66. *New York Times,* January 23, 1937. See Appendix B.

67. *Press Releases,* September 17, 1938.

68. *Ibid.,* December 24, 1938.

69. Hull to Caffery, September 21, 1938 (SD File No. 852.00/232a: tel.).

70. Caffery to Hull, September 28, 1938 (SD File No. 852.48/253: tel.).

71. Ambassador Bowers to President Roosevelt, December 6, 1938 (FDR Official Files, No. 422A).

72. President Roosevelt to Ambassador Bowers, December 6, 1938 (FDR Official Files, No. 422A).

73. Roosevelt to George MacDonald (asking MacDonald to be Chairman of the Committee), December 21, 1938 (FDR Official Files, No. 422D). See also Mrs. Rita Wallach Morgenthau to Roosevelt, January (n.d.), 1939 (FDR Official Files, No. 422D).

74. *New York Times,* February 14, 1939.

75. *Press Releases,* March 6, 1937.

76. *New York Times,* March 12, 1937.

77. "Is the State Department Favoring Franco?" *Nation,* CXLIV (March 13, 1937), 285. At that time the Roosevelt Administration was deeply involved in an effort to alter the structure of the United States Supreme Court.

78. *Press Releases,* March 20, 1937.

79. Harry Gannes, *How the Soviet Union Helps Spain* (New York, 1936), pp. 3-6.

80. *Ibid.,* p. 15.

81. *New York Times,* June 5, 1937.

82. *Ibid.,* January 2, 1937.

83. *Ibid.,* August 19, 1936.

84. *Ibid.,* October 24, 1936.

85. *Socialist Call,* August 31, 1936.

86. *New York Times,* August 15, 1936.

87. Norman Thomas, "Spain: A Socialist View," *Nation,* CXLIV (June 19, 1937), 700.

88. *Socialist Call,* November 13, 1937.

89. *New York Times,* August 15, 1936.

90. American Federation of Labor, *Proceedings of the Fifty-Sixth Annual Convention, 1936* (Washington, 1936), pp. 296, 578-80.

91. The A.F.L. later regretted this stand taken in regard to Spain. In 1946 both the A.F.L. and the C.I.O. demanded that the United States take the initiative in having the United Nations investigate charges against General Franco. A joint statement issued by the two organizations declared that the United States paid bitterly for its nonintervention policy during the Spanish Civil War. *New York Times,* March 31, 1946. This attitude was reaffirmed in 1950 when the A.F.L. Executive Council voted to adhere firmly to the policy of nonrecognition of the Franco Government. The Council stated: "Recognition of the Franco Government only paves the way for extensive financial aid to a despicable despotism now in the throes of a crisis which, if not alleviated by outside aid, can only lead to its doom." *New Orleans Times-Picayune,* February 6, 1950.

92. Supporters of General Franco pointed out that left-wing labor groups such as the National Maritime Union and the International Garment Workers Union were most active in aiding the Loyalist cause.

93. George Gallup and Claude Robinson, "American Institute of Public Opinion Surveys, 1935-1938," *Public Opinion Quarterly,* II (July, 1938), 389. See also F. S. Wickware, "What We Think About Foreign Affairs," *Harper's Magazine* (New York), CXXIX (September, 1939), 397-406.

94. Elmo Roper, "Fortune Survey," *Fortune Magazine* (New York), XV (April, 1937), 204.

95. Thomas A. Bailey, *The Man in the Street. The Impact of American Public Opinion on Foreign Policy* (New York, 1948), p. 10.

96. Gallup and Robinson, "American Institute of Public Opinion Surveys, 1935-1938," p. 389.

97. Parry, "The Spanish Civil War," p. 163. Parry had access to unpublished records of the National Opinion Research Center, Denver, Colorado.

98. "Public Opinion Survey," *Public Opinion Quarterly,* III (October, 1939), 600.

99. *Commercial and Financial Chronicle,* CXLIII (August 22, 1936), 1142-43.

Chapter Seven

A Holy War

The precarious position of the Catholic Church in Spain was an issue which for many people throughout the world transcended the political implications of the Spanish Civil War. Pope Pius XI openly sympathized with the Spanish Nationalists as it was his belief that the Loyalists were attempting to destroy the Church and convert Spain into a communistic state. The Pope declared that of all the perils which confronted human society, "the first, the greatest and now the general peril, is certainly communism in all its forms and degrees."[1] Accordingly, Pius XI charged that spreading Bolshevist propaganda in Europe caused the Spanish Civil War:

Satanic preparation has relighted — and that more fiercely — in neighboring Spain that hatred and savage persecution which have been confessedly reserved for the Catholic Church and Catholic religion as being the one real obstacle.

Our benediction, above any political and mundane consideration, goes in a special manner to all those who assume the difficult and dangerous task of defending and restoring the rights to honor God and religion.[2]

In May 1938 the Pope blessed General Franco, stating, "We send from our hearts the apostolic blessing, propitiator of divine favors";[3] and in April 1939, when the Nationalist army emerged victorious, the Pope telegraphed Franco: "Lifting up our heart to God, we give sincere thanks with your Excellency for Spain's Catholic victory."[4] Nor did Ambassador Bowers believe that the Pope was neutral in the Spanish struggle. In a letter to President Roosevelt

143

the Ambassador wrote that he was amused at the suggestion of Camille Chautemps, the French Premier, that the Pope was neutral in his feelings. Bowers declared: "He is just as neutral as he was in the case of Abyssinia. He is a very loyal Italian always. He has been favorable to the fascist cause in Spain, supported by 70,000 of Mussolini's army, throughout."[5]

In the United States a large majority of the supporters of General Franco were Catholics. This seemed to indicate that religion was the chief factor in determining their attitude.[6] Shortly after the outbreak of the Spanish Civil War the *Catholic World* published an article which reflected the views already prevalent among many Catholics in this country. This article, reprinted from the *Catholic Herald* of London, described the Madrid Government as communistic and stated that it was evident that the Soviet Union would attempt to interfere in the Spanish War. "Under these circumstances the anti-communist governments may reasonably hesitate to pledge themselves for an indefinite period of nonintervention." Although communism was an enemy of the Church, this writer sounded an apologetic note when he stated that Catholics could not view with satisfaction the dependence of Catholic institutions and culture on the protection of the anti-Communist dictators or the leaders of the military revolt in Spain. It was only an accident, he said, that Catholics and dictators had the same enemy — communism. In a Communist dictatorship hostility to Catholic life is complete and only anti-Communist dictators afforded a military shield for the Church against communism.[7]

The editors of the *Catholic World* were much more vigorous in the denunciation of the Loyalist Government than had been the writer in the *Herald*. They charged that the Madrid regime was "an anti-clerical government that has unleashed its fury against the Church." The editors asserted that priests and nuns were killed while all the churches, convents, monasteries, religious schools, and private chapels in Barcelona had gone up in flames. Thus in view of this open hostility to Catholicism, Catholics must unite to save the Church from its avowed enemies who were then in control of the Government.[8] The *Tidings*, official organ of the Los Angeles Archdiocese, warned that the Spanish Popular Front Government would drive the United States into war and the world would be endangered by the spread of communism.[9]

Other Catholics visited Spain and brought back news of "what is really happening" in that war-torn country. Rev. Karl J. Alter, Bishop of Toledo (Ohio), said that wherever he went, "Americans, including many non-Catholics, approached him and urged him to tell the American people . . . the truth about Nationalist Spain." That the struggle was "really . . . a war to save religion, morality and civilization itself." In describing conditions in Toledo (Spain) Bishop Alter stated that

> only five of the original 28 canons of the Cathedral are still alive, the rest have been slain by the Reds; from the Cathedral and other churches valuable manuscripts, chalices, ciboria, monstrances, etc., have been stolen by the Reds; Red airplanes have daily dropped explosives on towns of no military value; churches, altars, shrines, etc., have been needlessly and ruthlessly destroyed, bodies exhumed and valuables on the corpses removed. . . side altars of the Church were hacked and smashed, the main altar had been set afire, and that in an adjoining convent crypts had been opened and the bodies of nuns dragged out and left on the floor.[10]

Regarding his own feelings on the Spanish issue the Bishop told his congregation that

> I am not neutral. I don't want to be neutral. I want to be fair, objective and intelligently honest. According to the facts, there is only one side in Spain that can be intelligently and conscientiously approved — and that is Nationalist Spain. The other side is guilty of crimes that will seem fantastic when the American people learn of them.[11]

Certain Protestant groups were distressed by the antagonism exhibited by the Catholics toward the Spanish Republican Government. In their eyes support for Franco meant support for Hitler and Mussolini; thus the Catholic Church in America became the object of much criticism. A large number of Protestants saw the strife in Spain as a struggle between fascism and democracy and it was difficult for them to understand the position taken by most Catholics. Nor was it felt that the Catholics were being wholly fair in their interpretation of events in Spain. The *Christian Century* commented that

to a great extent the church [Catholic] has thrown the weight
of its influence upon the side of Franco and the insurgents.
Italian troops have gone into the war with banners blessed by
the church. It has played its part in representing the conflict
as one between atheistic bolshevism and the crusading forces of
Christianity. It has striven to create the impression that the
loyalists were murderous ruffians whose most characteristic
activities were desecrating altars, slaughtering priests and raping nuns, while the rebels and their invading allies were practically advancing on their knees.[12]

Advance, an organ of the Congregational Church, charged that all
Catholics who supported the Loyalist Government were severely
censured by the Catholic hierarchy. The editors warned the Catholics, however, that such a position was shortsighted and likely to
drive many liberals away from the Church.[13] A prominent religious
writer declared that the attitude of the Catholic Church in regard
to Spain was the "height of spiritual arrogance," and that the
Church was "too blind to see that it is defending a corrupt and
unjust civilization against a rising passion for justice."[14]

One of the most formidable controversies of the Spanish War
developed between Protestants and Catholics in the United States
over a joint pastoral letter prepared by the Catholic hierarchy in
Spain which justified the revolt against the Spanish Government.
The Spanish prelates stated that "false opinion created abroad,
particularly by a certain group of Spanish Catholics necessitated
the letter."[15] There were five principal points in the argument of
the Spanish bishops: (1) The Church did not want the war in
Spain although "thousands of her sons have taken arms on their
personal responsibility to save the principles of religion and Christian justice." (2) Since the Spanish Republic was proclaimed in
1931 the legislative and executive power in Spain had changed
Spanish history in a manner contrary to the needs of the national
spirit. (3) The elections of February 1936 were unjust. Although
the Right and Center parties received 500,000 more votes than the
parties of the Left, the former group elected 118 fewer deputies
because of the arbitrary annulment of votes in all the provinces.
(4) The Communist International had armed a revolutionary
Spanish militia so that Spain was virtually an armed camp when
the war broke out. (5) The civil war was legitimate because

five years of continued outrages of Spanish subjects in the
religious and social fields had endangered the very existence
of public welfare and had produced enormous spiritual unrest
among the Spanish people; and because when the legal means
were exhausted the idea entered the national conscience that
there was no other recourse except force to maintain order and
peace. Also because interests opposed to legitimate authority
had decided to overthrow the constituted order and establish
communism through violence. Finally, because, through the
fatal logic of facts, Spain had only this alternative: either to
perish under the precipitate assault of destructive communism,
already prepared and decreed, as has happened in the area
where the Nationalist Government has not triumphed, or to
attempt with titanic force to get rid of this frightful enemy
and save the fundamental principles of our social life and
national characteristics.[16]

Four conclusions were drawn by the prelates: (1) "The Church
could not remain indifferent in a fight, in which on one side, God
was renounced, while on the other side, notwithstanding human
defects, the fight was for the preservation of the old Spain and
Christian spirit." (2) The Church, however, "does not associate
herself with acts, tendencies, and intentions that figure in the
noble physiognomy of the Nationalist movement." (3) The civil-
military uprising "deepens in the people's consciousness two roots;
one of patriotism, and the other of religious sentiment." (4) There
is no other hope that Spain may again have justice and peace
except through the Nationalist movement.[17]

The letter from Spain provoked a heated exchange of statements by Protestant and Catholic leaders in this country. In a
letter prepared by Dr. Guy Emery Shipler, editor of the *Churchman,*
an independent Episcopal paper, and signed by 150 Protestant
clergymen, educators, and laymen, the Spanish hierarchy was
denounced for its stand. The Protestants stated that it was hard
to believe that the letter had been written in the twentieth century,
and charged that by the opinions expressed the Catholic hierarchy
in Spain demonstrated their "open hostility toward the popular
principles of freedom of worship and separation of church and
state." They characterized as "alarming" the bishops' "attempt
to justify a military rebellion against a legally elected government."
In so doing, they asserted, the hierarchy acted as "the apologists

for reaction and fascism." The letter continued: "Certainly the hierarchy can hardly expect to gain sympathy there, either for itself or for the Catholic religion with a declaration that treats with contempt principles that are the precious heritage of the American people." The Protestants were also disturbed by the fact that "no leaders of the Catholic Church in America have raised their voice in repudiation of the position taken by the Spanish hierarchy," and added that "they too seem to have given their blessing to General Franco and his Fascist allies." They declared that the pastoral letter approved of resort to violence, rejected not only the Popular Front Government of Spain, but also democratic institutions and the Spanish Republic itself. "It is clear," they maintained, "that the Spanish conflict is between the forces of democracy and social progress, on the one hand, and the forces of special privilege, and their Fascist allies on the other." Conceding that there had been excesses on the Loyalist side, the letter asserted that the Madrid regime had made every effort to prevent such occurrences, while on the Insurgent side Franco had encouraged violence. The Protestants stated that the Spanish hierarchy was indifferent to the actual facts of brutality and atrocities on the Rebel side. They claimed that priests and nuns had been murdered within National-ist territory, and the Protestant missions had been destroyed by the Insurgents.[18]

This document led to an immediate response by American Catholics. The Reverend Francis X. Talbot, editor of the Jesuit weekly, *America*, declared that the Protestants signing the letter were "misinformed of the facts" and were voicing opinions that had long been discredited. The open letter "neither establishes the point that it proposes nor engenders faith in the honesty of its authors or signatories." Father Talbot then declared that the

Protestant Christians of the United States, if they are to remain faithful to the principles of Christ, must repudiate the anti-Christ propaganda and practices of the Loyalist government, composed as it is of Communists, anarchists, syndicalists, and atheistic groups in Spain. By such an open letter published over their signatures they foster atheism and agnosticism.[19]

A similar expression was voiced by Reverend John J. O'Conner, acting managing editor of the *Commonweal*, who said that "if the distinguished gentlemen still believe that the struggle in Spain 'is between the forces of democracy and social progress on the one hand and the forces of special privilege and their Fascist allies on the other,' we can only express our regret that they have been so completely and so thoroughly hoodwinked."[20] Msgr. Michael J. Ready, General Secretary of the National Catholic Welfare Conference, commented that he could "only express astonishment that so large a number of intelligent and presumably fair-minded American Protestants, so far removed from the scene of the conflict and the sources of true information, could be stampeded into so harsh and hostile a diatribe against the harassed and suffering bishops of Spain."[21]

Ten days after the open letter of the Protestants was published 175 Catholics officially replied that the letter "misrepresented the facts and issues in Spain." The Catholic statement charged the existence of a "campaign of misrepresentation, errors and deliberate lies" against the Insurgents and challenged the Protestants to say whether they accepted and approved of a regime "which has carried on a ruthless persecution of the Christian religion since February 1936." The statement asserted that Catholics who supported Franco did so as private citizens and not as members of the Church. It was argued that the Communists seized power and attempted to institute a "Soviet Dictatorship," and were violating civil rights in Spain before the Army rose in revolt. The Catholic spokesmen stated that the reason Catholics supported the insurrection was to "save themselves from destruction and annihilation, not only as Catholics but as citizens." Charges of Insurgent atrocities were denied while it was maintained that the Communists had burned "all" the Catholic churches in the area they controlled, had destroyed "all" religious objects, and had "massacred virtually all priests in an attempt to destroy the Catholic religion." In conclusion the statement asserted that the Madrid Government then ruling Spain did not represent the will of the people, as two thirds of the Spaniards had "freely and enthusiastically acclaimed loyalty and allegiance to General Franco."[22]

In discussing the controversy over the Spanish prelates' letter, the editors of the *Nation* commented that American Catholics were placed in a very embarrassing position as "the savage tactics of the Christian Knight [Franco], his employment of Moors, and his close association with the neopagan, Catholic-baiting followers of Hitler has spread much doubt among the faithful." They added that the Catholics must speak out or accept fascism as the protector of the faith.[23] The editors of the *New Republic* described the pastoral letter of the Spaniards as a "boomerang," and claimed that it was not well received by Catholics throughout the world.[24] James T. Shotwell, Professor of History at Columbia University, in a letter to the *New York Times*, declared that the Spanish bishops have been blind to the social changes that have occurred in Spain which were unrelated to communism. It was Shotwell's belief that the "prelates have neither proved their case against their enemies nor justified their own."[25] In an effort to ameliorate the controversy Bishop Robert L. Paddock stated that he had signed the letter written by the Protestants, but did so "with no malice or intent to misrepresent, and certainly with no unfriendliness to the Roman Catholics in this country." He suggested that at least in matters concerning religion, "may we avoid calling each other names and feel and show a brotherly spirit."[26]

On October 19, 1937, an open invitation was extended by Spanish Ambassador de los Ríos for a mixed commission representing both Catholic and Protestant groups to go to Spain and visit both sides in order that "the whole question could be objectively clarified." Bishop Paddock, speaking as a member of the Protestant group, accepted the invitation, but no official Catholic reply was made.[27] In February 1939 a second invitation was extended by the Ambassador to prominent American Catholics to visit Loyalist Spain. No Catholics accepted this offer and Archbishop Michael Joseph Curley declined with the statement: "I guess he would have me come over wearing my clerical collar — and get murdered. . . . Any word or action of the Spanish Loyalist Government friendly to the Church . . . must be taken as a sign of fraud, or of self-deception, or of the repudiation of its principles."[28]

There were many Catholics in the United States who felt that it was their religious duty to defend publicly General Franco and the "holy cause" for which he was fighting. There is evidence which would seem to indicate that members of the Church sometimes acted as pressure groups to influence American opinion and official policy toward the Spanish Civil War. J. David Stern was threatened with a Catholic boycott for printing in the *Philadelphia Record* an editorial supporting the Popular Front Government in Spain, and better relations were not restored with Catholic leaders until a second editorial was printed correcting some of the impressions created by the first.[29] Michael Williams, editor of the *Commonweal*, felt so strongly about the alleged distortion of facts printed in the *Record* concerning the Spanish conflict that he challenged Stern to a public debate on the subject.[30] The *New Orleans Times-Picayune*, apparently pro-Loyalist in its sympathies, was warned by the editors of *Catholic Action of the South*:[31]

> No intelligently directed newspaper wants to offend the majority of its readers. . . because we feel that the *Times-Picayune* considers the goodwill of the Catholics in its field to be of value to its business, hence would not attempt, even if they were not in sympathy with Catholic feelings, to consistently carry headlines and phraseology describing happenings in Spain in a manner that is most offensive to Catholics and to all liberty loving citizens.

It was suggested that the *Times-Picayune* "check up on its information and instruct its headline writers and news story writers at least to consider the feelings of most of the newspaper's readers."[32]

Another writer reported that Catholic students in St. Louis wrote hundreds of letters to the *St. Louis Post-Dispatch* because of its editorial stand on Spain.[33] Lawrence Fernsworth, who was a Catholic and one of the Spanish correspondents for the *New York Times*, charged in a public lecture that "political forces in the Roman Catholic Church both here and abroad brought constant pressure on him to distort his reporting from Loyalist territory during the Spanish War." He stated that Father Talbot, editor of the Jesuit weekly, *America*, warned him that, as a Catholic, it was his duty to express his opinions to the hierarchy in Spain before writing his dispatches.[34]

Nor were Catholic pressure tactics confined to the press; they extended to the motion picture industry as well. The Walter Wanger film, "Blockade," which was a sermon against the slaughter of noncombatants in the Spanish Civil War, created much controversy. Although the producer prefaced the film with a statement that it was not intended as propaganda for either side in Spain, even the most casual observer could not fail to identify the carefully unspecified enemy as the forces of General Franco bombing cities, sinking food ships, and destroying hospitals. The Catholic Church launched a drive against the film on the ground that it presented a case for the "Communists" in Spain and was therefore atheistic. The National Legion of Decency, which had behind it the authority of the Catholic Church, did not specifically ban the picture but placed it in a special category with the observation that "many people will regard this picture as containing foreign political propaganda in favor of one side in the present unfortunate struggle in Spain."[35] Pressure was exerted on the Catholic manager of Radio City Music Hall to prevent him from exhibiting the film;[36] in Boston the City Council adopted a resolution condemning the film, but later the mayor permitted its showing with two deletions; the commissioner of licenses in Providence, Rhode Island, banned the picture on a second run after it had already made one appearance; and the Fox West Coast Theater chain refused to exhibit the film, which — in view of the movie's financial success elsewhere — was apparently the result of outside pressure.[37]

"Blockade" was also denounced in the Catholic press. The *Catholic News* predicted that it would "stir up prejudice, bad feeling, and contention," while the *Brooklyn Tablet* demanded "Blockade 'Blockade.' "[38] The Jesuit weekly, *America*, declared that the picture was significant because it was "the first picture to raise the question of propaganda issuing from Leftist brains in Hollywood."[39] Joseph Lamb, deputy of the New York Council, Knights of Columbus, denounced the movie as "subtle pro-Loyalist propaganda"; while Martin Carmody, Supreme Knight of Columbus, speaking for the 500,000 members of his organization, declared that the film was historically false and intellectually dishonest.[40] On the other hand the *Nation, New Masses*, the *American Guardian*, and other liberal and leftist publications urged their readers to crown "Blockade" with "box office success."[41] There were also several other motion pictures about the war in Spain which were condemned by many Catholics. The Pennsylvania censor board banned the film, "Spain in Flames," from the theaters of that state on the grounds that the picture was recruiting propaganda for the Loyalists, while the documentary film, "Spanish Earth," received similar treatment in Detroit.[42]

It is interesting to note, however, that the political views of the Catholic hierarchy were not binding on all Catholics. Many well-known Catholics such as Kathleen Norris, Westbrook Pegler, George M. Schuster, Shaemas O'Sheel, Lawrence Fernsworth, and millions of lesser known individuals, particularly those in trade unions, were either opposed to Franco or actively pro-Loyalist. Unpublished polls of the American Institute of Public Opinion disclosed that despite hierarchy pressure only four out of ten Catholics were sympathetic with the Franco regime.[43] In observing the Gallup reports which revealed that 76 per cent of those Americans expressing an opinion favored the Loyalists, the editors of *Catholic Action* remarked that "we cannot escape the deeply disturbing fact that . . . some Catholics — and in numbers to have real significance — voted . . . for the Spanish 'Loyalists.' "[44]

Many Catholics feared that a possible identification of fascism with Catholicism in Spain might have very unfortunate effects on Catholicism in all democratic countries. One Catholic writer denounced the hierarchy for its support of the Franco Government and fascism, pointing out that the political views of the bishops or even the Pope were not binding upon individual Catholics. This writer stated that non-Catholics should not make the mistake of assuming that all Catholics have "lined up with Franco at the snap of the ecclesiastical whip," and added that Catholics "need to be told that they are not repudiating the Church of Christ when they repudiate politically the hierarchy."[45] Another Catholic, the syndicated columnist Westbrook Pegler, had his column dropped by many regular subscribers, including the *New York World-Telegram,* when he told his readers that he could not "see why the working class Catholics are expected to be indignant against the government side in Spain. . . . If I were a Spaniard who had seen Franco's missionary work among the children I might see him in hell but never in the Church."[46] George M. Schuster apologized for his Church and stated that the reason Catholics in the United States defended Franco was because of "minorityitis." He explained that Catholics felt very insecure in their position and when the bulk of American opinion supported the Loyalists, "Catholic resentment rose up against deeply ingrained non-Catholic instinct." Then, taking a middle course, Schuster said that on a recent tour of Europe he found but few who sympathized with either side "but the majority believed that Spain would recover only if some way were found of arbitrating the dispute."[47]

Perhaps the most spectacular indictment of the Church's attitude toward the Spanish Civil War was made by an alleged Catholic priest who wrote under the pen name of Peter Whiffin.

He asserted that many Catholics tried to blame everything anti-religious on Russian communism, but "that's just trying to pass the buck." When a Cardinal, said the priest, blamed the Spanish conflict on sixty Russians attempting to spread the Communist doctrine, then, that Cardinal

> succeeds only in making a most damning indictment of the Spanish Church and clergy. For, if 60 Russians in three years could overturn the entire Spanish Church, after all her centuries of domination, with all her thousands of priests and religious, with all her millions of Catholics, and with all her power and organization and wealth — and overturn her so completely that she needed a counter-revolution and thousands of black soldiers and the substantial help of Italy and Germany to put her back on her feet — then surely there must be something very foul about the Spanish Church. There is no other explanation.[48]

Father Whiffin was subjected to extreme criticism by many Catholics and the Catholic press, so much that several months later in a paid advertisement the priest altered many of his views. He did not, however, retract his indictment of the Catholic hierarchy and its attitude toward the Spanish Civil War.[49]

The Catholic position regarding the Spanish conflict was further weakened when in June 1938 a very influential Catholic journal reversed its stand regarding the war in Spain. The *Commonweal*, after a change of editors, adopted an impartial attitude between the two opposing sides and asked that its readers do likewise.[50] In an editorial defending this new policy, the editors stated that it was hard to learn the truth of what had happened in Spain. Information from both sides had been so generally characterized by propaganda that the American people did not have sufficient knowledge of the whole situation. They asserted that Spain had to choose between two governments "whose characters were mixed and impossible to know." One side permitted the murder of priests and nuns and maintained a close alliance with Russia; the other side bombed defenseless cities, held totalitarian views, and were allied with Fascist nations. The only duty of Americans, the *Commonweal* declared, was to alleviate distress and suffering on both sides while working for peace. The editorial stated that the wisest policy for Americans was "positive impartiality" with sanity of judgment toward both sides.[51]

Michael Williams, the former editor, wrote an article the same week which took issue with the new editorial policy, asserting that a Franco victory would be beneficial to the cause of Christian civilization. Although admitting uncertainty in the news, he stated that all reports from Spain were not propaganda, and the fact was not to be denied that the Popular Front Government was attempting to destroy the Catholic Church.[52]

Three weeks later the editors of the *Commonweal* reviewed the sentiment that had been expressed concerning their revised attitude regarding Spain. They stated that there was no overwhelming support either for or against the new policy. The letters they had received were rather equally divided in sentiment and raised issues which could be listed under three separate categories. First, there was the problem of evidence. The readers inquired if the editors were taking a proper or improper attitude toward the evidence available. Secondly, they were asked if all Catholics were not obliged to support Franco. Finally, the question of "positive neutrality" was raised, what it was and what it meant for Americans.[53] Editorial comment in the Catholic press was generally critical. The Jesuit publications, *America* and *Blackfriars*, strongly criticized the attitude of the *Commonweal* and condemned the Loyalist activities against the Church. The *New World*, official organ of the Chicago Archdiocese, agreed that war was a strong possibility in Europe and that America should maintain a policy of strict neutrality, but expressed sympathy for the Catholic forces in Spain fighting communism.[54] The *Catholic Worker* was one Catholic journal, however, that applauded the new policy of the *Commonweal*. The *Worker* was unique among Catholic papers. It was published in New York and to its 75,000 subscribers preached a sort of "Catholic communism," but rejected violence, class war, revolution, and international war. Throughout the course of the Spanish War the editors advocated a policy of sympathy and support for the Loyalist regime in Spain.[55]

Although a majority of the people in the United States reviewed events across the Atlantic as not involving them directly, there were many Catholics who continued to be agitated over incidents concerning the Spanish conflict. One such incident occurred in January 1938 when sixty members of Congress sent a telegram of congratulations to the Loyalist Cortes meeting in Valencia:

We, the undersigned Members of the Congress of the United States, are happy to send our greetings and good wishes to the Spanish Parliament on the occasion of its regular session convened in accordance with the provisions of the Constitution of 1931. For you to meet again in the face of trying and tragic circumstances of the present demonstrates that the Spanish people and their representatives stand firm in their faith in democratic government.

We, who cherish freedom and democracy above all else, realize the significance of your heroic and determined fight to save democratic institutions in your country from its enemies both within and without Spain. Your struggle sets a stirring example to all democratic peoples. As members of one democratically elected parliament to another, we salute you.[56]

Certain Catholic leaders immediately condemned the message. Monsignor Michael J. Ready, Chairman of the National Catholic Welfare Conference, asserted that it was incredible "to believe that the duly elected representatives of our American democracy, sworn to uphold the right of religious liberty, could place themselves on record as sympathetic with a government which has absolutely proscribed the exercise of religion in the territory which it governs."[57] Bishop James E. Walsh declared that he was "amazed" at the message sent to a Communist government that was responsible for "Catholic massacres,"[58] while the National Catholic Alumni Federation issued a public statement strongly criticizing the signers of the telegram.[59] This feeling was reflected on the local level when, for example, the Lafayette (Louisiana) Diocesan Council of Catholic Women wrote Senator Allen J. Ellender (D-Louisiana) that they were "deeply grieved as Christians and Americans at the report of your having signed the greeting"; and the Holy Name Society of Holy Ghost Parish (Hammond, Louisiana) objected to Ellender's "sympathizing and encouraging a government which has shown itself to be little more than a puppet of Communist Russia."[60]

On February 10, 1938, an N. C. W. C. dispatch announced: "Sixty Congressmen Turn Out to be 17; 'Message' Backfires on Red Publicists." One of the news agency's staff correspondents made a canvass of the sixty Senators and Representatives who had signed the message and disclosed that four retracted their endorsement of the document, twenty-six did not intend to express sympathy with the Loyalist Government but signed the message only as a "Greeting to Democracy," four had nothing to say on the subject, seventeen declared that they had meant to express sympathy to the Spanish Republican Government, while the comments of five of the signers were listed as unclassified. The National Catholic Welfare Conference announced that this investigation proved: (1) That the message was not in the slightest degree spontaneous with the Congressmen, but was promoted by outsiders sympathetic to "leftist" Spain. (2) That four Senators retracted their signatures. (3) That half of the signers did not mean by their signatures to favor the Barcelona Government. (4) That actually less than a third were definitely willing to say that they meant their endorsement to express sympathy with the Loyalist regime. (5) That some of the signers charged trickery was used to obtain their signatures.[61]

Representative Fred Hildebrandt (D-South Dakota) explained that many groups in his constituency had called for an explanation of his motives in signing a message of greeting to the Spanish Parliament, the assumption being that he had publicly allied himself with one of the opposing factions in Spain. Hildebrandt stated that he was sorry this "innocent gesture" of greeting was diverted to propaganda uses. "I am sympathetic to the feeling of shock suffered by those religious groups in this country who, by the universality of their creed, have more than an academic interest in the outcome of the Spanish war." The Congressman charged that a second paragraph was later added to the document that he had signed since he "would not knowingly lend whatever prestige my name conveys to one belligerent group as against another, whether it be in Spain, Ethiopia, or China."[62]

Representative Burdick (R-North Dakota) likewise announced that he had made a serious mistake in signing the petition. Burdick declared that he had signed the message because he felt that a Fascist regime was attempting to overthrow a democratic government, but that one thousand letters had arrived from his home state expressing "surprise and sadness" that he had signed the document. The Congressman stated that the main argument expressed in the letters written to him was that the revolution in Spain was a religious upheaval and that the Barcelona Government had attempted to destroy the Catholic religion. Burdick declared that since he was not acquainted with the actual conditions in Spain, and since he did not wish to be a party to a religious controversy, "I must, in good conscience, say I made a mistake and withdraw my endorsement."[63] Similar action was taken by Senator Prentiss Brown (D-Michigan) and Senator Clyde Herring (D-Iowa).[64]

Another incident that aroused considerable agitation among certain Catholic groups was the plan announced by a group of American liberals to form a Board of Guardians for Basque Refugee Children and bring five hundred young Basques to the United States for the duration of the Spanish Civil War. Leaders of the movement, Gardner Jackson, Chairman of the American Friends of Spanish Democracy, New York Representative Caroline O'Day, President Mary Emma Woolley of Mt. Holyoke College, Professor James T. Shotwell of Columbia University, and Dr. Frank Bohn, Secretary of the American Board of Guardians of Basque Children, described the plight of these young victims of war and stated that offers had been received from 2,700 American homes to care for the children.[65] The Spanish Chargé d'Affaires informed Under Secretary of State Welles that a group of Spanish Basques who owned a large Mexican hat factory in St. Louis had made known their desire to care for some of the children should they be permitted to enter the United States.[66] Mrs. Eleanor Roosevelt was also very interested in the welfare of these children and at her insistence Ambassador Bowers was made chairman of a committee to help provide for their relief.[67]

In the United States Catholic reaction was very strong in opposition. Even though predominantly Catholic, the Basque people had vigorously supported the Republican Government and had caused the American Catholics no little concern in explaining the alliance between the atheistic "Reds" and Catholic Basques. Cardinal O'Connell denounced the "ill advised plan" because "other means of relief so readily suggest themselves."[68] Representative John W. McCormack (D-Massachusetts) saw the plan as a smokescreen for Red propaganda and complained that Basque children previously sent to England and other countries had not necessarily been placed in Catholic homes.[69] McCormack also wrote to President Roosevelt asking to see him concerning the matter.[70] The Secretary of the Massachusetts State Council of the Knights of Columbus likewise wrote to President Roosevelt that "this rash and foolish plan is a real danger to the established neutrality policy of this nation. The unfortunate war victims . . . might easily be used for propaganda purposes by groups actively seeking sympathy for the Communist-Socialist regime of the Madrid-Valencia government."[71] A similar letter was written to the President by Joseph A. Callahan, High Chief Ranger, Massachusetts Catholic Order of Foresters, who claimed that the children should be sent to France or other countries closer to their home.[72]

President Roosevelt was influenced, however, probably by Ambassador Bowers and Mrs. Roosevelt, to consult the State Department concerning the possibility of allowing these children to enter the United States for the duration of the Spanish strife. Under Secretary Welles wrote Marvin McIntyre (the President's personal secretary) that the question of permitting the Basque children entrance into the United States was one for the Secretary of Labor to decide. Welles stated that it was his personal view that they should not be brought to this country but should be taken to some country nearer their parents.[73] In any event, despite considerable planning and several public announcements by the American Board of Guardians for Basque Refugee Children, none were ever brought to the United States.

That the succor of children who were the innocent victims of internecine civil war should have become the subject of heated controversy in the United States gives a measure of the temperature of the heated religious controversy engendered by the Spanish conflict.

NOTES

1. *Commonweal*, XXIV (June 5, 1936), 9.
2. *New York Times*, August 17, 1936.
3. *Time* (New York), XXXI (May 16, 1938), 9.
4. *Christian Century*, LVI (April 12, 1939), 467.
5. Bowers to Roosevelt, August 11, 1937 (FDR Official Files, 422C).

6. A prominent psychologist conducted a survey at several colleges to determine if there was a definite religious split in the students' sympathies toward the opposing sides in Spain. The percentage of responses to the attitude statement, "I hope the Loyalists win the war," was as follows: Bennington College, agreed 82; uncertain 12; and disagreed 8; Catholic University of America, agreed 11; uncertain 13; disagreed 76. The researcher found that at Bennington College, a liberal arts school in Bennington, Vermont, there had been repeated lectures, movies, and discussions — all with a heavily pro-Loyalist emphasis; while at Catholic University most of

the activities had indicated a strong pro-Rebel bias. Theodore M. Newcomb, "The Influence of Attitude Climate Upon Some Determinants of Information," *Journal of Abnormal and Social Psychology* (Princeton), XLI (July, 1946), 291-302.

7. *Catholic World*, CXLIII (September, 1936), 747-48.

8. *Ibid.*, 748. See also G. M. Godden, "How Communism Attacked Spain," *ibid.*, CXLIV (November, 1936), 403-07.

9. *Tidings*, January 1, 1937.

10. "Our Common Catholic Interests," *Catholic Action*, XX (September, 1938), 5-6.

11. *Ibid.* The editors of *Catholic Action* commented: "Bishop Alter deserves the thanks not only of the Catholic body of America, but the entire citizenry of the United States for authenticating facts previously reported mainly in the Catholic press concerning the war of the Spanish Reds against religion and morality and the equally determined fight of the Nationalists to save Spain for the Spanish people." *Ibid.*

12. *Christian Century*, LV (June 29, 1938), 804-05.

13. *Advance*, CXXVIII (December 1, 1936), 691.

14. Reinhold Niebuhr, "Arrogance in the Name of Christ," *Christian Century*, LIII (September 2, 1936), 1157-58.

15. The Spanish Catholics to whom the letter referred presumably were those in the Basque provinces who were bitterly opposed to the Insurgent regime of General Franco.

16. The full text of the letter is printed in the pamphlet, *Joint Letter of the Spanish Bishops to the Bishops of the Whole World: The War in Spain* (New York, 1937), pp. 1-27. See also *New York Times*, September 3, 1937.

17. *Ibid.*

18. *New York Times*, October 4, 1937. Among the signatories were Bishops James Chamberlain Baker and Robert L. Paddock, Reverend Harry Emerson Fosdick, Professors George S. Counts, John Dewey, Robert S. Lynd, Franz Boas, and William Allan Neilson, and President Walter Dill Scott of Northwestern University.

19. *New York Times*, October 5, 1937.

20. *Ibid.*

21. *Ibid.*, October 6, 1937.

22. *Ibid.*, October 14, 1937. Signing the letter were former Governor Alfred E. Smith; Chancellor James Byrne of the University of New York; Martin H. Carmody, Supreme Knight of the Knights of Columbus; Michael Williams, editor of the *Commonweal*; Professor Carlton J. H. Hayes; former New York Supreme Court Justice Daniel F. Cohalan; John M. Dealy, National Commander, Catholic War Veterans; Louis Kennedy, President, National Council of Catholic Men; and the editors of virtually every well-known Catholic periodical and newspaper throughout the country.

23. *Nation*, CXLV (October 9, 1937), 363.

24. *New Republic*, XCII (October 13, 1937), 254.

25. *New York Times*, September 7, 1937.

26. *Ibid.*, October 15, 1937.

27. *Ibid.*, October 19, 20, 1937.

28. *Catholic Action*, XXI (February, 1939), 5.

29. Riegel, "Press, Radio, and the Spanish Civil War," p. 133.

30. *Commonweal*, XXV (May 21, 1937), 85-87. Williams suggested that William Allen White act as impartial judge and that the jury be chosen from representatives of the Associated Press, United Press, and other noted journalists. Although Williams offered a side bet of $1,000 on the outcome of the debate, no reply seems to have been made by Stern.

31. Official organ for the Archdiocese of New Orleans; Diocese of Lafayette, Louisiana; and Diocese of Natchez, Mississippi.

32. *Catholic Action of the South*, January 14, 1937. This warning seemed to have little effect on the editorial policies of the *Times-Picayune*. Although advocating a policy of strict neutrality for the United States, ideologically speaking, the editors were sympathetic to the Republican Government throughout the course of the conflict.

33. Leo H. Lehman, "The Catholic Church in Politics: Censorship by the Church," *New Republic*, XCVII (November 23, 1938), 64.

34. *New York Times*, January 24, 1940. For other comments concerning pressure exerted by Catholics on the secular press, see Heinz Eulau, "Proselytizing in the Catholic Press," *Public Opinion Quarterly*, XI (Summer, 1947), 189-97; also George Seldes, *The Catholic Crisis* (New York, 1945), pp. 184-210. This book must be used with caution, however, because of the author's strong anti-Catholic bias.

35. *National Legion of Decency List*, June 30, 1938.

36. *Nation*, CXLVII (July 9, 1938), 38-39. The picture was shown, however, and enjoyed a large box office success.

37. Thorp, *America at the Movies*, pp. 203-10. Although Catholics exerted pressure through direct intervention, these tactics were not dissimilar from those of other denominations or special interest groups.

38. *New York Times*, June 17, 1938.

39. *America*, quoted in, *Catholic Action of the South*, June 30, 1938.

40. *Ibid.*, June 20, 1938. See also *Propaganda Analysis*, I (July 16, 1938), 1.

41. *Ibid.*

42. See extension of remarks by Leon Sacks (D-Pennsylvania), in the *Congressional Record*, 75 Cong., 1 Sess., LXXXI (May 10, 1937), A1107-08; Thorp, *America at the Movies*, p. 210.

43. Parry, "The Spanish Civil War," p. 373. The result of the survey among Catholics was as follows: 39 per cent pro-Franco; 31 per cent neutral; and 30 per cent pro-Loyalist. The poll among Protestants disclosed that 48 per cent were pro-Loyalist, 43 per cent neutral, and 9 per cent pro-Franco.

44. *Catholic Action*, XXI (February, 1939), 8.

45. Mary M., "A Catholic Speaks Her Mind," *Nation*, CXLV (December 18, 1937), 683-85.

46. *Time*, XXXI (May 16, 1938), 44. Since this column was omitted by so many of Pegler's syndicated papers, it was printed by the *New Republic* as a service to its readers. *New Republic*, XCV (May 11, 1938), 19.

47. George M. Schuster, "A Catholic Defends His Church," *New Republic*, XCVII (January 4, 1939), 246-48.

48. Peter Whiffin, "A Priest Warns the Church," *Forum* (New York), XCVII (April, 1937), 195-201.

49. ——————, "Peter Whiffin Tells the Whole Truth," *ibid.* (June, 1937), x-xi.

50. Michael Williams, the founder and former editor, relinquished his editorship to an editorial board. He was retained on the staff as special editor but no longer controlled editorial policy.

51. *Commonweal*, XXVIII (June 24, 1938), 229-30.

52. *Ibid.*, 241-42.

53. *Ibid.* (July 15, 1938), 324-25.

54. *Ibid.*, 326; *New York Times*, June 28, 1938.

55. See Eulau, "Proselytizing in the Catholic Press," pp. 189-97.

56. *Congressional Record*, 75 Cong., 3 Sess., LXXXIII (March 10, 1938), A959-60. The message was signed by twenty-six Senators and thirty-four Representatives. The list of Senators included Democrats, Republicans, and one Progressive. The signatories included Warren R. Austin, Harry F. Byrd, Arthur Capper, Tom Connally, Robert M. LaFollette, Jr., Kenneth McKellar, and Claude Pepper. The House signatories, mostly men of liberal tendencies, included twenty-seven Democrats, two Republicans, two Progressives, and three Farmer-Laborites. Also see *New York Times*, January 31, 1938.

57. *New York Times*, February 1, 1938. A similar statement was made by Ready in *Catholic Action*, XX (February, 1938), 5.

58. *New York Times*, February 2, 1938.

59. *Ibid.*, February 4, 1938.

60. *Catholic Action of the South*, February 24, 1938.

61. *Ibid.*, February 10, 1938.

62. *Congressional Record*, 75 Cong., 3 Sess., LXXXIII (March 10, 1938), A959-60.

63. *Ibid.* (February 28, 1938), A800-01.

64. *New York Times*, February 3, 1938.

65. *Time*, XXX (June 7, 1937), 75.

66. Sumner Welles, June 15, 1937 (SD File No. 852.48/123: memo.).

67. Bowers to author, February 15, 1954.

68. *Commonweal*, XXVI (June 18, 1937), 198.

69. *Ibid.*

70. McCormack to Roosevelt, June 10, 1937 (FDR Official Files, No. 422C). Roosevelt must have been in a quandry with the politically powerful McCormack advocating one course of action and his wife another.

71. *Time*, XXX (June 18, 1937), 75.

72. Callahan to Roosevelt, May 25, 1937 (FDR Official Files, No. 422C).

73. Sumner Welles to Marvin McIntyre, June 18, 1937 (FDR Official Files, No. 422C: memo.).

Chapter Eight

The Embargo Controversy

Probably the leading problem facing the American Government during the Spanish War was that of determining whether arms, ammunition, and implements of war should be allowed to go to Spain during the course of the hostilities. The Spanish arms embargo had been adopted in 1936 for two principal reasons: (a) to keep the United States out of a possible European conflict; and (b) to cooperate independently with England and France to shorten and localize the Spanish War by preventing American supplies of arms from reaching either side. This embargo, however, subsequently became the subject of violent controversy in American public and official circles. Those who sympathized with the Loyalist Government argued that the embargo should be repealed since it operated against a friendly democracy — the legally recognized Government of Spain; while the supporters of General Franco urged with equal vehemence that American policy remain unchanged. Intensive campaigns were conducted during the spring of 1938 and again during the early part of 1939 to secure repeal of the embargo. The question became a momentous issue for the American people in their championship of the contending factions in Spain.

By the early months of 1938 the sweeping successes of General Franco's well-equipped forces had brought victory almost within their grasp. During the first six months of the war the Insurgents had occupied half of metropolitan Spain and had reached the gates of Madrid only to be stalled by a desperate defense of the capital by the Loyalists. Although the struggle reached a stalemate on this front, the Nationalists subsequently enjoyed victory in other

163

parts of Spain. Málaga fell in the South, and during the period between April and October 1937, the Insurgents conquered the Asturias and Basque provinces. In December 1937 the battle began which resulted in the capture of Teruel by the Rebels, and on March 9, 1938, the Insurgents launched a new offensive along the Aragon front with the objective of capturing Barcelona and forcing the highly industrialized area of Catalonia out of the war. It was during this critical phase of the fighting that supporters of the Spanish Government in the United States launched a vigorous and well-organized campaign to secure repeal of the arms embargo against Spain.

The Republican Government, despite a numerical superiority in manpower, was never able to overcome the Insurgent's supremacy in trained troops and experienced officers, or to match Franco's strength in planes, artillery, and other technical equipment, most of which came from Germany and Italy. The Loyalists had received substantial aid, partially from France, but primarily from the Soviet Union. Russian planes and tanks were invaluable in the defense of Madrid, and Marcel Rosenberg, Soviet Ambassador to Spain, was reported to have had a large military staff acting in the capacity of technicians and advisers to the Spanish Government.[1] Russians fighting in Spain, however, never did reach a very large number. The Counselor of the American Embassy in Valencia wrote Secretary Hull that within Spanish Government forces individual Russian officers and men were only occasionally reported with the total probably not exceeding 2,000.[2] Ambassador Bowers, in reflecting upon Russian activity in Spain, did not believe the number exceeded 450 and these, he stated, were held in some distrust by the Spaniards because all they did was "eat and drink and run after Spanish girls." Bowers observed that the Loyalists needed every fighting man they could get and "they accepted this kind of Russian aid that we were delighted to accept in the war when the same Fascism that was fighting the Spanish Democracy was fighting ours."[3]

Nevertheless, the Axis powers were not to be denied a victory in Spain. In February 1938 Hitler exclaimed: "The German Government would see the introduction of bolshevism in Spain as not only an element of unrest in Europe, but also as upsetting the European balance of power."[4] Likewise, Mussolini's own newspaper, *Popolo d'Italia,* declared that "Italy has not been neutral in this conflict, but has fought, and victory will be hers. Madrid will fall, as Bilbao fell, and Spain will be the tomb of Bolshevism, not of Fascism."[5] Thus Germany and Italy continued to pour sufficient numbers of arms, supplies, and men into Spain to insure a fascist victory for General Francisco Franco.

The policy of nonintervention promoted by Great Britain and France had proved to be unsuccessful and had only provided a cloak of secrecy for the continuous flow of arms and men into Spain. Repeated efforts to use official observers and naval patrols met with failure and in actual practice had been a disadvantage for the Loyalists while aiding the Insurgents. The Madrid Government was prevented from receiving any sizable amount of arms, while Franco was well supplied by Germany and Italy in defiance of the nonintervention agreement. Count Ciano, the Italian Foreign Minister, complained to Hitler that Franco had originally asked for twelve transport planes to win the Spanish War, but that before the war ended, these twelve aircraft had become more than one thousand planes, six thousand dead, and fourteen billion lire.[6]

The Spanish Government not only complained to Germany and Italy concerning their activities in Spain but protested to the League of Nations as well. The League, still shocked by the Abyssinian fiasco, questioned its jurisdiction in the matter on the grounds that the Spanish Civil War was an internal affair and not subject for the League to handle. The League Council shelved the matter, thus leaving any possible action in the hands of the Nonintervention Committee. The Council applauded the efforts of Great Britain and France to restore international order and recommended to League members on the Nonintervention Committee "to spare no pains to render the nonintervention undertakings as stringent as possible, and to take appropriate measures to insure forthwith that the fulfillment of the said undertakings is effectively supervised."[7]

In May 1937 the League was confronted with a *Spanish White Book* which contained over one hundred documents attempting to prove Italian and German intervention.[8] Nevertheless, noninterference remained a League policy since the Council refused to take any action. The United States, not being a member of the League of Nations, took no part in these discussions or the formulation of League policy, but the American Consul at Geneva and other diplomatic officials in Europe kept the State Department fully informed of League activities.

Periodically throughout the conflict the Spanish Government launched vigorous protests against the embargo policy of the United States. In October 1937 Ambassador de los Ríos pointed out to Under Secretary Welles that this "was the first time in the history of the civilized world where a legally constituted government had been prevented from obtaining the materials it required in its own legitimate self-defense."[9] Welles informed the Ambassador that those European powers geographically closer to Spain and more directly involved in the situation had assumed primary jurisdiction of the difficulties encountered through the Nonintervention Committee. Therefore, the United States was determined to remain aloof from these negotiations and the conflict in Spain.[10]

In November 1937 the Spanish Ambassador formally protested against the American embargo on the grounds that it represented the negation of two essential principles of international law. First, the embargo represented the breaking of a treaty by a unilateral act and this action conflicted with statements by the President and Secretary of State on the sanctity of treaties and their modification by mutual agreement.[11] Second, it was the negation of the right of a legitimate government to acquire the means of defense against those who rise against authority and law.[12]

A few weeks later de los Ríos advised Assistant Secretary of State Wilson that he had delayed making this formal protest because he felt that American public opinion was so strongly set on the subject that argument was futile. The Ambassador noted, however, that recent signs of a change had been observed which gave hope that the United States was ready to distinguish between the aggressor and the assaulted.[13] For example, the Ambassador cited the nonapplication of the Neutrality Act in the Sino-Japanese War then raging as indicative of a shift in public opinion.[14] Upon being informed by Wilson that "there was not the faintest hope" that the embargo would be lifted, the Ambassador inquired if there were not "a possibility of its application in terms less rigid than the past?"[15]

On December 21, 1937, Secretary Hull replied to the formal protest lodged against the United States by the Spanish Government. He declared that because of the troubled state of the world and the well-known desire of this country to keep out of war, this Government had, under specific provisions of law enacted by Congress, pursued a policy of refusing to permit the export of arms, ammunition, and implements of war to warring nations. Moreover, the Secretary added, "I must definitely state my conviction that the question of the control of . . . implements of war from the United States to foreign countries is a domestic question to be decided by this Government alone." He concluded by asserting that "this Government does not concur in the thesis that it is obligated under international law to provide arms to either or both of the parties to a war or a civil conflict."[16]

In April 1938, while the fight to lift the embargo was raging in the United States, Álvarez del Vayo[17] called on the Counselor of the American Embassy in Barcelona. It had been reported, del Vayo declared, that President Roosevelt was favorably disposed toward the movement in the United States to abolish the Spanish embargo but felt that such action would be inadvisable since the Loyalist cause was nearly lost. del Vayo asserted that any such belief on the part of the President or the Secretary of State was not supported by the military situation in Spain. Notwithstanding Rebel victories, he continued, the Government could and would carry on the war for many months; that in all the major centers such as Madrid, Albacete, Ciudad Real, and Valencia the officers and troops were enthusiastic and were determined to fight until victory. He concluded by requesting that the United States reverse its policy and permit the duly recognized Government of Spain to purchase arms for its defense.[18] This plea was reiterated by Ambassador de los Ríos a few weeks later when he told Pierrepont Moffat, Chief of the Division of European Affairs, that any feeling that Loyalist resistance was about over was "entirely erroneous." The Ambassador also developed the theory that the Western democracies had best awaken to the dangers of the Italian and German occupation of Spain.[19] Although these efforts were futile, the Spanish Government through its diplomatic representatives never ceased to plead for a change in American policy.

During the successive diplomatic crises in Europe the people of the United States had for almost three years lived under a law drafted and adopted in the hope that it would keep this country at peace regardless of events in other parts of the world. The Neutrality Act of 1935, broadened in scope in 1936 and 1937, was designed to keep the country out of war by prohibiting the shipment of military supplies or the granting of credits to belligerent nations, and by forbidding American vessels to travel in war zones. The law was to be applied without favor, which meant that the President would not have the authority to discriminate between the aggressor and the attacked. Consequently, if a democratic state were the victim of aggression it would be barred from obtaining weapons for its defense in this country. Supporters of the Spanish Republic, however, were given new hope by President Roosevelt's "Quarantine" speech delivered in Chicago on October 5, 1937. The Administration departed somewhat from the trend of isolationism and compulsory neutrality when the President stated that "the moral consciousness of the world . . . must be aroused to the cardinal necessity . . . of putting an end to acts of aggression." He added that an "epidemic of world lawlessness" was spreading, and that "when an epidemic of physical disease starts to spread, the community approves and joins in a quarantine of the patients to protect the health of the community against the spread of the disease."[20]

American opinion was gradually shifting ground, and with each new crisis American dislike of the European dictators was becoming more pronounced. This did not mean, of course, that there was any great weakening of sentiment for keeping out of foreign entanglements on the part of the great mass of American people. Nevertheless, by late 1937 it became apparent to many persons that the Spanish arms embargo was not neutrality but the precise opposite, since it operated to the exclusive disadvantage of the Loyalist Government. Even as staunch an isolationist as Senator Nye became restive when he saw how the American arms embargo was working out in Spain, and he endeavored to have the law modified. The Senator and others seemed to have felt that the only practical effect of the embargo was to prevent the democratic, legally recognized Government of Spain from purchasing arms in this country while its antagonists were kept supplied by certain European governments. Supporters of the Loyalists urged repeal of the embargo to remove this discrimination. They argued that a victory for the Nationalists would be a victory for fascism and for Hitler and Mussolini; that it would endanger the friendly democracies in Europe; and that the success of General Franco would increase the threat of fascism in South America.[21]

The President was beset by pressures and informal legal opinions from all sides urging that the embargo on arms to Spain be removed. According to one syndicated column, "Washington has seen all kinds of lobbying . . . but seldom before has Washington seen people spend money to come from all over the country on a cause from which they would receive no material benefit."[22] Eight hundred women paraded in Washington and left a petition at the State Department which demanded that the United States sell arms to the democratically elected Government of Spain so that the Spanish people could defend themselves "against the invading armies of Hitler and Mussolini."[23] Prominent citizens lent the influence of their names in an effort to convince President Roosevelt that American Spanish policy should be revised. In February 1938 sixty persons, including former Secretary of State Stimson and former Ambassador to Germany William E. Dodd, sent a petition to the White House stating that the policy of the United States toward Spain had assisted the insurrection and had prolonged a war "fought with great danger to democratic institutions." The petitioners declared that "a consideration of the matter will disclose that the shipment of war materials to the established government of Spain would not threaten or endanger the peace of the United States," and that the amendment sought is "grounded in well-recognized principles of international law and is strictly in accordance with historic American foreign policy."[24]

In April 1938 fifteen prominent scientists, men who do not ordinarily deal in politics, sent a letter to President Roosevelt asking that the embargo be lifted to "save the world from a fascist gulf." They stated:

It is our belief that you have in your power today to make for the United States a great contribution to the democratic cause which you, like ourselves, espouse. We believe that giving the Spanish Republicans an opportunity to defend their country more effectively against the spread of fascism would be to act in defense of world democracy and American freedom.[25]

A more cosmopolitan group expressed the view that

to continue the embargo against Spain means a further implementation of British policy which today stands naked to the world as a policy of collaboration with predatory fascism. The democratic American people have never made such a choice, nor will they ever support such a policy. . . . Our embargo against Spain, originally intended to apply equally against both sides in collaboration with a European concert, has become a weapon against the people of Spain. The American embargo has contributed greatly to the tragic spectacle of a democratic people facing the attacks of a foreign invader and the faithlessness of its friends. American honor is at stake. . . . We can no longer withhold from the recognized government of Spain the right of free access to the American markets under the pretense that this is 'neutrality.'[26]

There were similar expressions of opinion on many college campuses. Seventy-five members of the Vassar College faculty, headed by Dean Mildred Thompson, asked the President to end the Spanish embargo, asserting that it had "worked against the very end that it was intended to accomplish."[27] Forty-two members of the Princeton University faculty, including Albert Einstein of the Institute for Advanced Study, sent a petition to the White House urging that the embaigo be revoked;[28] while a lengthy telegram from sixteen hundred students and faculty of the University of Chicago made a similar plea.[29]

The question aroused additional public interest when the issue of neutrality was discussed on the radio program, America's Town Meeting of the Air. Participants in the discussion were Raymond L. Buell, President of the Foreign Policy Association, Senator Nye, and Josephine Schain, Chairman of the National Committee on the Cause and Cure of War. Buell called the Spanish embargo "unjust and unneutral," and stated that he favored repeal because "this act has worked to help fascist dictatorship in every part of the world." Miss Schain wanted the Neutrality Law amended because it was "too rigid and inflexible; it operates in favor of the treaty-breaking nations; it throws us against our will on the side of the wrongdoer; and experience has shown that it operates against the best interest of our country." Senator Nye also called the Spanish embargo "unneutral" and declared that he would like to see civil war removed from the provisions of the Neutrality Law.[30]

There were also many left-wing groups that strongly favored repeal of the embargo. While the proposals to lift the embargo were receiving serious consideration by certain lawmakers, the *Socialist Call* printed a banner headline calling on the working classes to "DEMONSTRATE YOUR SOLIDARITY FOR THE WORKING CLASS OF SPAIN: INSIST THAT ROOSEVELT

LIFT THE EMBARGO AGAINST THE LOYALISTS."[31] A statement was sent to President Roosevelt by Roy E. Burt, National Secretary of the Socialist party, which declared:

> The Socialist Party of the United States insists that you at once lift the embargo now applied against Loyalist Spain. . . .There is yet time for the lifting of the embargo. Every American tradition of justice, liberty, and democracy, to which you pledge allegiance, demands this action. . . .
>
>   ❋   ❋   ❋
>
> From the very first the Socialists protested the embargo. We insisted then as we insist now that the embargo worked against a friendly people and was a distinct and invaluable aid to the enemy.[32]

In Moscow the Comintern issued a manifesto calling for removal of the arms embargo. "Proletarians of the United States," the Communists declared, "demand a policy of bridling the fascist violators of universal peace, a policy worthy of the traditions of Lincoln and Washington. Demand immediate removal of the embargo on the export of arms to Spain."[33] Earl Browder told a mass meeting at Madison Square Garden that "the shameful embargo is a disgrace that can only be wiped out by complete reversal of this treacherous policy";[34] and the National Lawyer's Guild, which has been regarded as left-wing, in a national referendum voted 702 to 67 in favor of lifting the embargo.[35]

Many other groups also felt that American policy toward Spain was unneutral. In New York three hundred pastors of the East Annual Conference of the Methodist Episcopal Church adopted a resolution requesting that the Spanish embargo be repealed;[36] while Rabbi Stephen S. Wise in a peace rally at Madison Square Garden called upon the United States to lift the arms embargo and denounced all who had prayed for Franco.[37] The editors of *Current History* declared that the American people were caught in a "sore dilemma" in regard to the Spanish situation and asked, "Can This be Neutrality?"[38] A similar viewpoint was presented by the *New York Times,* whose editors asserted:

> It is obvious by now that the neutrality law does not keep us neutral as it has served to aid one antagonist against the other. The whole experiment has been discredited and there is little

doubt in the minds of thoughtful Americans that our policy in this respect needs consideration and revision. A law which makes us unneutral and at the same time ties our hands is the worst possible solution of our most urgent international problem.[39]

An early indication of the Administration's attitude toward repeal of the Spanish embargo was revealed in the correspondence between Buell and Secretary of State Hull. Buell had written Hull on March 18, 1938, urging the revocation of the Proclamation of May 1, 1937, which prohibited the export of arms and other implements of war to Spain. In support of this request he cited provisions of the existing Neutrality Act which authorized the President to revoke the Proclamation of May 1, 1937, whenever "in his judgment the conditions which have caused him to issue said proclamation have ceased to exist." Buell expressed the opinion that these conditions had ceased to exist and that while the civil strife in Spain continued, it did not threaten the security of the United States.[40] Several days later Secretary Hull sent the following reply to Buell:

After careful consideration I am of the opinion that there has been no change in the situation in Spain to warrant the President taking such a step. Furthermore, the Joint Resolution of Congress approved January 8, 1937, is still in effect which is a definite arms embargo against Spain: Even if the Proclamation of the President of May 1, 1937, was revoked, the prohibition upon the export of arms, ammunition, and implements of war to Spain laid down in the Joint Resolution of January 8, 1937, would still remain in effect.[41]

Thus in view of unsettled world conditions and indications that any attempt to repeal the neutrality law would provoke a fight in Congress, the State Department threw its influence against considering any revision of American policy at that time.

The Spanish Republicans had many sympathizers in Congress, however, and in spite of this statement by Hull, which seemed to indicate Administration opposition, Representative Byron Scott (D-California) introduced a resolution (H. J. Res. 640) on April 5, 1938, calling for repeal of the Spanish arms embargo.[42] On May 2 Senator Nye introduced a similar resolution (S. J. Res. 288) in the Senate.[43] In support of his resolution Scott forwarded a letter to President Roosevelt, signed by 206 members of the American bar, which urged "immediate reconsideration of the policy of the United States Government toward the republican Government of Spain." They declared that "the embargo legislation, in denying to the established Government of Spain the right to purchase from citizens of the United States the means of self-defense against insurrection, constitutes an unprecedented repudiation of well-settled principles of international law as well as a reversal of traditional American foreign policy."[44]

In the Senate, Nye told his colleagues that he was "not prompted by the interest of either side involved in Spain," but was "prompted only by a desire to right an injustice growing out of the embargo program — an injustice which reflects upon our country because of the departure from age old principles." He maintained that American Spanish policy was "partial to one side and against the side of a friendly recognized government." The Senator also argued that American policy was contrary to the Havana Convention of 1928, the declared purpose of which was "to prohibit the traffic of arms and war materials, except when it is destined to a Government, so long as the belligerency of the rebels has not been recognized, in which case the rules of neutrality shall be applied." Nye's resolution was so drafted that it would have allowed the lifting of the embargo only insofar as it applied to the Spanish Government, since the ban on shipments to the Insurgents would not have been affected. He also inserted a provision forbidding American ships from participating in the proposed traffic. Thus American citizens would be allowed to sell arms to the Loyalists but might not incur the risks of delivery.[45]

Representative Bernard strongly urged that Congress repeal the Spanish embargo. He declared that 150,000 Americans from every section of the country had gone on record favoring the selling of arms to the legally elected Government of Spain which was defending its democratic institutions.[46] A similar opinion was voiced by Representative Amlie who inserted in the *Congressional Record* numerous resolutions from interested persons favoring the Nye and Scott proposals.[47]

Although Secretary Hull had opposed repeal of the Spanish arms embargo in his letter to Raymond Buell, there is some evidence that by May 1938 the State Department had changed its attitude. On May 3 Hull called his advisers together to consider the Nye resolution to lift the Spanish embargo. Present were Sumner Welles, Judge R. Walton Moore, Green Hackworth, Adolf Berle, Jr., and James Dunn. After some discussion it was agreed that the lifting of the embargo should apply to both sides in Spain but that some discretion should be left to the Chief Executive regarding details of the new policy. This conclusion was sent to Senator Pittman, Chairman of the Senate Foreign Relations Committee, with the understanding that a formal statement would be sent to the Committee within thirty-six hours.[48] Based on these reports, Arthur Krock, the usually reliable Washington observer for the *New York Times*, reported that the Administration would support the Nye resolution with the prospect that it would be passed before Congress adjourned. Krock stated that Hull and Pittman had already reached an agreement to proceed with the resolution and that a canvass of the Senate showed that a large majority would vote for the legislation.[49]

However, President Roosevelt, who was on a fishing trip in the Caribbean, immediately wired Secretary Hull to delay any further action on the matter until he had returned to Washington because the proposed change in policy had aroused a storm of controversy. High Catholic functionaries were reported to have appealed to the President, while Ambassador Kennedy cabled from London that such a step might endanger the European nonintervention policy and increase the likelihood that the war would spread beyond Spanish frontiers.[50] Krock later observed that the background influences which prompted the President to delay action until his return were to be found in the domestic political situation, and particularly the various groups engaged in acrimonious controversy over raising the embargo against Spain.[51]

Soon after Roosevelt returned to Washington he held a conference of high officials to discuss the new developments. It was apparently agreed that American policy would remain unaltered, since immediately after the conference Representative Sam Rayburn, presumably an Administration spokesman in the House, told a reporter that he was "opposed to taking up the question of amending the Neutrality Act now," and then added, "It would be a funny thing if we changed the Neutrality Law after such a short operation."[52] The final decision came on May 13, 1938, when Secretary Hull clearly stated that the Administration would not recommend any action on the measure. In answer to Senator Pittman's inquiry as to the attitude of the State Department concerning the Nye resolution, Hull made the following statement:

In recent years this Government has consistently pursued a course calculated to prevent our becoming involved in war situations. In August, 1936, shortly after the beginning of the civil strife in Spain, it became evident that several of the great powers were projecting themselves into the struggle through the furnishing of arms and war materials and other aid to the contending sides, thus creating a real danger of the spread of the conflict into a European war, with the possible involvement of the United States. . . . Twenty-seven Governments of Europe took special cognizance of that fact in setting up a committee designed to carry out a concerted policy of non-intervention in the conflict. In view of all these special and unusual circumstances, this Government declared its policy of strict non-interference in the struggle and at the same time announced that export of arms from the United States to Spain would be contrary to such policy.

    ✿   ✿   ✿

The fundamental reason for the enactment of the Joint Resolution, January 8, 1937, was to implement this policy by legislation. . . . Even if the legislation applied to both parties, its enactment would still subject us to unnecessary risks we have so far avoided. . . . In view of the continued danger of international conflict arising from the circumstances of the struggle, any proposal which at this juncture contemplates a reversal of our policy of strict non-interference. . . would offer a real possibility of complications. From the standpoint of the best interests of the United States in the circumstances which now prevail, I would not feel justified in recommending affirmative action on the Resolution under consideration. . . . If reconsideration is to be given to a revision of our neutrality legislation, it would be more useful to reconsider it in its broader aspects in the light of the practical experience during the past two or three years, rather than to rewrite it piecemeal to cover a particular situation.[53]

Senator Pittman's committee agreed to follow the suggestion of Secretary Hull, and action on the Nye resolution was indefinitely postponed.[54]

A final campaign to repeal the Spanish arms embargo was launched after Congress convened in January 1939. Former Secretary of State Henry L. Stimson wrote Cordell Hull that in regard to the Spanish crisis the United States "should take decisive action and that by so doing this country may well be able to ward off serious consequences to the whole world." Stimson cited long legal arguments for lifting the Spanish embargo and pleaded with Hull to discuss the matter personally with President Roosevelt.[55]

Stimson also wrote a letter to the *New York Times* on January 23, 1939, in which he gave nine basic reasons governing his views on the Spanish question. (1) When the United States recognized the Spanish Republican Government as the true Government of Spain, that country was acknowledged as a member of the family of nations and vested with the conventional rights and privileges accorded friendly powers. (2) One of the most important of these rights, which a nation like Spain could expect from a friendly government, was the right of self-defense against rebellions which challenged its authority. Such a nation torn by domestic strife, had the exclusive right to the friendly assistance of its neighbors by being permitted to purchase in their markets the necessary supplies and munitions to suppress the rebellion. (3) It had been the general policy of the Government of the United States to sustain this general right of a nation against which civil strife or rebellion had broken out. (4) Former Secretary of State Robert Lansing had pointed out that because the United States was a peaceful and generally unarmed nation, this government had always relied upon the right to use the markets of the world to purchase the means of defense. (5) Under the rules of international law governing cases of insurrection against a government whose status has been recognized by its neighbors, the government was the only party permitted to purchase arms and munitions abroad. (6) The foregoing was the well-established world practice governing rebellions when the revolt in Spain broke out against the recognized Republican Government. (7) Had the United States continued its former practice and permitted the Government of Spain to make purchases of arms in this country, there is little danger that those purchases would have aroused resentment of other countries. (8) If the Loyalist Government was overthrown, it would be because it had been denied arms and munitions necessary for defense. (9) The embargo should be lifted at once by the President because the change in the international situation during the past two years would justify such action by him. The embargo, which by the terms of the law authorizing it as a protection against conditions which would endanger the peace of the United States, is now shown by the events of the past two years to be itself a source of danger to that peace. Any danger that may come to the people of the United States from the situation in Spain would arise not from any lawful sale of munitions in our markets to the Government of Spain, but from the assistance which our embargo has given to the enemies of Spain. It is the success of the lawless precedents created by those enemies which would constitute our real danger. There is no reason why we should ourselves facilitate and accentuate that danger. There is still less reason why we should violate our own historic policy to do so. The prestige and safety of our country will not be promoted by abandoning its self-respecting traditions, in order to avoid the hostility of reckless violators of international law in Europe.[56]

Several days after the Stimson letter had been published, the *New York Times* printed a letter received from Martin Conboy, a member of the New York bar, in which the opposite view was presented. Conboy stated that he considered the primary reason for retaining the Spanish embargo to be that it conformed to the national neutrality policy, and furthermore, the embargo could only be removed by Congressional repeal of the joint resolution adopted January 8, 1937. He maintained that Stimson ignored the purpose of American neutrality, which was to keep this country free of European disputes. "It does not make the slightest difference," Conboy asserted, "whether the situation is a state of war between two nations or a state of civil war, where aiding by supplying arms to either or both parties to the war will be productive of danger to our peace." He concluded by stating that it was hard to understand why it was demanded that legislation designed to keep this country at peace should be replaced by legislation that would lead to war.[57]

A third letter to the *New York Times* published on January 31, 1939, contained a reply by Charles C. Burlingham, prominent New York attorney, and Philip Jessup, Professor of International Law at Columbia University, to the charges made by Conboy. Burlingham and Jessup argued that American neutrality statutes have always applied to civil wars but only when the United States had recognized the belligerency of the contending forces. In the case of Spain this government had not recognized the belligerency of the Franco or the Loyalist forces. They cited precedents to prove that the policy of the United States in foreign civil wars had always been, when the strife was in Europe, to do nothing in the way of restricting the commerce in arms, and when the war was in Latin America, to prevent arms from reaching the rebels but to assist the legally recognized government in obtaining them. The letter stated that President Roosevelt issued the neutrality proclamation in regard to Spain because of the efforts of the Nonintervention Committee and the belief that the United States might become involved in the affairs of Europe should this country work against that cooperative policy and thus cause its defeat. They added, however, that this

> effort has been defeated by Mussolini and Hitler; the basic conditions have changed and the revocation of the embargo by the President would be fully in accord with the statute. It would further mark a return to our historic policy of avoiding intervention in European civil wars by following a strict hands-off policy instead of taking affirmative action which, as events have demonstrated, inevitably affects the outcome of a struggle in which we profess not to be concerned.[58]

There were many others who argued, as did Burlingham and Jessup, that lifting the Spanish embargo could not be considered an act of interference because the belligerency of the Rebels had not been recognized and the ordinary rules of neutrality were not applicable. Thus the United States was justified in extending aid to the recognized Spanish Government. Opponents, however, contended that although the belligerency of the Rebels had not been formally recognized, it had been tacitly recognized by the application of an impartial arms embargo against both sides. The position of the United States was somewhat anomalous since this country had persistently refused to recognize the belligerency of the Franco forces, while at the same time had treated both sides on an equal basis. Of course, there is no rule which forbids one state from rendering assistance to the legitimate government of another state, yet whether such aid shall be rendered is a matter of policy or expediency and is not to be concerned with the question of right and duty according to international law.[59]

Nevertheless, certain groups and individuals continued to urge lifting of the embargo on the shipment of arms to the Spanish Government. After the capture of Barcelona the editors of the *Christian Science Monitor* declared that only speedy aid could prevent a complete "fascist" victory in Spain;[60] while Paul Kellogg, editor of *Survey Graphic*, asked the President to revoke the "unjust" Spanish embargo which was a "blot on Americans in a critical period for democracy."[61] The *Socialist Call* reported that the messages of 250,000 workers had "swamped the offices of the lawmakers urging them to execute the will of the American people,"[62] and the New York State Socialist party adopted a resolution stating:

It is on record that the chief influence on placing and continuing the iniquitous Spanish embargo has been President Roosevelt. . . . It was the influence of the White House that has kept the embargo in effect as against the obvious wishes of the American people. We condemn this conduct of President Roosevelt and the entire administration as opposed to our best interests.[63]

Parades by Communists in New York City and demonstrations by the American Law Students Association and the National Student Union also protested the embargo against Spain.[64] James Baker, national secretary of the Negro Committee to Aid Spanish Democracy, urged members of Congress to "throw the full weight of American democracy on the side of world democracy by lifting the embargo."[65] Two hundred and fifty Protestant and Jewish clergymen from thirty-five different states sent a telegram to President Roosevelt urging that the embargo be revoked,[66] and an organization known as the National Council to Lift the Embargo Against the Spanish Republic was formed.[67]

Not all the reasons advanced for lifting the embargo were ideological. There was increasing pressure to resume normal economic relations with Spain. Before 1936 Spain had been a large consumer of American goods, and many persons in the United States were anxious that this trade be continued. Senator Robert Reynolds (D-North Carolina) told the Senate that the South needed additional foreign markets for cotton and urged that normal commercial relations be resumed with Spain.[68] Senator Nye presented a resolution adopted by the legislature of North Dakota which asked that the embargo be lifted to provide further markets for the wheat surplus and thus improve the economic position of the American farmer.[69]

The State Department, however, refused to alter its previous position and declined to recommend that President Roosevelt consider revision of American Spanish policy. Nor was Congress moved to take any immediate action. Perhaps this may be explained by the imminence of a Franco victory in Spain and a fear of reprisals against American interests.[70] At any rate, it was soon too late for the United States to take steps to aid the Republican Government, for by the middle of February 1939 Loyalist leaders had indicated their readiness for peace. Madrid fell to the Nationalists on March 28, 1939, and one of the most destructive civil wars in history had come to a close.

The Spanish arms embargo was in effect from January 8, 1937, until April 1, 1939. During this period the arms export licensing system, under the control of the National Munitions Control Board, facilitated prevention of violations of the law and the detection of efforts to make indirect shipments to Spain. The Spanish Government made repeated efforts to purchase aircraft and other war supplies from the United States through a third country. Secretary of the Treasury Morgenthau stated that Spanish Ambassador de los Ríos had $15,000,000 in a safe deposit box at the Riggs National Bank in Washington but was never able to use the money to buy arms for his government.[71] Despite a careful system of control there is some evidence that a few shipments of American war material actually reached the Loyalists. The German Ambassador accredited to Franco Spain reported to his government: "It is stated with certainty that the automatic weapons which the Red Spaniards have received . . . come not only from Mexico but also from the United States and that the volume of shipments from there continues to grow considerably."[72] The Italian newspaper *Popolo d'Italia* charged that such war goods were sent from the United States to Spain via Russia. "In the month of September [1937]," the paper asserted, "the United States exported arms and munitions totaling upward of $20,000,000 of which nearly $10,000,000 was bought by the Soviet Union, which in turn sent the arms and munitions to Red Spain."[73] There were also various news dispatches that reported American arms being used by the Loyalists, and one American reporter in Spain stated that he saw many weapons which had been made in the United States.[74]

Many such weapons, however, were only of American design and were not manufactured in the United States. Other weapons, although produced in this country, were shipped to other countries prior to the January 1937 embargo and then transshipped to Loyalist Spain by interested third parties. Secretary Hull stated that manufacturing rights for certain types of Boeing, Curtiss, and Martin planes had been sold by these companies to the Soviet Union. The Secretary indicated that reports involving American planes in Spain were false and that the State Department was convinced that the only planes of American origin to reach Spain since the outbreak of civil strife were six used transports which were shipped to France in December 1936, then transshipped to Spain.[75] In October 1938 Consul Charles Bay reported from Seville that American war material, including 17 armored cars, 38 field guns, 680 machine guns, 3,480 rifles, and 11,700 projectiles was allegedly captured by the Insurgents.[76] Acting Secretary Moore replied that the Department of State and War Department had made a careful study of the report and "it is extremely unlikely that any of these arms, ammunition, and implements of war were exported from the United States after January 8, 1937." He pointed out that all the equipment listed was old and obsolete, then added, "it is not believed . . . that any private American manufacturers could have exported any guns of this type to Spain since the embargo went into effect."[77]

It is doubtful if any American war supplies reached the Nationalists. In December 1938 President Roosevelt asked the State Department to investigate the reported shipments of shells and hand grenades to General Franco via Belgium, Holland, Germany, and England.[78] Under Secretary Welles replied that the

Department has investigated all alleged shipments of arms to Franco and has in each case found the allegation without foundation. The Department has no reason whatsoever to believe that arms of any kind exported from this country since January 8, 1937, have reached the rebel forces in Spain.[79]

Ambassador Bowers cabled Secretary Hull that many complaints had been made to him concerning the purchase of war material in the United States by Germany and Italy for transshipment to the Spanish Rebels.[80] The Secretary replied that the exports of arms to those countries had been in "negligible quantities" and he concluded by stating: "The Department has no reason to believe that any arms, ammunition, or implements of war exported from the United States since January 8, 1937, to any foreign country have reached Spain."[81]

Although the National Munitions Control Board attempted to prevent all shipments of American war material from reaching Spain, there were a few cases where shipments of American aircraft eluded the authorities and reached the Spanish Government by way of Mexico, Canada, and France. Despite an earlier promise by the Mexican Government to prevent transshipment of arms from the United States to Spain, in December 1937 ten planes out of a shipment of twenty-two, which had been illegally exported from this country, left Vera Cruz for Barcelona.[82] In another case approximately forty fighter planes, manufactured in the United States by the Grumman Engineering Corporation and the Brewster Aeronautical Corporation, reached the Spanish Government after the parts were shipped to a Canadian company for assembly there and then reshipped to Spain by way of Turkey and France.[83] Documents authorizing the export of these aircraft were later discovered to be forgeries. This demonstrates that the licensing system was not infallilible; nevertheless, it was very effective in most cases in preventing the shipment of war supplies from the United States to Spain.[84]

There is considerable evidence to support the conclusion that President Roosevelt was personally sympathetic to the Loyalist cause and perhaps wanted to revoke the Spanish embargo but was prevented from doing so by strong pressures both within and outside of the Administration. Mrs. Eleanor Roosevelt commented that

> Franklin frequently refrained from supporting causes in which he believed because of political realities. There were times when this annoyed me very much. In the case of the Spanish Civil War, for instance, we had to remain neutral though Franklin knew quite well he wanted the democratic government to be successful. But he also knew that he could not get Congress to go along with him. To justify his action, or lack of action, he explained to me, when I complained, that the League of Nations had asked us to remain neutral. By trying to convince me that our course was correct, though he knew I thought we were doing the wrong thing, he was simply trying to salve his own conscience, because he himself was uncertain.[85]

Even after the President had refused to lend his support to the Nye resolution in May 1938, he seriously considered the issue. Both Secretary Ickes and Secretary Morgenthau strongly urged Roosevelt to revoke the Spanish embargo. Ickes wrote the President that he personally favored lifting the embargo. He declared that the joint resolution of May 1, 1937, repealed the January 8 resolution, and "in view of the changes that have occurred in the conditions existing on May 1, 1937, the President is authorized by the statute to revoke the May 1 proclamation without further act by Congress."[86] Morgenthau likewise pleaded with Roosevelt to overrule Hull and the State Department and permit the Spanish Government to purchase arms in this country.[87]

Secretary Ickes wrote a second letter to Roosevelt in November 1938, enclosing a "Petition of Members of the American Bar to the President of the United States — With Accompanying Memorandum on the Embargo Against Spain." Ickes asked the President to consider carefully this petition and suggested that the Lawyer's Committee on American Relations with Spain be received at the White House.[88] Roosevelt forwarded the letter to Sumner Welles and asked his opinion on the matter.[89] A similar memorandum was sent to Attorney General Homer S. Cummings instructing him to "please study the Spanish Embargo situation from a legal point of view and talk to me about it." Cummings was advised that the "State Department lawyers and the Secretary of State believe that if I were to revoke my proclamation of May 1st, the original prohibition of January 8th would still remain in force. The other side claims that the resolution of May 1st cancelled out the resolution of January 8th — and I think there is some merit to this contention. What do you think?"[90] In reply to the President's memorandum, Welles stated that "the decision was reached here that even if you were to revoke your proclamation of May 1, 1937, the original prohibition upon the export of arms, ammunition, and implements of war to Spain laid down by the Congress on January 8, 1937, would still remain in force."[91]

President Roosevelt followed the advice of the State Department and steadfastly refused to undertake any efforts which would alter American policy toward Spain. By the spring of 1939, however, the President did favor a general revision of American neutrality laws through Congressional action. Senator Pittman, who was to pilot the bill through Congress, advised Roosevelt that outright repeal was impossible but that some changes might be made in the existing law. Pittman also told the President that he was "exceedingly apprehensive" lest the debate reopen the "highly controversial issue" of American policy toward the Spanish Civil War and the project be lost in a partisan conflict.[92] Nevertheless, it was agreed that Administration efforts would concentrate on repeal of the arms embargo and to permit export of war materials to belligerents on a "cash and carry" basis. The bill was introduced by Pittman in March 1939 when the Spanish Civil War was drawing to a close, but it was not until after the outbreak of the war in Europe in September 1939 that the revision was made.

This reversal of Administration policy apparently was a tacit admission of its incorrectness. The arms embargo was retained and zealously defended through 1938, yet by early 1939 President Roosevelt was willing to permit the sale of arms to belligerents. This suggests that Roosevelt may have realized that he was wrong in his attitude toward the Spanish question, but adopted such a policy because of strong pressures.

Despite such pressure the President conferred on November 7, 1938, with Assistant Secretary of State A. A. Berle, Jr., as to the possible role the United States could play in at least securing an armistice in the Spanish strife.[93] Berle replied that it probably would be necessary to associate with the South American countries; and, if possible, make it a unanimous act of the Lima Conference.[94] Berle added that such a move had a good chance of success. He felt that Loyalist Spain would accept and that Franco might, but if the Generalissimo did not, the knowledge that he had declined would liberate forces which might bring peace within a few months. Furthermore, the Assistant Secretary concluded, if Franco did refuse "it would clear the way for changing our position in the matter of the Spanish embargo."[95] There was no unanimity of sentiment, however, among the twenty-one republics concerning this matter. Secretary Hull was apparently opposed and the President's hopes were never realized.

One of the most important sources of pressure on the President came from Secretary Hull and the State Department. Hull strongly defended the Spanish embargo on the grounds that it helped prevent the war from spreading beyond Spanish frontiers; it bettered relations with England and France; it avoided encouraging the

Axis to intervene openly in Spain; and it might be construed an act of open interference to revoke the embargo during the course of the war since this country had maintained such a policy for almost two years.[96] These arguments are not convincing, however, because the war was not prevented but postponed, and there is no proof that American Spanish policy actually bettered relations with England and France. It is also doubtful if the American embargo discouraged the Axis from intervening openly in Spain, while the United States could hardly be charged with intervention since no legal status of belligerency existed and the rules of neutrality did not apply. Nevertheless, Hull has strongly defended his position in stating that it is "hard to see how we could have pursued any other course."[97] He consistently advised the President to retain the Spanish embargo and criticized other of the President's advisers who advocated a different policy.[98] Secretary Morgenthau commented that Roosevelt's primary motive in refusing to lift the embargo was "less a fear of alienating organized pro-Franco groups in the country than a desire not to force the hand of his Secretary of State." He added that the President "could not afford, for the sake of a single issue, to weaken Hull before Congress, where his popularity often won the Administration a narrow victory on major fights."[99] Ambassador Bowers has stated that Roosevelt's sympathy was entirely with the Loyalists and that the President "squirmed" a great deal over American policy. Bowers asserted, however, that our policy in Spain was "imposed" on Roosevelt by Secretary Hull; and Hull got his advice from James C. Dunn, Chief of the Division of European Affairs and Adviser on Political Relations. The Ambassador believes that the President's domestic program would have been endangered had he taken a stand in conformity with his ideas because of the Catholic influence.[100]

Perhaps the strongest foreign influence behind the American embargo came from England and was a part of Neville Chamberlain's appeasement program.[101] Thus the United States in retaining the Spanish embargo supported the policy of appeasement and must to a certain extent share responsibility for it. This policy resulted in the United States, England, and France becoming active collaborators with the Axis in their avowed purpose of destroying the legally constituted Government of Spain.

Ambassadors Kennedy and Bullitt were likewise sources of pressure on the President. Kennedy, a well-known Catholic layman, openly and consistently defended Chamberlain's course and together with Bullitt he supported a policy of causing no offense to the Axis.[102] In May 1938 Kennedy cabled Secretary Hull that with all its faults "nonintervention has contributed towards the preservation of peace in Europe. Settlement of the Spanish problem would seem to be an essential prerequisite to any scheme for general European appeasement. The interjection of any new factor into this already overcharged and delicate situation, might have far-reaching consequences."[103] Both Bullitt and Kennedy corresponded directly with the President and repeatedly urged him to retain the Spanish embargo so as not to embarrass the nonintervention efforts of Britain and France. Roosevelt indicated that he was influenced by this argument when he stated that the leading powers of Europe had adopted a program of nonintervention and that the democracies at least were determined to adhere to that policy. Some of these democracies and the League of Nations, Roosevelt added, "urged very strongly upon us the importance of our arms embargo in the interests of world peace, pointing out the likelihood of a general conflict in Europe unless the Spanish Civil War were kept strictly within the boundaries of Spain."[104]

Perhaps one of the major reasons Roosevelt refused to support the Nye resolution and failed to mention it for the record was the influence of certain big city machine politicians and party bosses who regarded the Spanish Civil War as a "hot" issue. It is possible that the President felt that a Catholic defection of votes might have defeated the Democrats in the presidential election of 1940, and he did not want to alienate this large segment of voters. The pro-Loyalists were rather equally divided between Republicans and Democrats, while pro-Franco Catholics were mostly Democrats largely found in the eastern cities. The local leaders in the Democratic party thus did not want the Administration to raise an issue whereby religious feelings might be translated into political pressure. Then, too, James A. Farley, an outstanding Catholic layman, was at the height of his political career and may have advised the President of possible political implications should the Spanish embargo be revoked.[105] At any rate Secretaries Ickes and Morgenthau and even Mrs. Roosevelt might urge the Loyalist cause but they could not deliver the votes.

There is little doubt, however, that the fight to have the embargo retained was spearheaded by certain groups within the

Catholic Church. In late January 1939, when the war in Spain was obviously drawing to a close, the *Christian Science Monitor* concluded that "one consideration and only one prevented that action. That consideration was the attitude of the Roman Catholic hierarchy."[106] The moderately liberal *Washington Times* noted that "it is a cold political fact that the Catholic Church has taken a determined stand in favor of General Franco,"[107] while Pearson and Allen described the Catholic pressure that had been exerted against the Nye resolution.[108] Although this Catholic pressure was an open secret, the President, State Department, and most of the daily press were discreetly silent on the subject.[109]

In December 1938 the National Council of Catholic Men sponsored a "Keep the Spanish Embargo Committee" whose "members . . . had committed themselves but to one thing in accepting membership, namely, *keeping the Spanish Embargo*."[110] The editors of *Catholic Action* commented that the committee "has already elicited an expression of public opinion in favor of the retention of the embargo to the extent of more than two million petitions addressed to the President and the Congress of the United States," and urged "all those interested in preserving the peace and security of the United States . . . to continue their support of the National Council of Catholic Men in this important matter in order that the very highest degree of united action may be achieved."[111] It was reported that twenty of the most important Catholic lay organizations with a combined membership of four million adult Catholics "stood four-square against any proposed action of this government to aid the persecutors of Christianity in Spain and were quick to lend their strength to appropriate action."[112]

The new organization received wide publicity in the Catholic press and purchased advertising space in various secular newspapers.[113] Appeals were made from the pulpit as in Philadelphia where Denis Cardinal Dougherty directed all Catholics "to sign immediately protests and letters and forward them to Congress protesting against the removal of the embargo on munitions to Spain."[114] George Cardinal Mundelein, Archbishop of Chicago, described by one writer as a "strategic length between Catholic reaction and New Deal realism," was reported to have frequently consulted with the President and advised him not to support any effort to revoke the embargo.[115]

A legal study was made by Dr. Herbert Wright, Professor of International Law at Catholic University of America, in which he stated that if the civil strife in Spain were restricted and not apt to involve the United States, then the American Government would be free, as a matter of policy, to grant or withhold assistance to the Loyalists. He asserted, however, that the President's Proclamation of May 1, 1937, stated that the peace of the United States was endangered and therefore "the United States is bound by international law to abstain from assisting either the Loyalists or Franco — whether actively or passively." Wright added that since Germany and Italy had recognized the Insurgents as the *de facto* Government of Spain, then those countries were free to grant or withhold assistance to Franco as they saw fit.[116]

Many prominent Catholics and Catholic sponsored organizations sent messages to the White House requesting that the President refrain from taking any action that would alter American policy toward Spain. One group declared that "we commend the United States for consistently refusing to lift the embargo against Spain. We hope that such refusal will be rigidly adhered to."[117] On January 16, following a radio appeal by Father Coughlin, it was reported that more than 100,000 telegrams opposing repeal of the embargo had been sent to members of Congress.[118] Senator Pat McCarran (D-Nevada), a Catholic and the father of two nuns, warned that any attempt to lift the Spanish embargo would be remembered by a long Senate fight against it.[119] The Knights of Columbus at their annual convention in New York passed a resolution urging retention of the embargo, and Dr. Joseph F. Thorning charged that all agitation to lift the embargo was Communist inspired.[120]

Thus because of these many and varied pressures and the belief that the overwhelming sentiment of the American people was against the sale of military supplies, President Roosevelt refused to revoke the Spanish embargo. It is entirely possible, however, that Roosevelt overestimated the strength of the isolationists and supporters of General Franco, and had he chosen to alter American policy toward Spain it would not have materially affected his position. On the contrary, the President by a different policy might have weakened the appeasement policies of the European democracies and decreased the strength of isolationism in the United States. Certainly, American opinion would not have countenanced any form of interference by the United States in the Spanish conflict; nevertheless, positive public opinion and a large part of the press favored the Republican Government of Spain and probably would not have objected had the Loyalists purchased arms in this country to defend themselves against Fascist invasion.

Roosevelt mistakenly felt that a vast majority of American Catholics were behind Franco, but indications are that such convictions were largely confined to the hierarchy and that numerous Catholics actually saw the wisdom of repealing the embargo. They knew that many British Catholics, and the bulk of the French Catholics were sympathetic with, and the Basque Catholics were fighting for, the Spanish Government. The fact that Franco was "saving" Spain with Nazi pagans, infidel Moors, and Italian Fascists was revolting to many of the faithful. Discipline within the Church was strict, however, and few American Catholics openly expressed pro-Loyalist sentiments. In any event, although Roosevelt had some misgivings concerning American Spanish policy, he refused to act and so must share responsibility with Britain and France in contributing to the advent of the Second World War by appeasing Fascist aggressors in Spain.

NOTES

1. *Times* (London), January 7, 1937. Perhaps the most detailed published account of Russian activity in Spain is contained in W. G. Krivitsky, "Stalin's Hand in Spain," *Saturday Evening Post* (Philadelphia), CCXII (April 15, 1939), 5-6, 115-22. There has been some question concerning General Krivitsky's true identity. The *New Masses* has called him an imposter, claiming that he had never served in the Soviet Army. The *Post,* however, insists that the General was former Chief of Soviet Military Intelligence in Western Europe and fled to America as a political refugee.

2. Thurston to Hull, October 26, 1937 (SD File No. 852.00/6955).

3. Bowers to author, February 15, 1954. The reports that the Spanish Government was under the domination of Moscow were largely unfounded. Ambassador Bullitt cabled from Paris in January 1938 that "Communist influence had diminished enormously and at the moment the Spanish Government, while radical, was by no means Communist and was definitely hostile to Moscow." Bullitt to Hull, January 25, 1938 (SD File No. 852.00/7254: tel.).

4. *New York Times*, February 21, 1938.

5. *Ibid.,* June 27, 1937. The Fascist Grand Council, in observing the "liberation" of Catalonia from "barbarous bolshevist oppression," declared in February 1939 that it sends "ardent greetings to the heroic Spanish warriors and Italian Legionnaires, the solid factors in the victory, and makes known to all that the volunteer forces of fascism will not abandon the struggle

before it has ended, as it must end, with Franco's victory." *Ibid.,* February 5, 1939.

6. Department of State, *Spanish Government and the Axis* (Washington, 1946), p. 19. In February 1941, Stefani, the official Italian news agency, reported that Italy had sent Franco a bill for 7,500,000,000 lire to pay for Italian aid during the Spanish Civil War. This amount covered the cost of 763 planes, 1,414 motors, 1,672 tons of bombs, 9,250,000 rounds of ammunition, 1,930 cannon, 240,747 small arms, 7,514,537 artillery shells, 324,900,000 rounds of small arms ammunition, and 7,668 motor vehicles. The report also stated that 91 Italian warships were engaged in the Spanish War; 92 Italian cargo vessels ferried the matériel; and Italian submarines sank 72,800 tons of "hostile" shipping. *New York Times,* February 28, 1941. A year later Franco ordered transferred to Italy 5,000,000,000 lire (a lire at that time was worth 5.05 cents) in Spanish treasury bonds in partial payment of Spain's war debt to Italy. *Ibid.,* February 6, 1942. For documentary accounts of German aid to Franco Spain, see Appendix C. Foreign intervention in Spain is also fully treated in Hubbard, "British Public Opinion and the Spanish Civil War," pp. 76-119.

7. League of Nations Assembly, Sixth Committee, *Situation in Spain and Connected Questions* (Geneva, 1937), pp. 1-27. See also Francis O. Wilcox, "The League of Nations and the Spanish Civil War," *Annals of the American Academy of Political and Social Science,* CXCVIII (July, 1938), 65-72.

8. Spanish Foreign Office, *The Italian Invasion of Spain* (Washington, 1937).

9. Sumner Welles, October 18, 1937 (SD File No. 852.00/6771: memo.).

10. *Ibid.*

11. The treaty referred to was the Spanish-American Treaty of Friendship and General Relations signed at Madrid, July 3, 1902.

12. de los Ríos to Hull, November 19, 1937 (SD File No. 711.00111/1582).

13. The Ambassador was probably referring to the President's "Quarantine" speech delivered in Chicago, October 5, 1937.

14. Hugh R. Wilson, December 8, 1937 (SD File No. 711.00111/1582: memo.).

15. *Ibid.*

16. Hull to de los Ríos, December 21, 1937 (SD File No. 711.00111/1582).

17. At that time he held no office in the Spanish Government; he was later appointed Minister of State in the reorganization of April 5, 1938.

18. Thurston to Hull, April 3, 1938 (SD File No. 852.00/7671: tel.).

19. Pierrepont Moffat, April 21, 1938 (SD File No. 852.00/7803: memo.).

20. *New York Times,* October 6, 1937. The Spanish Ambassador was so gratified at hearing the President's speech that he immediately called upon Under Secretary Welles to inquire if Roosevelt's speech did not require the active participation of the United States on the side of the democracies of the world? The Ambassador declared that the present situation in Spain was an instance where the influence of the United States could be exerted in behalf of democracy. Sumner Welles, October 18, 1937 (SD File No. 852.00/6771: memo.).

21. Paul Kellogg, "Between Going to War and Doing Nothing," *Survey Graphic* (New York), XXVIII (March, 1939), 226-28.

22. Drew Pearson and Robert S. Allen, "Washington Daily Merry-Go-Round," *New Orleans States*, May 9, 1938.

23. *New York Times*, April 5, 1938.

24. *New York Times*, February 16, 1938.

25. *Ibid.*, April 28, 1938. The letter is also printed in *Science News Letter* (Washington), XXXIII (May 7, 1938), 298. Among the signers of the petition were Harold C. Urey, Arthur H. Compton, Harlow Shapley, F. R. Moulton, Robert A. Millikan, and Oswald Veblen.

26. *New York Times*, March 6, 1938. Signers included Bishop Francis J. McConnell, Dr. Guy Emery Shipler, A. F. Whitney, Francis J. Gorman, Rockwell Kent, Dr. Walter B. Cannon, Harold C. Urey, Robert Lynd, Franz Boas, Henry Pratt Fairchild, Maxwell Anderson, Theodore Dreiser, and Van Wyck Brooks.

27. *Ibid.*, June 10, 1938.

28. *Ibid.*, May 8, 1938.

29. Sixteen hundred students and members of the faculty at the University of Chicago to President Roosevelt, May 4, 1938 (FDR Official Files, No. 422C: tel.). This was only one of hundreds of such communications examined by the author at the Roosevelt Library in Hyde Park. One amusing note was scrawled as follows: "For God's Sake! *Lift that Embargo to Spain.* Look what happened to us." Signed: "Ghost of Czechoslovakia." *Ibid.* (n.d.).

30. Wolcott D. Street (ed.), "Should Our Neutrality Law be Repealed or Revised?" *Bulletin of America's Town Meeting of the Air* (New York), IV (December 26, 1938).

31. *Socialist Call*, April 23, 1938.

32. *Ibid.*

33. *New York Times*, May 1, 1938.

34. *Ibid.*, July 20, 1937.

35. *Ibid.*, May 29, 1938.

36. *Ibid.*, May 18, 1938.

37. *Ibid.*, April 5, 1938.

38. *Current History*, XLIV (November, 1937), 25-28.

39. *New York Times*, May 10, 1938.

40. Buell to Hull, March 18, 1938, quoted in *Press Releases*, March 26, 1938.

41. Hull to Buell, March 22, 1938, *ibid.*

42. *Congressional Record*, 75 Cong., 3 Sess., LXXXIII (April 5, 1938), 4810.

43. *Ibid.* (May 2, 1938), 6030.

44. *Ibid.* (March 29, 1938), A1229-30.

45. *Ibid.* (May 2, 1938), 6030.

46. *Ibid.* (June 2, 1938), A2310-11. Bernard stated that objectors to American Spanish policy included Henry L. Stimson, ex-Secretary of State; Jerome Davis, President of the American Federation of Teachers; William E. Dodd, former Ambassador to Germany; Dr. Albert Einstein, the Institute for Advanced Study, Princeton, N. J.; Sherwood Anderson, writer; Professor Franz Boas, Columbia University; Walter Lippman, columnist; Dorothy

Thompson, columnist; Dr. Harvey Cushing, Yale Medical School; A. F. Whitney, President, Brotherhood of Railway Trainmen; Bishop Francis J. McConnell; Bishop G. Bromley Oxnam; Rabbi Stephen S. Wise; Helen Keller; Kathleen Norris, writer; and Bennett Cerf, publisher.

47. *Ibid.* (June 16, 1938), A2933.

48. Pearson and Allen, *New Orleans States*, May 11, 1938. Secretary Hull does not mention this conference in his *Memoirs*, nor does Sumner Welles in his various writings; however, the incident is described in Bendiner, *The Riddle of the State Department*, pp. 59-62.

49. *New York Times*, May 5, 1938. The front-page story announcing the change in policy was preceded by the headline: "Roosevelt Backs Lifting Arms Embargo on Spain; Congress Agrees it Fails."

50. Pearson and Allen, *New Orleans States*, May 11, 1938; Kennedy to Hull, May 9, 1938 (SD File No. 852.24/631: tel.); see also, Bendiner, *Riddle of the State Department*, pp. 60-62.

51. *New York Times*, May 14, 1938.

52. *Ibid.*, May 10, 1938.

53. Hull to Pittman, May 12, 1938 (SD File No. 852.24/708). See also Hull to Roosevelt, May 11, 1938 (FDR Official Files, No. 422C). This memorandum contains the full text of the letter to Pittman with a marginal note: "O. K., FDR, 5-12-38."

54. *New York Times*, May 14, 1938. Pearson and Allen reported that the move to vote down the Nye resolution in the Senate Foreign Relations Committee was "railroaded" through by Pittman, with the aid of Senators Walter F. George (D-Georgia), Pat Harrison (D-Mississippi), and Hiram W. Johnson (R-California). The two columnists also asserted that Senator Borah, the principal supporter of the resolution, was late in arriving because he had not been promptly notified of the meeting. When Borah did arrive the vote had already been taken. Pearson and Allen, *New Orleans States*, May 18, 1938.

55. Stimson to Hull, January 18, 1939 (FDR Official Files, President's Secretary's File Box 52).

56. *New York Times*, January 24, 1939. See Appendix A for the complete text of this letter. Arthur Krock commented that Stimson had often advised Hull and had gone along with him on certain policies, but "it may be that for the first time in their relations Mr. Stimson is giving the Roosevelt government inconvenience and anxiety instead of holding its hand." *Ibid.*, January 25, 1939.

57. *Ibid.*, January 26, 1939. See Appendix A for the complete text of this letter.

58. *Ibid.*, January 31, 1939. See Appendix A for the complete text of this letter. Conboy replied to Burlingham and Jessup reaffirming his argument that even if the President should revoke his May 1, 1937, proclamation pertaining to the Spanish arms embargo, munitions could not be shipped to Spain because the joint Congressional resolution of January 8, 1937, would still remain in effect. *Ibid.*, February 2, 1939.

59. Vernon A. O'Rourke, "Recognition of Belligerency and the Spanish Civil War," *American Journal of International Law*, XXXI (July, 1937), 398-413; James W. Garner, "Questions of International Law and the Spanish

Civil War," *ibid.* (January, 1937), 66-73; and Edwin Borchard and William Potter Lage, *Neutrality for the United States* (New Haven, 1940), p. 355.

60. *Christian Science Monitor,* January 27, 1939.

61. Kellogg, "Between Going to War and Doing Nothing," pp. 226-28.

62. *Socialist Call,* February 4, 1939. This figure is probably very accurate. Senator Pittman reported on January 25, 1939, that the Senate Foreign Relations Committee, during the preceding week, had received 35,000 letters on the question of the Spanish embargo. *New York Times,* January 26, 1939.

63. *New York Times,* February 14, 1939.

64. *Ibid.,* February 2, 25, 26, 1939.

65. *Ibid.,* February 8, 1939.

66. Protestant and Jewish clergymen to President Roosevelt, January 24, 1939 (FDR Official Files, No. 422C: tel.). The author examined literally hundreds of communications at the Roosevelt Library protesting the Spanish embargo. One of the telegrams was signed by 5,000 persons, while there were numerous others with at least 2,000 signatures.

67. *New York Times,* January 9, 1939.

68. *Congressional Record,* 76 Cong., 1 Sess., LXXXIV (March 27, 1939), 3353-54.

69. *Ibid.* (February 16, 1939), 1455.

70. Counselor Thurston cabled Secretary Hull that lifting the Spanish embargo would be construed as an act tantamount to intervention in the conflict and in the event of a Rebel victory our large investments and frozen exchange acounts in Spain might be adversely affected. Thurston to Hull, April 4, 1938 (SD File No. 852.00/7671: tel.).

71. Henry Morgenthau, Jr., "The Morgenthau Diaries: III," *Colliers,* CXX (October 11, 1947), 79.

72. Department of State, *Documents on German Foreign Policy, 1918-1945,* III, 646.

73. *Popolo d'Italia,* quoted in the *New York Times,* October 17, 1937. Soviet Ambassador Alexander A. Troyanovsky denied the charges, declaring: "A statement like that is somebody's pure invention." *Ibid.,* October 19, 1937.

74. *Ibid.,* November 5, 1937; February 5, 1939.

75. Hull to Bay, August 17, 1937 (SD File No. 852.00/6178).

76. Bay to Hull, October 18, 1938 (SD File No. 852.00/8623).

77. Moore to Bay, December 23, 1938 (SD File No. 852.00/8747).

78. Roosevelt to Welles, December 3, 1938 (FDR Official Files, No. 422C: memo.).

79. Welles to Roosevelt, December 6, 1938 (FDR Official Files, Sumner Welles File).

80. Bowers to Hull, March 25, 1938 (SD File No. 711.00111/1716: tel.).

81. Hull to Bowers, March 29, 1938 (SD File No. 711.00111/1716: tel.).

82. *Third Annual Report of the National Munitions Control Board* (Washington, 1939), p. 83.

83. *Ibid.,* pp. 85-86. See also *New York Times,* January 10, 1939.

84. The Munitions Board, operating under the State Department, was vigorously supported by Secretary Hull and Foreign Service officers abroad.

4

On one occasion the Department refused to issue an export license covering the purchase in the United States of two bullet-proof limousines for the President and Premier of Spain. This evoked a strong word of protest from Ambassador de los Ríos. de los Ríos to Hull, November 19, 1937 (SD File No. 711.00111/21: memo.). For several case histories of attempts to send war matériel to Spain indirectly, see *New York Times*, March 22, 1940; *Press Releases*, October 29, 1938; and the *Fourth Annual Report of the National Munitions Control Board* (Washington, 1939), p. 111.

85. Eleanor Roosevelt, *This I Remember* (New York, 1949), pp. 161-62. Mrs. Roosevelt was very interested in the Spanish War and often spoke with the President concerning American policy. On one occasion she protested that American arms were being shipped to General Franco by way of Germany and England. When Roosevelt received assurances from Welles that such reports were false, Mrs. Roosevelt was promptly notified. President Roosevelt to Mrs. Roosevelt, December 6, 1938 (FDR Official Files, Sumner Welles File: memo.).

Mrs Roosevelt also relates an instance of disagreement with Winston Churchill concerning the Spanish Civil War. When she was visiting England in October 1942, Mrs. Roosevelt remarked at a dinner given in her honor that "we should have done something to help the Loyalists during their Civil War." Prime Minister Churchill was very annoyed over her views on Spain and replied that both he and Mrs. Roosevelt "would have been the first to lose our heads if the Loyalists had won." Roosevelt, *This I Remember*, p. 274.

86. Ickes to Roosevelt (n.d.) (FDR Official Files, No. 422A).

87. Henry Morgenthau, Jr., "The Morgenthau Diaries: III," *Colliers*, CXX (October 11, 1947), 79. Although Hull objected, Morgenthau, as Secretary of the Treasury, purchased large amounts of Spanish Government silver. *Ibid.*

88. Ickes to Roosevelt, November 23, 1938 (FDR Official Files, No. 422C). The lawyers argued that "the Embargo against Spain is an act in violation of a solemn treaty of the United States with Spain [Spanish-American Friendship Treaty of 1902; see Malloy, *Treaties and Conventions*, II, 1701]. The embargo is an abandonment and repudiation of traditional American Foreign Policy; the Embargo was not justified by any actual or threatened danger of war; the Embargo does not achieve either impartiality or neutrality, but is in actual effect an aid to insurgents seeking to disestablish the legitimate government. The effect of the Embargo has been to injure the established government of a friendly nation, to aid insurrection, to encourage armed revolt against an established government and to assist foreign aggression." Therefore: "The Embargo legislation affecting civil strife should be revoked immediately; and the United States should return to its honorable and historic policy in conformity with international law."

89. Roosevelt to Welles, November 25, 1938 (FDR Official Files, No. 422C: memo.).

90. Roosevelt to Homer S. Cummings, November 28, 1938, *ibid*. The Attorney General must have discussed this matter personally with the President since no written reply seems to have been made.

91. Welles to Roosevelt, November 25, 1938, *ibid*.

92. Langer and Gleason, *Challenge to Isolation*, p. 79.

93. A. A. Berle, Jr., November 19, 1938 (SD File No. 852.00/8654½: memo.).

94. The Eighth Pan-American Conference held in Lima, Peru in December 1938.

95. A. A. Berle, Jr., November 19, 1938 (SD File No. 852.00/8554½: memo.).

96. Hull, *Memoirs*, I, 517.

97. *Ibid.*

98. In November 1938, when Roosevelt, at the request of Ickes and Morgenthau, was seriously considering the embargo question, Hull wrote the President: "I herein enclose the Act of Congress imposing an embargo on shipments of arms, ammunition, and implements of war to Spain. This makes it clear, I think, that only Congress can change our embargo policy as contained in this act." Hull to Roosevelt, November 18, 1938 (FDR Official Files, Secretary Hull's File: memo.).

99. Henry Morgenthau, Jr., "Morgenthau Diaries: III," *Colliers*, CXX (October 11, 1947), 79.

100. Bowers to author, February 15, 1954.

101. The record suggests, however, that British public opinion was much more in sympathy with the Spanish Republicans than His Majesty's Government. On four occasions the British Institute of Public Opinion conducted polls on the Spanish Civil War with the following results: (1) January 1937, "Do you consider that Franco's junta should be recognized as the legal Spanish Government?" Yes, 14 per cent; no, 86 per cent. (2) March 1938, "In the present war in Spain are you in sympathy with the Government, with Franco, or with neither?" Government, 57 per cent; Franco, 7 per cent; neither, 36 per cent. (3) October 1938, "In the present conflict in Spain between Franco and the Government are your sympathies with Franco or the Government?" Government, 57 per cent; Franco, 9 per cent; no opinion, 34 per cent. (4) January 1939, in answer to the same question, Government, 72 per cent; Franco, 9 per cent; and no opinion, 19 per cent. Parry, "The Spanish Civil War," p. 287. For an analysis of British public opinion, see Hubbard, "British Public Opinion and the Spanish Civil War."

102. Morgenthau, "Morgenthau Diaries: IV," *Colliers*, CXX (October 18, 1947), 16; Dodd and Dodd (eds.), *Ambassador Dodd's Diary*, pp. 371-72.

103. Kennedy to Hull, May 9, 1938 (SD File No. 852.24/631: tel.).

104. Samuel I. Rosenman (ed.), *The Public Papers and Addresses of Franklin D. Roosevelt*, 13 vols. (New York, 1941), VI, 192.

105. The editors of the *Nation* suggest that he did, but Farley in his autobiography remains silent on the issue. *Nation*, CXLVI (May 28, 1938), 607; James A. Farley, *Jim Farley's Story* (New York, 1948), Robert E. Sherwood, *Roosevelt and Hopkins* (New York, 1948); and James F. Byrnes, *Speaking Frankly* (New York, 1947), also fail to mention the Spanish Civil War.

106. *Christian Science Monitor*, January 26, 1939.

107. *Washington Times*, cited in the *Nation*, CXLVI (May 28, 1938), 609.

108. Pearson and Allen, *New Orleans States*, May 11, 1938.

109. Perhaps most papers did not wish to become involved in a group conflict such as the *Philadelphia Record* experienced.

110. "Our Common Catholic Interests," *Catholic Action*, XXI (February, 1939), 3-6.

111. *Ibid.*

112. *Ibid.*

113. For example see the half-page advertisement that appeared in the *Washington Post*, January 8, 1939.

114. Michael Francis Doyle to Marvin McIntyre, January 15, 1939 (FDR Official Files, No. 422C).

115. Max Lerner, "Behind Hull's Embargo," *Nation*, CXLVI (May 28, 1938), 608. The *Christian Science Monitor* reported that Cardinal Mundelein telephoned Roosevelt at the White House and prevailed upon the President not to support the Nye resolution. *Christian Science Monitor*, January 26, 1939.

116. *New York Times*, April 10, 1938. Professor Wright's statement evoked a strong response from Raymond Buell, who declared that "the so-called neutrality policy of the United States as applied to Spain thus injures not only the sense of justice but the interests of the American people." He recalled that prior to January 1937 it had always been the policy of the United States to sell arms to friendly governments engaged in suppressing revolts, and added that the only possible justification of the Spanish embargo was the belief that the Nonintervention Commission could prevent arms from reaching both sides in Spain. This policy of nonintervention had failed, Buell asserted, and the American embargo had proved to be an instrument of intervention against the Loyalist Government. He did not believe that if the Proclamation of May 1, 1937, was revoked, the Embargo Act of January 8, 1937, would remain in effect. Buell stated that there was every indication that Congress intended to supersede the specific embargo of January 8 by the May Neutrality Act. He argued that the fact that President Roosevelt had deemed it necessary to issue a proclamation in May reimposing the embargo would support the claim that the January 8 Act had been superseded. *Ibid.*, April 17, 1938.

117. *Ibid.*, November 25, 1938. In examining the Roosevelt files at Hyde Park, the writer thought it strange that while there were hundreds of communications urging repeal of the Spanish embargo, not one telegram or letter was noted which urged retention of the embargo. This matter was discussed with members of the library staff and despite their special efforts no such messages were found.

118. *Ibid.*, January 17, 1939.

119. *Time*, XXXIII (January 23, 1939), 36. Until his death in September 1954, McCarran remained one of the strongest supporters of General Franco. The Nevada Senator repeatedly urged Spain's admittance into the United Nations and was the driving force behind recent U. S. loans to the Spanish Government. See Pat McCarran, "Why Shouldn't the Spanish Fight for Us?" *Saturday Evening Post*, CCXXIII (April 28, 1951), 25, 136-38.

120. *New York Times*, January 9, 10, 1939.

Chapter Nine

Recognition

By the end of 1938 General Franco had launched a vigorous offensive in Catalonia, a highly industrialized area whose ports and munition plants made it the heart of Loyalist resistance. The German and Italian dictators continued to ignore the nonintervention agreement and gave effective aid to the Spanish Nationalists, insisting at the same time that the Western democracies adhere to the nonintervention accord and remain aloof from the conflict. The Insurgent drive into Catalonia was crowned with success when on January 26, 1939, the Nationalist forces captured the Loyalist capital of Barcelona without fighting a single major engagement.[1] The Government and remaining Loyalist troops in this region took refuge in France; and only the small area around Madrid and Valencia remained in the hands of the Spanish Government.

As Catalonia had been the life source of the Republican Government, its occupation by the Nationalist forces made it apparent to all but a few that the world must prepare for a new order in Spain. In Germany and Italy the news that Barcelona had fallen was greeted with great enthusiasm. The Führer sent a telegram of warm congratulations to El Caudillo;[2] and in Rome, Il Duce told thousands of cheering Fascists about the achievements of "our famous legionnaires" by whose aid Spain was being "completely liberated from the infamies of the Reds."[3] Great Britain and France, however, were not so elated over the impending Fascist victory in Spain. Premier Édouard Daladier told his countrymen that the British and French governments were in complete agreement on the "necessary measures" to be taken in the event Mussolini refused to withdraw his troops from Spain at the end of the civil war.[4] Foreign

Minister Georges Bonnet added strength to this statement by announcing that in event of war, the two great European democracies would join in a program of mutual defense.[5]

The occupation of Barcelona met with varying response in the United States. The editors of the *Christian Science Monitor* remarked that it would seem that the democracies would awake to the moral and practical implications of a Franco victory and end the "farce" of nonintervention. They added that although the democracies had not helped Spain, "the liberty loving men and women of Spain have helped us. By their courage and determination to withstand tyranny, they have inspired free people everywhere."[6] The editors of the *New York Times* stated that "whatever else lies ahead for unhappy Spain and troubled Europe, it is clear from the point of view of American opinion the first acid test of the Burgos government will be provided by its ability to exercise restraint at Barcelona and to prevent . . . measures of retaliation."[7]

The editors of the *Commonweal* conducted a survey of press comment regarding the fall of Barcelona and reported that the American press was apparently unconcerned as to the effects of the war on the Spanish people.[8] In reviewing the editorial comment, the *Commonweal* further stated that the *Christian Century* foresaw Axis influence in Spain as a danger to the democracies; the *New York Sun* asserted that only mopping up operations remained for Franco to become master in Spain; the *New York Herald Tribune* commented that in spite of Franco's fascist victory, guerrilla warfare was likely to continue; the Catholic weekly, *America*, declared that the war was over in Spain, but the Loyalists were trying to prolong the contest against the best interests of the Spanish people; *Echo,* a Catholic paper of Buffalo, expressed the fear that now the war was practically over, Mussolini would not evacuate his troops from Spain; the *Baltimore Sun* observed that it was a victory for the dictators and Italian Fascists; the *New Republic* warned that Germany and Italy were in Spain to stay and would prove to be a great danger to France; the *Chicago Daily News* likewise saw danger to the democracies and felt that Mussolini would make stronger moves in the Mediterranean; and the *Brooklyn Tablet,* a Catholic paper, stated:

A victory for the Nationalists will mean an end to the clamoring and shouting that has disrupted us in the working out of our national problems. It will avert the most dangerous threat of becoming involved in foreign wars to which the United States has been exposed since 1917. It will eliminate the source of confusion, disunion, and misunderstanding that disrupts united Catholic action.[9]

By late February 1939 the Insurgents had gained control of over three-fourths of Spain and the Loyalist Government was in the process of dissolution. President Azaña resigned and Premier Negrín was ousted from office, thus leaving very little which could be called a Spanish Republic. The remaining Loyalist authorities sought assurances from Franco that he would guarantee clemency to political refugees, rid Spain of foreign domination, and permit the people through a plebiscite to choose the next form of Spanish Government.[10] The General refused, however, to accept these terms of surrender and prepared to launch new offensives against the only remaining Loyalist strongholds, at Madrid and Valencia.

One of the most destructive civil wars in history came to an end on March 28, 1939, when Madrid fell to the Nationalists. Hundreds of thousands of men had died during the struggle and the property damage amounted to millions of dollars. Crisis after crisis had brought Europe to the brink of a general war during the almost three years the Spanish conflict was in progress. Outside interference by the Great Powers, particularly Italy and Germany, and to a lesser extent Russia and France, had long delayed the outcome of the war and had tended to consolidate a new alignment in Europe, an alignment of the totalitarian states against the democracies. In Spain General Franco was at the height of his power and dictatorship ruled supreme.

Even before the occupation of Madrid the Nationalists had achieved new successes on the diplomatic front. Within a month after the fall of Barcelona thirty states had recognized the Franco regime and had established relations with it. On February 27, 1939, Great Britain and France recognized the Nationalist organization as the *de jure* Government of Spain, and thus destroyed the last hope of the Loyalists for foreign aid.[11] No doubt the British and French were interested in the commercial advantages to be secured by early recognition and hoped that German and Italian influence would vanish from Spain once normal relations were established. The United States, however, delayed extending recognition to the new Spanish regime until it was apparent that the Loyalist Government had ceased to exist.

President Roosevelt moved with caution and carefully surveyed the Spanish situation. He remarked to one friend that "at this moment things look like a victory for one side. We know that such things do not always work out well. What a pity it could not have been a negotiated peace. In any event I hope that the good people will not suffer, whatever the result may be."[12] Later, the President told a press conference that no steps had been taken to recognize the Insurgent Government and that the United States still maintained relations with the Loyalists.[13] Nevertheless, the United States was confronted with the fact that the Franco regime had gained complete control of Spain, and the State Department was faced with the necessary decision as to whether recognition would be accorded to the Nationalist Government.

Secretary Hull told the press as early as February 27, 1939, that the United States was considering recognition of Franco Spain but the matter would have to be given serious consideration.[14] The State Department had already rejected the suggestions of several Latin-American republics that all the American nations present a united front on the question of recognition. Under Secretary Welles remarked that in considering this proposal the Department adhered to the traditional policy of the United States in exercising independent action in relations with other countries and added that since the twenty-one republics in this hemisphere were not a unit in their attitude toward the Spanish Civil War, it was doubtful if such a program could have succeeded, even with the cooperation of the United States.[15]

While President Roosevelt and the State Department were somewhat hesitant in following the immediate steps of Britain and France in recognizing the Nationalist Government, the supporters of General Franco in the United States Congress launched a strong movement to influence American Spanish policy. Senator Dennis Chavez (D-New Mexico) remarked that he earnestly urged that this country take immediate steps to recognize the Nationalist Government of General Franco. "I do this," he stated, "because of the sincere belief that it will contribute to the immediate peace of the world and tend to restore normal relations between the United States and a great country of Europe and add to our own immediate prosperity."[16] In support of his plea for recognition Chavez discussed the Spanish Civil War at length and presented a staunch defense of the Nationalist Government and its "fight against communism." He stated that it was time the people in the United States gained a true picture of what had happened in Spain since most Americans had been "misled by international propaganda." The Senator declared that if the people in this country were acquainted with the facts of the case, "they would see the striking similarity between the Nationalist movement and their own struggle for freedom." He asserted that Americans in their crusade against fascism had overlooked communism in Spain, and he added that the only possible objection to Franco was that "we do not agree with his form of government but," he continued "I am not willing to concede that the government of Franco will be Fascist by any sense of the term." Chavez concluded his argument by stating that he favored recognition because "it will be only by restoring the normal relations between the nations [the United States and Spain] that we can hope to restore our lost trade. . . . Conditions in our own nation do not warrant our passing up any opportunities for trade."[17]

Senator Reynolds (D-North Carolina), in arguing for immediate recognition of Franco Spain, likewise emphasized the trade advantages the United States would acquire by taking such a step. " Every country of the world is looking to getting business in Spain," he said. "I say that we should do likewise."[18] The Senator reminded his colleagues "that all the nations of the earth interested in sundry products are selling now to the duly constituted Government of Spain, and in view of the fact that we of the South have millions of bales of cotton to sell, I hope we will soon bring about recognition of that Government."[19] Nor did Reynolds overlook the ideological considerations, stating that he did not see how it could "be seriously contended that the communists, anarchists, and syndicalists who were fighting for the loyalist cause were truly interested in democracy as we have hitherto understood the meaning of the word?"[20]

Senator David I. Walsh (D-Massachusetts) tacitly lent his support to the movement for recognition by inserting in the *Congressional Record* a "scholarly analysis" of the Spanish situation written by Dr. Joseph B. Code, Professor of History at Catholic University of America. Professor Code declared that during the civil war in Spain certain officials and a large part of the American press "have done much to alienate the affections of the Spanish people" by the "pursuance of a policy sympathetic toward those who would have destroyed the last vestige of Spanish culture." Code presented seven points in arguing for immediate recognition of the new regime in Spain: (1) The friendship of the Spanish people should be sought. (2) Franco was in control of more than 80 per cent of the people and territory of Spain. (3) Both Britain and France had extended recognition. (4) The United States would lose trade advantages by not extending recognition. (5) Argentina and Brazil had expressed intention of granting *de jure* recognition. (6) Recognition should be granted "to get Spain's assistance in insuring South American cooperation in New World matters." (7) There is no evidence that Spain will not live up to its international obligations.[21]

Perhaps the leading advocate in the House for American recognition of Franco Spain was Representative John W. McCormack (D-Massachusetts). In a letter to the Secretary of State, McCormack stated that "to extend . . . recognition at this time is the acceptance of the *de facto* status of that government and cannot be fairly interpreted by any other nation as an unfriendly act." He added that the "interests of American institutions and representative government require the neglect of no opportunity to exercise in a friendly manner our influence during the period of reconstruction."[22] Later, McCormack told the House that the "communist" Government of "so-called loyalist Spain" no longer existed and he posed the question as to what Government Ambassador de los Ríos represented.[23] The Congressman suggested four reasons why the United States should recognize the Franco Government: (1) Such action would gain the friendship of the people of Nationalist Spain. (2) The Government of Nationalist Spain was not the "vicious and destructive" type as found in Soviet Russia. (3) The Nationalist Government represented a great majority of the Spanish people and it was "not our prerogative to dictate to the people of other nations the form of government they shall possess." (4) It would add to American prestige in Central and South America. Thus, McCormack concluded, "a clear case for recognition exists. . . . It is my opinion and the opinion of millions of Americans, that such action should be taken at once."[24]

There were numerous other individuals and organizations urging the recognition of Franco Spain. Merwin K. Hart, Chairman

of the American Union for Nationalist Spain, wrote President
Roosevelt that "we believe Nationalist Spain . . . will commence
the building of a great state that within ten or fifteen years will
have become one of the great states of Europe."[25] Dr. Joseph F.
Thorning told the Maryland Chapter of the International Federation
of Catholic Alumnae that "the time has come for every convinced
believer in God to bring to the notice of the Honorable Franklin
D. Roosevelt . . . and the Honorable Cordell Hull . . . that patriotism, international law, and love of religious liberty all suggest
early recognition of the defeat of the Soviet Union in Spain."[26]
Dr. Thorning also told an audience at Fordham University that
recognition would be "a step toward world peace and prosperity."
He declared that Franco "believes in liberty of conscience for
Protestant, Catholic, or Jew; [he] . . . guarantees the right of trial
by jury, [he] . . . is thoroughly competent and socially progressive,
liberal and representative of the best elements of the nation."[27]
The New Mexico House of Representatives adopted a resolution
favoring recognition of the Nationalist Government on the grounds
that such action was advocated by Senator Chavez and that General
Franco was supported by the Catholic Church.[28]

The movement to withhold recognition from the Franco Government by no means assumed the proportions of the drive to revoke
the Spanish embargo. There was no concerted effort in Congress
to oppose recognition. Senator Nye, however, commented that "it
is first necessary that Franco establish a civil government; then we
can see what type of government he will present to the world." He
added that recognition should be withheld if Franco organized a
government along totalitarian lines.[29] Even strong pro-Loyalist
papers such as the *Washington Post* and *Christian Science Monitor*
recognized that the Republican Government of Spain had been
defeated. The editors of the *Post* stated that

> the sooner the fact of Nationalist dominance in Spain is ac-
> cepted the quicker that unhappy country will be able to con-
> centrate on the enormous task of reconstruction. . . . The de-
> mocracies cannot save the Spanish Republic by withholding
> recognition from Franco. That would merely insure that his
> government would have to depend on German and Italian
> aid.[30]

A similar viewpoint was expressed by the editors of the *Monitor,* who declared:

> Starting as a representative government the loyalists have gradually lost the right to speak for more than a fraction of the nation and have no stronger moral claim than the original military insurgents. It would be well now to recognize that their democratic ideals, insofar as they transcend personal or partisan interest, will be best worked out in peaceful lines. The tenacity with which the Republic has hung on proves that those ideals have vitality and gives hope that they will revive in Spain, whomever controls the Government.[31]

After the State Department had been officially notified that Britain and France had recognized Franco's Government, Secretary Hull suggested to the President that Ambassador Bowers be ordered home "for consultation" so as to clear the way for establishment of relations with the Nationalists should it be deemed advisable.[32] For more than two and a half years Ambassador Bowers had personally written and sent voluminous reports on every phase of the struggle to the State Department and President Roosevelt. His opinions were as follows:

(1) That after the first days of considerable confusion, it was plainly shown to be a war of the Fascists and the Axis powers against the democratic institutions of Spain.

(2) That the Spanish war was the beginning of a perfectly thought-out plan for the extermination of democracy in Europe, and the beginning of a Second World War with that as the intent.

(3) That the Nonintervention Committee was a shameless sham, cynically dishonest, in that Germany and Italy were constantly sending soldiers, planes, tanks, artillery, and ammunition into Spain without an interference or real protest from the signatories of the pact.

(4) That Germany and Italy were using Spanish towns and people for experimental purposes in trying out their new methods of destruction and their new technique of terrorism.

(5) That the Axis, in preparation for the continental struggle, was using Spain to see how far it could go with the silent

acquiescence of the great democracies and to test their spirit, courage, and will to fight in defense of their ideals.

(6) That the Axis powers believed that with the conversion of Spain into a Fascist state, it could, and would, be used as an entering wedge in South and Central America. . . .

(7) That the purpose was manifest in a book prepared for use in the schools bitterly attacking democracy in general and that of the United States and Britain in particular.

(8) That the attacks, ridicule, and insults aimed at the United States and England by the Franco press left no possible doubt as to its position.

(9) That while the Axis powers poured in armies, planes, tanks, artillery, technicians, and engineers for Franco, the Nonintervention Committee of the European democracies and our own embargo were making a powerful contribution to the triumph of the Axis over democracy in Spain; that whereas the war on China was being waged by the Japs alone, on Czechoslovakia by Nazi Germany alone, on Abyssinia by Fascist Italy alone, the first country to be attacked *by the Axis — Germany and Italy together — was Spain* [*italics his*].

(10) That it was my opinion, long before Munich, that the next attack would be on Czechoslovakia, because of the bitter abuse of her, without apparent reason, by Germans and Italians who crossed the Spanish border for food in Saint-Jean-de-Luz and Biarritz.

(11) I had informed Washington that our interests, ideologically, commercially, and industrially, were bound up with those of democracy in Spain, whose government we recognized as the legal constitutional government, and that the victory of Franco would be a danger to the United States. . .[33]

Upon arriving in the United States Bowers was not surprised to find a powerful public sentiment favorable to the Loyalists, but it was then too late to realize that the American embargo had been an important factor in giving victory to Franco. The Ambassador stated that a cleavage in the higher strata of the State Department prevented a more sympathetic consideration to his point of view. He believed that Assistant Secretary George S. Messersmith and Under Secretary Sumner Welles supported his views but Secretary Hull and James C. Dunn, Chief of the Division of European Affairs, actually determined American policy.[34]

After arriving in Washington, Ambassador Bowers called the President by telephone and proposed that an appointment be made that very night for the purpose of making a report on the situation in Spain. Roosevelt suggested, however, that the Ambassador had best see Secretary Hull first. Bowers stated that his visit with Hull was cordial but the Secretary seemed "disinclined to discuss the Spanish situation, the solution of which had [already] been determined. . ."[35] A few hours later Ambassador Bowers was ushered into the executive office of the President where he found Roosevelt ". . . more serious and graver than I had ever seen him before." Before Bowers could take his seat the President declared, "We have made a mistake; you have been right all along." The President added that he had been deluged with too much contradictory information about what had transpired in Spain. Roosevelt then stated that he could see no reason to be in any hurry about recognition and that he would let the victor "stew in his juice" for awhile.[36]

That evening Bowers visited Senator Key Pittman, Chairman of the Foreign Relations Committee, author of the Spanish embargo, as well as an old personal friend. During the ensuing conversation, Pittman declared that he was "afraid we made a mistake in Spain." He then added that in the beginning he thought the embargo necessary because it would keep the other nations out and localize the war. Bowers agreed, but added that when it became apparent that the Axis powers were sending war matériel to Franco, the embargo might well have been lifted and the Spanish Government given its rights under international law.[37]

Several days later Ambassador Bowers was invited to appear before the House Foreign Affairs Committee to give his impressions of Spain. He spoke for more than an hour relating his frank opinions. Bowers told the Committee that he felt the American embargo had "unquestionably" contributed to the Fascist triumph. At the conclusion, the Ambassador said, "I had the feeling that the committee was sympathetic to my view."[38]

Secretary Hull, however, argued in favor of immediate recognition. He stated that since the Spanish conflict was of a domestic character and did not involve seizure of territory by an aggressor nation, the primary considerations by the State Department were whether Franco actually controlled the civil administration, whether the Spanish people supported the new Government, and whether the Nationalists were willing and able to discharge their international obligations.[39] After having been assured on these matters,[40] and with Roosevelt's approval, Hull cabled the Insurgent Foreign Minister Francisco Jordana that it was the disposition of this Government to establish diplomatic relations with the Nationalist Government of Spain.[41] On the same day President Roosevelt revoked the proclamation issued May 1, 1937, in regard to the state of civil strife which existed in Spain, and declared that the joint resolution of Congress approved January 8, 1937, had ceased to apply.[42] The State Department also rescinded the rules and regulations concerning the embargo as well as the restrictions on contributions and financial assistance.[43]

American recognition of Franco Spain was bitterly attacked by many persons in the United States. Representative John Coffee (D-Washington) declared that he was "astounded" to learn that the United States had recognized Franco since this country "has repeatedly said that it would not recognize governments that were established through the use of force." Coffee maintained that

it was on this theory that we have not recognized Manchuria, Ethiopia and the German conquests of Austria, Checko-Slovakia and Memel. But now we recognize Spain and lift the embargo. Why? In the past when we asked to lift the embargo our voices fell upon deaf ears. Now, no sooner than democracy is driven from Spain than we join the dictators of the world. Why? So that our arms may be helpful in mopping up the discordant elements. I hate to see my government fight democracy at the behest of perfidious Albion or of Franco.[44]

A similar expression was voiced by 473 Protestant clergymen who wrote President Roosevelt that the "crowning mistake on our part has been the official recognition of the Franco regime by the United States." They added that "a decent self-respect, not to speak of a concern for our own welfare, should have prevented us from recognizing a government which announced and is carrying on a program of brutal reprisals against Republican leaders."[45] Also, the editors of the *Socialist Call* angrily asserted that "a government which had assisted French and British imperialism strangle Loyalist Spain could not be expected to follow any other course," and added: "American, French and British democracy murdered the Loyalist regime [and then] joined the Fascists at the final blood feast."[46]

The *New York Times,* however, expressed an opinion that was probably representative of the attitude adopted by most of the secular press. The editors stated that

> American recognition of the Franco regime was sooner or later inevitable. Such recognition does not imply political sympathy or moral approval. It is a simple recognition of a state of fact that Franco is now master of Spain, and that there is not even a rival government to dispute these claims. Those who think our action hasty should recall that we are the last of the major western powers to take the step.[47]

The *New York Post* likewise commented that the recognition of the Nationalists in Spain "should neither shock nor surprise anyone, because recognition does not imply approval of a government."[48]

Thus the Spanish question receded into the background to be overshadowed by the threatening war clouds in Europe. The Spanish Civil War had proved to be but a dress rehearsal for the great conflict that was to follow. By a shortsighted policy the world's great democracies had allowed the Spanish Republic to be destroyed by the dictator Franco and his Fascist allies, Germany and Italy. Many liberals in the United States had protested such a policy but public opinion was largely indifferent, preferring to hide behind a curtain of neutraltiy legislation which actually worked against the best interests of the United States.

Even President Roosevelt's warmest supporters cannot fail to see and admit his errors and deficiencies. The Administration's Spanish policy of 1936-1939 has been called the cardinal blunder of American foreign policy during the Roosevelt era,[49] and from the standpoint of farsighted statesmanship it was a blind and tragic course which not only permitted a dictatorship to be imposed on the Spanish people, but was the nightmarish product of appeasement which led to war. As President Roosevelt spoke so often about defending democracy, his lack of action in regard to Spain is difficult to understand and explain. It may have been, as one writer has stated, that the whole affair was a skeleton in the Roosevelt closet — faintly unpleasant or unimportant in the light of larger events.[50]

Nevertheless, such a policy made inevitable the humiliating appeasement of Franco during the Second World War.[51] It created in Spain a den of fascism which has continued to plague the body politic of Europe long after the Axis dictators were removed from the scene. Even the tardy withdrawal of the American Ambassador from Madrid in 1946 did little to repair a policy inaugurated a decade earlier.[52] The fact remains, however, that few people in the democratic countries wished to risk the possibility of war to save the Spanish Republic. Contrary to their national interests, the democracies consented to a policy of nonintervention that enabled the Axis powers to intervene in favor of the insurrection and establish a friendly dictatorship in Spain. Viewed in retrospect, the Spanish episode represented one phase in the attempt of the Fascist powers to obtain a strategic victory and political influence in Europe. Great Britain, France, and the United States were not prepared militarily or psychologically to abandon their efforts toward maintaining peace or to contest the interests of the Fascist powers. Although Americans might draw some consolation from the fact that the war in Spain had come to an end without spreading beyond Spanish frontiers, the possibility of a Fascist Spain was viewed with apprehension, and the prospects of world peace had been rendered more uncertain.

NOTES

1. Barcelona had become the Loyalist capital after the Spanish Republican Government had withdrawn first from Madrid, and later from Valencia.

2. *Times* (London), January 28, 1939.

3. *New York Times*, January 27, 1939.

4. *Ibid.*

5. *Ibid.*

6. *Christian Science Monitor*, January 27, 1939.

7. *New York Times*, January 26, 1939.

8. *Commonweal*, XXIX (February 10, 1939), 439-40.

9. *Ibid.*

10. Whitney H. Shepardson (Council on Foreign Relations), *The United States in World Affairs, 1939* (New York, 1940), pp. 14-16.

11. *New York Times*, February 28, 1939. David Low drew a very amusing cartoon which pictured Chamberlain observing Franco, Hitler, and Mussolini dressed in Spanish costumes performing a Spanish dance. The caption stated: "Honest, mister, there is nobody here but us Spaniards." David Low, *A Cartoon History of Our Times* (New York, 1939), p. 81.

12. Roosevelt to Admiral Mark Kerr, January 24, 1939 (FDR Official Files, No. 1504).

13. *New York Times*, March 8, 1939.

14. *Ibid.*, February 28, 1939.

15. *Press Releases*, February 17, 1939.

16. *Congressional Record*, 76 Cong., 1 Sess., LXXXIV (March 1, 1939), 2051.

17. *Ibid.*, 2056-64.

18. *Ibid.* (March 14, 1939), 2720.

19. *Ibid.* (March 27, 1939), 3353-54.

20. *Ibid.* (March 14, 1939), 2720.

21. *Ibid.* (March 13, 1939), A961.

22. *New York Times*, January 29, 1939.

23. Representative Charles Anderson (D-Missouri) retorted that "he [de los Ríos] has about the same status as the Ambassador from Ethiopia." *Congressional Record*, 76 Cong, 1 Sess., LXXXIV (March 10, 1939), 2569-70.

24. *Ibid.* Irked at press reports of 75,000 telegrams sent to President Roosevelt in protest against the possible recognition of General Franco, McCormack told the House that this was an organized propaganda drive which indicates "how far some people and organizations will go to manufacture a false public opinion." The Congressman stated that the Washington drive was under the leadership of the Washington Friends of Spanish Democracy. He asserted that his office had obtained a copy of the telegram in advance together with a memorandum of the Washington Friends of Spanish Democracy which stated: "This is a sample of the 2,500 telegrams we are sending President Roosevelt as Washington's quota of the national 100,000 wire campaign. The telegrams cost only 10 cents each. They must reach the President by Sunday night, March 19. This is a rush order, but imperative. Can you make yourself responsible for at least 10 signatures and 10 dimes and get the signatures into this office immediately? The telegrams will be sent from here." McCormack denounced these tactics and reaffirmed his demand for immediate recognition of the Nationalists in Spain. *Ibid.* (March 20, 1939), 2977.

25. *New York Times*, January 28, 1939.

26. *Ibid.*, March 20, 1939.

27. Extended remarks of Senator David I. Walsh, *Congressional Record*, 76 Cong., 1 Sess., LXXXIV (March 13, 1939), A962.

28. *New York Times*, March 5, 1939.

29. *Ibid.*, March 8, 1939.

30. *Washington Post*, February 28, 1939.

31. *Christian Science Monitor*, March 9, 1939.

32. Obviously, because of his strong pro-Loyalist bias and support of the Republican Government, Ambassador Bowers would not have been acceptable to General Franco.

33. Claude G. Bowers, *My Mission to Spain* (New York, 1954), pp. 411-12.

34. *Ibid.*, p. 414.

35. *Ibid.*, p. 418. Actually Bowers and Hull were close friends and their differences on Spanish policy were political and not personal.

36. *Ibid.*, pp. 418-19. In a letter to the author (February 15, 1954) Bowers reiterated these same statements.

37. *Ibid.*, p. 419.

38. *Ibid.*, pp. 419-20.

39. Hull, *Memoirs*, I, 616-18.

40. These assurances were received by Ambassador Bullitt, who, on orders from the State Department, negotiated informally with the Franco representatives in Paris. *Ibid.*

41. *Press Releases*, April 1, 1939.

42. The text of the proclamation on Spain issued April 1, 1939, declares in part: "Now, therefore, I, Franklin D. Roosevelt, President of the United States of America, under and by virtue of the authority conferred on me by the aforesaid joint resolutions, do hereby proclaim that in my judgment the state of civil strife in Spain described in said joint resolution of January 8, 1937, and the conditions which caused me to issue the said proclamation of May 1, 1937, have ceased to exist and I do hereby revoke said proclamation of May 1, 1937. Accordingly, the provisions of the said joint resolution of January 8, 1937, and of the said proclamation of May 1, 1937, no longer apply." *Press Releases*, April 1, 1939.

43. *Ibid.* Ambassador Bowers returned to Madrid to supervise the packing of his belongings. Upon returning to the United States he was appointed Ambassador to Chile; a post he retained until his retirement in 1953.

44. *New York Times*, April 2, 1939.

45. *Ibid.*, April 28, 1939. The names of the clergymen, including nine bishops, represented eleven religious denominations from thirty-six states.

46. *Socialist Call*, April 8, 1939.

47. *New York Times*, April 3, 1939.

48. *New York Post*, March 16, 1939. The United States has never wholly approved of the Franco Government. President Roosevelt wrote Norman Armour, the American Ambassador at Madrid, in March 1945 that "having been helped to power by Fascist Italy and Nazi Germany, and patterned itself along totalitarian lines, the present regime in Spain is naturally the subject of distrust by a great many American citizens, who find it difficult to see the justification for this country to continue to maintain relations with such a regime." The President added that the "fact that our Government maintains formal diplomatic relations with the present Spanish regime should not be interpreted by anyone to imply approval of that regime and its sole party the Falange, which has been openly hostile to the United States and which has tried to spread its Fascist party ideas in the Western Hemisphere." *New York Times*, September 27, 1945. Similarly, President Harry S. Truman stated at his weekly press conference on February 7, 1952, that "he was far from enthusiastic about bringing Spain into the North Atlantic Treaty." Truman quite frankly declared that he was "not fond" of the present Government of Spain. *Ibid.*, February 8, 1952.

Within the past two years, however, the United States has embarked upon a new Spanish policy when Washington decided that Spain was necessary to American defense; that her position between the Atlantic and Mediterranean and between Europe and Africa was strategically desirable. With both the United States Air Force and Navy clamoring for bases on the Iberian peninsula long, difficult negotiations ended on September 26, 1953, with the signing of three agreements:

(1) The Spanish gave the United States the right to prepare bases for mutual defense and for joint usage. The bases remain Spanish and the Spanish flag flies over them.

(2) In exchange the United States agreed to modernize to a certain extent Spain's armed forces.

(3) It was also agreed to provide Spain's economy with a limited amount of assistance in the form of loans.

49. Welles, *Time for Decision*, pp. 57-61. Welles, with keen hindsight, argued that if the United States, in accordance with its traditional foreign policy, had permitted the legally recognized Government of Spain to purchase military supplies, possibly the Soviet Union would have rendered more aid, and Great Britain and France would have reconsidered their nonintervention policy. Thus Germany and Italy would not have defied such a large part of the world in giving Franco assistance. The former Under Secretary was of the opinion that had the Spanish Republican Government survived, Italy would have been less likely to attack France and events in Europe might have taken a different course.

50. Parry, "The Spanish Civil War," p. 376.

51. For an excellent account of American-Spanish relations during the Second World War, see Herbert Feis, *The Spanish Story: Franco and the Nations at War* (New York, 1948). For an apology for the Franco regime by the former American Ambassador to Spain and a prominent historian, see Carlton J. H. Hayes, *Wartime Mission In Spain, 1942-1945* (New York, 1945); and *The United States and Spain* (New York, 1951).

52. In 1946 the United Nations General Assembly adopted a resolution, which recommended that all member states withdraw their ambassadors and ministers from Madrid. *United Nations Bulletin* (Lake Success, N. Y.), I (December 24, 1946), 21-24. The American Ambassador was recalled in December 1946, and it was not until January 1951 that a successor was named.

Appendix A

Letters Published in the *New York Times*

PREFACE

Although the State Department consistently refused to alter American policy toward Spain, supporters of the Loyalists continued to urge the lifting of the embargo on the shipment of arms to the Spanish Government. During late January and early February 1939 a very interesting and informative series of communications was published in the *New York Times* expressing opinion both for repeal and retention of the Spanish embargo. The letters were written by former Secretary of State Henry L. Stimson, who advocated immediate lifting of the embargo; by Martin Conboy, a prominent Catholic layman and New York attorney, who replied to Stimson and opposed any embargo change; by Charles C. Burlingham, former president of the New York City Bar Association, and Philip C. Jessup, Professor of International Law at Columbia University, who challenged Conboy and elaborated on the Stimson point of view; and by Conboy, in a final rebuttal to Burlingham and Jessup. These letters were also read into the *Congressional Record* by Senator Gerald P. Nye (*Congressional Record*, 76 Cong., 1 Sess., LXXXIV [February 13, 1939], A507-12.)

DOCUMENT NO. 1

(From the *New York Times* of January 24, 1939)

TEXT OF STIMSON'S LETTER ON THE EMBARGO

To the Editor of the *New York Times*:

I have been asked for my views concerning the present situation in Spain and the duties of our own Government and people toward that situation. The basic reasons which govern my views

213

consist of simple and long-standing principles of American international conduct. They do not in the least depend upon ideological considerations which may or may not be involved in the conflict. On the contrary, they depend solely on the interest of our own country toward that conflict and its possible results.

First.   The republican government of Spain (commonly termed the Loyalist Government) has been recognized as the true Government of Spain by our Government. The same decision has been reached by Great Britain, France, and a number of other countries. The principles upon which our Government acts in making such a decision have been well understood since the beginning of our history. They do not depend in any degree upon the internal structure of the government recognized or the domestic theories which control its relations to its citizens, whether they be Communist, Fascist, monarchial, or democratic.

Such ideological internal relations are exclusively a domestic matter for Spain itself, into which foreign governments should not intrude. That is a fundamental rule of international relations. Thomas Jefferson expressed it well as long ago as 1792:

"We certainly cannot deny to other nations that principle whereon our own Government is founded, that every nation has a right to govern itself internally under whatever forms it pleases and to change these forms at its own will; and externally to transact business with other nations through whatever organ it chooses, whether that be a king, convention, assembly, committee, president, or whatever it may be." (Jefferson to Pinckney, *Works*, vol. III, p. 500.)

When our Government several years ago through our President determined that the Spanish Government in question had control of the administrative machinery of the state with the general acquiescence of its people and was able and willing to discharge international and conventional obligations, that Spanish Government became to us and all our citizens the true Government of Spain for the purpose of our respective international relations. By this decision we admitted it as a member of the family of nations which we recognized as our friendly neighbors in the world and vested it with all of the conventional rights and privileges which we accord to such friendly neighbors.

Second.   One of the most important of these rights which a state like Spain is entitled to expect from another government, which has recognized it as a friendly neighbor in the family of nations, is the right of self-defense against any future rebellions which may challenge its authority. History shows that almost every state, including our own, sooner or later in its history has to meet with the hazard of domestic strife within its borders, including an armed rebellion against its authority. In such a case the duty which the neighbor states owe to the member of the family whose authority has been challenged is perfectly well settled. It is that such a nation has the exclusive right to the friendly assistance of its neighbors by being permitted to purchase in their markets the necessary supplies and munitions for the purpose of putting down the rebellion: and, further, that no similar assistance shall be given to the rebels who have challenged its authority. Any such assistance to the rebels would be deemed a most unfriendly act — even a cause of war — against the mother state.

Third. No nation has gone further than the United States in sustaining this general right of a nation against which civil strife or rebellion has broken out. During our own great Civil War our Federal Government insisted that it alone has the right to purchase war materials in the world at large and made vitally needed purchases of war materials abroad.

"Had England undertaken to embargo arms to both the North and the South, the North might have lost the war." (Borchard, *Neutrality for the United States*, p. 337.)

In the case of rebellions among its neighbor states the United States has acted upon the same principle and has not only given assistance to their governments but has refrained itself from giving and has prevented its nationals from giving aid to the rebels. By the joint resolution of 1912, applying to this hemisphere and somewhat more widely extended in 1922, our President has been authorized to levy embargoes against supplying arms or munitions to rebels against the authority of friendly states. To mention only a few cases, such embargoes have been levied by our Government in the case of rebellions against Cuba in 1912, Mexico in 1912, 1923, and 1929, Nicaragua in 1921, and Brazil in 1930. In these and other cases we have recognized it as our duty to assist the government and to prevent assistance from our markets reaching rebels against that government.

Furthermore, in 1928 we executed and in 1930 ratified a general convention promulgated by the Sixth Pan American Conference between the American republics and covering generally this subject of the mutual rights and duties of states in the event of civil strife. This convention provided: "Article 1. The contracting states bind themselves to observe the following rules with regard to civil strife in another one of them.

* * *

"3. To forbid the traffic in arms and war material, except when intended for the government, while the belligerency of the rebels has not been recognized, in which latter case the rules of neutrality shall be applied."

This treaty made the previously existing traditional practice a binding rule of conduct among its signatories.

Fourth. During the Great War Secretary of State Lansing took occasion to point out why the United States was so insistent on maintaining this right of a government to buy arms and munitions in the markets of the world, whether in cases of domestic strife or of general war. As he pointed out, it was because our Nation, being a peaceful and generally unarmed nation, would have found any other rule of law most dangerous to its own safety.

"Secretary Lansing declared that the United States had from the foundation of the Republic . . . advocated and practiced unrestricted trade in arms and military supplies, because it had never been the policy of the Nation to maintain in time of peace a large military establishment or stores of arms and ammunition sufficient to repel invasion by a well-equipped and powerful enemy, and that in consequence the United States would, in the event of attack by a foreign power, be . . . seriously, if not fatally, embarrassed by the lack of arms and ammunition. . . . 'The United States has always' Lansing said, 'depended upon the right and power to purchase arms from neutral nations in case of foreign attack. This right which it claims for itself, it cannot deny to others.' He contended that a nation whose policy and principle it was to rely upon international obligations and international justice to preserve its political and territorial integrity might become the prey of an aggressive nation whose policy and practice it was to increase its military strength during times of peace with the design of conquest, unless the nation attacked could . . . go into the markets of the world and purchase the means to defend itself against the aggressor." (Hyde, *International Law Chiefly as Interpreted and Applied by the United States,* vol. 2, at p. 752.)

Fifth. Thus under the rules of international law governing cases of insurrection against a government whose status has been recognized by its neighbors, the government itself is the only party which will be permitted to purchase arms and ammunition abroad, and any assistance to the rebels would be a violation of such international law, an unfriendly act against their government. Until the insurrection has progressed so far and successfully that a state of belligerency is recognized by the outside nations, no rules of neutrality apply. The only party recognized as lawful is the mother government at which the insurrection is aimed. In the case of Spain no such belligerency has been recognized by us or by Great Britain or by France. Under such circumstances any attempt to treat the situation as embodying the duty of neutrality is based upon a complete misconception of the rules of international law. Prof. Edwin Borchard, in his study on *Neutrality and Civil Wars, Thirty-first American Journal of Law,* at pages 304 and 305, has thus expressed the situation:

"International law requires the United States to treat the elected government of Spain as the lawful government of Spain, and, until the belligerency of the rebels is recognized, as the only government entitled to receive the assistance of the United States in suppressing armed opposition. . . . This embargo against Spain was thought to be neutrality legislation, but it seems more likely the precise opposite."

Sixth. The foregoing was the well-established practice of the world governing rebellions which occurred in the family of nations, when on July 19, 1936, the present revolt in Spain broke out against the republican government which we had recognized. Instead of following the rules of law which has theretofore been established with practical unanimity, a series of novel experiments were attempted on both sides of the Atlantic. These have resulted in a complete reversal of the pre-existing law and practice.

In Europe the conflict in Spain excited apprehension for fear that other nations might either be dragged in or voluntarily come in to fish in troubled waters. The totalitarian states, both Fascist and Communist, were apprehended to be aggressive and likely to intervene. In fact, rumor attributed to them a share in the instigation of the Franco revolt. Accordingly, in September 1936, under the leadership of Great Britain, a special agreement of nonintervention was engineered among the neighboring nations to Spain in the hope that the conflict might be localized and the danger of its spread prevented. The first thing to be said about this agreement was that it was a complete abandonment of a code of practice which the international world had adopted through preceding ages as the best hope of achieving the same purpose and minimizing the spread of disorder. International law is the product of the efforts and experience of the nations aimed to promote peace and stability.

In the second place, however well intentioned it may have been, an experiment based upon the promises of the totalitarian states was more wishful than sensible. Those states had already progressed too far along the primrose path of treaty violation and the nonintervention agreement at once became a mockery and a failure. The only nations which have observed the nonintervention agreement have been the ones from whom the danger of nonintervention was not apprehended — Great Britain and France. Italy and Germany, while ostensibly accepting the obligations of the covenant, have continuously and flagrantly violated it. At the present moment Italy is openly avowing its effective participation on the side of Franco. She is openly pushing every effort to bring the strife to a conclusion in favor of the rebels.

Thus the nonintervention agreement has simply resulted in closing to the recognized government of Spain those world markets for supplies and munitions which under the law of nations she had a right to depend upon and to have open to her purchases. It has not prevented supplies from going to the rebels who, under international law, have no right to them. Not only have the rebels been receiving arms and munitions but, as everybody now knows, they have actually received organized Italian troops in large quantities conducting for them a very large share of the fighting.

Seventh. On our side of the Atlantic there has been even less excuse for a departure from law, for we have been far remote and our interests were very unlikely to be seriously affected by the war in Spain. If we had continued our former practice and permitted the Government of Spain to make purchases in this country of arms and munitions, as we had done in the many cases which I have cited, there was no real danger that those purchases would have aroused any resentment against us from which we need have any apprehension. As a matter of fact, our Government has continued under our silver purchase law to make large purchases of Spanish silver from the Spanish Government which undoubtedly have assisted that Government in its conduct of the war. Such purchases have not even attracted attention in the press, let alone aroused hostile acrimony against us.

In any event, we should have been following the law and could have given critics a perfectly good reason for our action. To assert that such a course of self-respecting adherence on our part to a historic policy of international law could have dragged us into war in Europe does not speak well for the balanced judgment of those who make the assertion.

But our Congress, not altogether unnaturally, may have been influenced by a desire to support the objectives of the nonintervention agreement which had just been entered into in Europe, and at that time Congress may not have foreseen that this agreement would not be faithfully observed. Congress may not have foreseen that instead of becoming a means of equal treatment toward both sides of the combatants in Spain, it would become an engine of glaring favoritism toward one side alone — the Rebels — and that the legitimate Spanish Government which by law was the only side entitled to buy arms would eventually become the only side which was unable to buy arms. At all events our Congress in January 1937 passed a temporary resolution applying an embargo to the sale of arms to both the combatants in Spain. And on May 1, 1937, this temporary resolution was superseded by Public Resolution No. 27. By the language of that resolution the exportation of munitions to any foreign State was prohibited on a proclamation by the President that "a state of civil strife exists . . . and that such civil strife is of a magnitude or is being conducted under such conditions that the export of arms . . . would . . . endanger the peace of the United States." On the same day, May 1, 1937, the President imposed the present embargo against Spain.

Eighth. The results have shown how futile as well as dangerous novel experiments in international law can be. The United States on its part has abandoned a traditional policy to which for a century and a half it had carefully adhered as a means of protecting the peace and stability of nations, which like itself, preferred to live not armed to the teeth. It is likely sorely to rue the day when that principle was abandoned and when it consented to a new precedent which may hereafter weight the scale in favor of a militaristic and thoroughly armed nation.

On the other hand; the progress of events during the past 2 years in Spain has served to demonstrate the vitality of the Loyalist Government and thus has tended to confirm the correctness of our Government's decision when we recognized that Loyalist Government as representative of the people of Spain.

To an extent which probably few anticipated, that Loyalist Government has succeeded in defending itself not only against a surprise attack by its own rebellious army, but against a powerful combination of aggressive interveners by land and sea and air. By so doing it has furnished strong evidence of its vitality and of the fact that it must be supported by the great mass of the people within its territory. Starting without an army of its own, forced to organize and train its raw militia, conspicuously lacking in the powerful modern guns, planes, and other munitions which have been available to its opponents, it has for many months been putting up a most surprising and gallant defense against opponents who have had every advantage in the way of land and naval organization and who are illegally aided both on land and on sea by powerful organized forces from Italy and Germany.

If this Loyalist Government is overthrown, it is evident now that its defeat will be solely due to the fact that it has been deprived of its right to buy from us and other friendly nations the munitions necessary for its defense. I cannot believe that our Government or our country would wish to assume such a responsibility.

Ninth. In short, I have come to the conclusion that the embargo imposed under the resolution of May 1, 1937, should be at once lifted by the President. By its terms I believe he has the power to take such action. The change in the international situation during the past 2 years would justify such action by him. The embargo, which by the terms of the law authorizing it was intended as a protection against conditions which would endanger the peace of the United States, is now shown by the events of the past 2 years to be itself a source of danger to that peace. Any danger that may come to the people of the United States from the situation in Spain would arise not from any lawful sale of munitions in our markets to the Government of Spain but from the assistance which our embargo has given to the enemies of Spain. It is the success of the lawless precedents created by those enemies which would constitute our real danger. There is no reason why we should ourselves facilitate and accentuate that danger. There is still less reason why we should violate our own historic policy to do so. The prestige and safety of our country will not be promoted by abandoning its self-respecting traditions, in order to avoid the hostility of reckless violators of international law in Europe.

Henry L. Stimson

New York, January 23, 1939.

DOCUMENT NO. 2

(From the *New York Times* of January 26, 1939)

MARTIN CONBOY'S LETTER IN REPLY TO STIMSON, OPPOSING EMBARGO
CHANGE

To the Editor of the *New York Times*:

In his letter to the *New York Times* published in your issue of today Mr. Henry L. Stimson presents his views "concerning the present situation in Spain and the duties of our own Government and people toward that situation." He adds that "the basic reasons which govern my views consist of simple and long-standing principles of American international conduct," and he advocates the lifting of the embargo on arms to Spain by Presidential proclamation. My own view of the matter differs in that I consider the American reason for keeping the Spanish embargo is that it conforms to our national neutrality policy, and further, that, irrespective of whether it should or should not be maintained, the embargo can only be removed by the repeal by Congress of a joint resolution of Congress adopted on January 8, 1937.

The neutrality policy of this country was established when the United States were formed as a separate nation. The policy was declared by the first President of the United States. It was enacted in one of the first laws adopted by the Congress of the United States. The policy has never been narrowed. Whenever there have been any modifications of it they have all been by way of enlargement to make it more effective.

The policy has been extended to include the prohibition of the sale of arms and munitions of war. Coming to recent instances, the neutrality law, passed August 31, 1935, made the export of arms, ammunition, and implements of war from the United States to any belligerent state unlawful whenever the President found that there existed a state of war between two foreign states. Within a month after this enactment the Italian attack on Ethiopia began. On October 5, 1935, President Roosevelt issued two proclamations, one forbidding shipment of munitions to the belligerents, the other giving notice that American citizens could travel on belligerent ships only at their own risk.

When civil war broke out in Spain, July 1936, the President had no authority to lay an embargo on the exportation of munitions and implements of war to Spain for the use of either side, because the then existing neutrality legislation did not apply to a condition of civil war.

Nevertheless, the established policy of the United States was opposed to such traffic and, accordingly, on August 7, 1936, the Assistant Secretary of State informed all American consular representatives in Spain that "in conformity with its well-established policy of noninterference with internal affairs in other countries, either in time of peace or in the event of civil strife, this Government will, of course, scrupulously refrain from any interference whatsoever in the unfortunate Spanish situation." No licenses were issued by the Federal Munitions Control Board and none, in fact, was sought, until December 1936. Then an American company applied for a license to export airplanes and engines to the Loyalist Government of Spain. The Board, which had refused licenses for the exportation of arms and munitions to Italy and Ethiopia during the war between those countries, was without authority in law to refuse licenses to ship such articles to Spain.

The editor of the *British Year Book of International Law,* 1937, commenting upon this situation, says:

"With evident regret, therefore, the board felt obliged to issue the licenses in the present case, and it did so. The President publicly expressed his disapproval of the action of the Cuse Co. in refusing to comply with the Government's nonintervention policy, although he admitted that the company was within its legal rights in shipping the airplanes and engines to the Spanish Government. At the same time he caused the various governments of Europe most directly concerned to be informed of his sincere regrets and of the intention of the Government of the United States to continue to pursue a policy of strict neutrality in the present civil war."

The President publicly characterized as "unpatriotic" such shipments as had been made and deprecated "the unfortunate noncompliance by an American citizen with this Government's strict nonintervention policy."

Thereupon, on January 8, 1937, Congress passed a joint resolution. This is a special act to stop the exportation of arms and munitions to Spain. It is founded on the well-established policy of the United States which had been violated by the shipments made before there was any statute prohibiting them. It reads —

"That during the existence of the state of civil strife now obtaining in Spain it shall from and after the approval of this resolution, be unlawful to export arms, ammunition, or implements of war from any place in the United States to Spain or to any other foreign country for transshipment to Spain or for use of either of the opposing forces in Spain."

The embargo specifically laid by this resolution can be lifted only upon proclamation by the President that the state of war has ceased to exist.

The next step in the expression by Congress of our well-established principle of neutrality was the writing into our neutrality statute by joint resolution adopted May 1, 1937, of a general provision relating to civil strife in any foreign country. The President was thereby authorized to establish an embargo by proclamation upon a finding by him that a state of civil strife existed in such country and "that such civil strife is of a magnitude or is being conducted under such conditions that the export of arms, ammunition, or implements of war from the United States to such foreign state would threaten or endanger the peace of the United States."

Upon the same day the President acting under the authority of that joint resolution issued a proclamation with relation to Spain admonishing all citizens and residents of the United States to abstain from the exportation of arms, ammunition, or implements of war from any place in the United States to Spain or to any other State for transportation to or for the use of Spain under the penalties provided for in this statute. This proclamation had no effect upon the embargo existing under the joint resolution of January 8, 1937, except to permit the President to invoke certain administrative powers given him by the later resolution which had not been contained in the earlier one.

Mr. Stimson, in his letter to the *Times*, refers to the joint resolution of January 8 as a "temporary resolution," which he says "was superseded" by that of May 1. Upon that assumption he continues by saying that "the embargo imposed under the resolution of May 1, 1937, should be at once lifted by the President. By its terms I believe he has the power to take such action." But Mr. Stimson ignores the fact that the President has not the power to lift the embargo which was imposed by Congress in its joint resolution of January 8, 1937, until the state of civil strife has ceased in Spain.

Secretary of State Hull, undoubtedly with the advice of the eminent legal staff in his office, and probably also under the advice of the Department of Justice, wrote, on March 21, 1938, to the president of the Foreign Policy Association, New York, the following:

"It is manifest that the state of civil strife in Spain described in the joint resolution of Congress of January 8, 1937, has not ceased to exist. Accordingly, even if the proclamation of the President of May 1, 1937, were to be revoked (lifting the embargo under the general resolution of that date) the prohibition upon the export of arms, ammunition, and implements of war to Spain laid down in the joint resolution of Congress approved January 8, 1937, would still remain in effect."

This conclusion necessarily follows from the well-settled rule of statutory construction that when there are two statutes upon the same subject, the earlier being special and the later general, the special statute remains in force in the absence of an express repeal or absolute incompatibility.

Mr. Stimson stresses what he claims to be the duty of this country toward "the recognized Government of Spain." In his argument based thereon he ignores the purpose of our neutrality policy, which is to keep us out of European disputes. It does not make the slightest difference whether the situation is a state of war between two nations or a state of civil war, where aiding by supplying arms to either or both parties to the war will be productive of danger to our peace.

There is a condition of civil war in Spain. After 2 years of fighting the insurgents are in control of 35 of the 50 provinces in Spain, and more than half of the population of the country is within the territory they control. Sympathy with one side or the other has no more to do with the invocation and applicability of our policy than would sympathy as between two warring nations. When two nations are involved in war it makes no difference, so far as our policy is concerned, whether we sympathize with one or the other. Our neutrality policy is to assist neither.

This is not the first time the United States has been urged to adapt its neutrality policy to the preference of some of our citizens for one or other of foreign combatants. Washington had to face exactly that difficulty. France had been on our side in the Revolution. France, at war with England afterward, presumed upon that friendship by acts inconsistent with our neutrality. And Washington refused to have our policy of neutrality so invaded.

So, likewise, when a condition of civil strife exists, our established policy of neutrality is equally applicable. The converse of neutrality is assistance to one or another of the belligerent parties. In short, the change demanded by those who favor the lifting of the present embargo under the circumstances would mean an affirmative act of aid and assistance in favor of one of the belligerent parties as against the other.

In the present instance insistence upon maintenance of the integrity of our well-established policy of neutrality and upon the lack of power of the President to lift the embargo imposed by Congress in its resolution of January 8, 1937, need not preclude us from inquiring whether, if the matter were one of mere temporary expediency, the President was well advised in affirming that the export of arms and munitions does tend to threaten or endanger the peace of the United States.

Within limits there can be no complaint against those who hold that the cause of one of the parties to the civil strife in Spain is better than the cause of the other party. Those who are endowed with sight and hearing are aware that the minds of men and women are occupied with the relative merits of the various political cults now popular in Europe.

Where might this lead us? Congress knew by experience how easy it is for the acts of citizens to get us into a situation in which the peace of the United States would be endangered. How to avoid being led into a situation of that kind was a more difficult problem.

We had been in very much the same position 20 years before when the World War started in 1914. We knew the United States had no part in the maneuvers that precipitated the declaration of war. And we know, also, that partly through what we did ourselves, and might have refrained from doing, we were drawn irresistibly into the war before it ended.

Just how and why the United States did get into the Great War has been the subject of innumerable volumes. But there were some facts concerning which Congress could not be in doubt.

We did take contracts for arms and munitions, and whether by our own choice or because the control of the seas left us no choice we did supply, without limit or restraint, arms, munitions, contraband of war, to one set of contestants. We did take pay for all this in securities of one set of belligerents. And we thereby exposed ourselves to the enmity of the other side. We had made ourselves in their eyes their potential enemies, and were exposed by our own acts to retaliation by them if the end of the war left them in position to retaliate.

When we had been drawn into the war by the inexorable logic of events and had come out of it as participants in victory, we found we were left with billions of debt. We paid, or we are still paying, a large portion of the cost of the war. What we lost in lives and in the wrecked lives of our wounded, and in the care of these latter, likewise go into the account.

We achieved nothing for ourselves, nor did we succeed in bringing peace to Europe as was evident in 1935 and is still more evident now.

Congress surely was justified in insisting that we must try to avoid like consequences of avoidable errors. They thought it well, while we could still do so without being under the influence of the passions that such a war in Europe must engender among us, even if we were not participants, to take thought about those actions of our own that could be identified as having in any considerable measure been contributory factors to our entry into that war. The legislation that resulted in 1935, amplified in 1937, undoubtedly represented the sober judgment of the American people.

We made these enactments in development of our well-established policy to safeguard the peace of the United States. We made them because we concluded, by our costly experience, that our established policy has to be extended.

We abandoned the profitable business of selling arms and munitions. We abandoned the more deceptive expectation of profits from lending money on Government securities. We put behind us the indignation aroused by loss of lives that came from traveling on ships of belligerent nations. We cut clear of all the disputes that came when a neutral nation tried to maintain its place on the sea against the action of belligerents. And we decided that the favor and profit to be drawn from belligerents benefiting by our arms, munitions, and credits was too dearly bought at the price of the threat and danger to the peace of the United States involved in such transactions.

It is true that in the neutrality legislation of 1935 and 1937 the major preoccupation of Congress was directed to the possibility of a world war. But as long ago as 1912, having in mind the supreme desirability of peace in this hemisphere, Congress provided for embargoes upon the exportation of arms or ammunition "whenever the President shall find that in any American country conditions of domestic violence exist which are promoted by the use of arms or munitions of war procured from the United States."

By an amendment of 1922 the resolution was extended to include, in addition, "any country in which the United States exercises extra-territorial jurisdiction," and the President's authority was broadened by authorizing him to include cases where conditions of domestic violence "are or may be" promoted by the use of munitions procured from the United States.

Under this law proclamations have been issued prohibiting shipments of arms to Mexico, to China, to Honduras, to Cuba, to Nicaragua, and to Brazil.

On May 28, 1934, the sale of arms and munitions of war to Paraguay and Bolivia, then engaged in armed conflict in the Chaco, was prohibited.

When these laws were adopted the United States was not the only possible purveyor of arms and munitions. But the United States did not make its policy contingent upon adoption of the same policy by others.

Need we be surprised, therefore, that when the Spanish civil war developed Congress expressed no concern for the fact that arms and munitions could be purchased elsewhere by one or both of the parties to the civil strife. The peace of the United States was held to be of greater importance than the competition in manufacture and sale of arms.

We are to suppose that Congress had in mind something other than a theoretical gesture, and that the President when he said he found a condition that would threaten and endanger the peace of the United States if we sent arms to Spain meant just what he said.

There is no need for doubt on that point.

There were present all the elements necessary to "threaten and endanger the peace of the United States" sooner or later, and to threaten and endanger it not in relation to Spain alone but to the much more potent forces that have transformed all Europe into armed camps.

So far as the United States could go to avoid being drawn into danger by acts of its own, Congress and the President were bound to go, and the people of the United States resolutely desired them to go.

If we were to seek evidence that the precautions then taken were well advised, we have only to recall the bare outlines of what has happened since. A Norwegian ship had been sunk in December 1936; a French ship bombed in January 1937; three British ships in February, and two French ships in March. The bombing of French and British ships in the harbors of Barcelona and Valencia has been a frequent feature of the news during the past 2 years.

We in the United States can be well content to have no immediate interest in such news. Nor can we limit this consideration to the civil strife in Spain as a separate entity. We must recall that week in September last when peace and war hung in the balance and when the frontier between France and Spain was plainly marked as one of the battlegrounds included in the plans of the two great rival forces that from hour to hour seemed likely to be engaged in a conflict by which European civilization would have been destroyed.

The threat of general war has not yet passed. And yet, with that danger facing us, with the prospect that the utmost exertion may be required to maintain the security of the United States in the midst of a toppling civilization, there are those who seriously and with unaccountable insistance demand that our well-established policy shall now be reversed.

It is demanded that legislation designed to keep this nation at peace shall be replaced by legislation that would lead to our again being trapped into war.

In my humble judgment, the people of the United States will have none of it.

Conditions that "would threaten and endanger the peace of the United States" are not to be lightly passed over, even if the desire of those who seek the change is to improve the chances of one of the contending elements in the Spanish strife.

Our preferences, either as to Spain or as the world at large, may be as the poles apart, but when it comes to endangering deliberately the peace of the United States over the quarrels of other peoples, the solid good sense of the American people is certain to prevail.

Yours truly,

Martin Conboy

New York, January 24, 1939.

———————

DOCUMENT NO. 3

(From the *New York Times* of January 31, 1939)

TEXT OF REPLY OF BURLINGHAM AND JESSUP TO CONBOY'S LETTER

To the Editor of the *New York Times*:

Martin Conboy's letter published in your issue of January 26, contains statements which cannot remain unchallenged as a basis for the immediate policy of the United States toward Spain or for the future policy of this country. Mr. Stimson's letter, which Mr. Conboy seeks to rebut, is in itself the answer to some of Mr. Conboy's arguments, but others of them are directed to points on which Mr. Stimson did not elaborate.

Mr. Conboy starts from the fundamental fallacy that the existing embargo on exportation of arms to Spain rests upon the historic neutrality policy of the United States. It is surprising that so able a lawyer should be thus misled by the confusing and inaccurate label of "neutrality act" which has been pinned on the joint resolution of May 1, 1937. The joint resolution of January 8, 1937, dealing specially with Spain, is not even popularly called a "neutrality act" and cannot be so considered.

It is elementary that the historic neutrality policy of the United States formulated by Washington and Jefferson was designed to protect the rights and to enforce the duties of the United States when we were neutral during a foreign war. The Spanish arms-embargo resolution sought neither to protect neutral rights nor to fulfill neutral duties. Our neutrality statutes as enacted from the earliest days of this country down to the present do, of course, apply to civil wars, but, with the exception of provisions to prevent organizing hostile expeditions in our country, only when the United States has recognized the belligerency of the contending forces.

Neither the United States nor other governments have recognized the belligerency of the Franco or the Loyalist forces. We know that Franco has repeatedly sought to obtain such recognition and that it has constantly been denied to him. When there is no belligerency there is no neutrality, and when there is no neutrality there is no neutral duty or neutrality policy.

In 1895 Attorney General Harmon gave an opinion concerning the shipment of arms to Cuba, where there was then a rebellion against Spain. He told the Secretary of State:

"International law takes no account of a mere insurrection, confined within the limits of a country, which has not been protracted or successful enough to secure for those engaged in it recognition as belligerents by their own government or by foreign governments. . . .

"Neither Spain nor any other country has recognized the Cuban insurgents as belligerents. They are, therefore, simply Spanish citizens with whom Spain is dealing within her own borders, and the fact that, by common report, they are engaged in armed resistance to her authority is merely a circumstance of suspicion to be considered in any inquiry which may be had concerning the conduct of persons within the United States who may be suspected of hostile intentions toward Spain. . . ."

Substitute "Franco" for "Cuban" and that opinion is applicable to the existing situation in Spain. Similarly, when civil war was raging in Mexico in 1912, Secretary Bryan wrote to the Mexican Ambassador as follows:

". . . I am constrained to call to your attention the obvious fact that since there is now no recognized state of belligerency in Mexico, the rules and laws governing warfare and the conduct of neutrals are not involved. In other words, under the present situation, so far as the commerce of Mexico with other countries is concerned, the status is one of peace and no interdiction of any kind exists against commerce in any form outside the jurisdiction of Mexico.

"The duties of neutrality under the law of nations cannot be either expanded or constricted by national legislation."

These statements represent the traditional policy and the sound legal position of the United States in regard to foreign civil wars. There have been a large number of revolutions and civil wars in European countries since the United States became a Nation, but in no one of them have we adopted an embargo act like the joint resolution of January 8, 1937. Far from being consistent with traditional American policy, it is a distinct departure from it.

In regard to Latin-American civil wars, our policy has been different; but it by no means fits the picture which Mr. Conboy paints. He refers to the joint resolution of 1912 which empowered the President to impose embargoes upon shipments of arms to Latin-American countries in which civil war existed. He refers also to the amendment of 1922, which extended this power to cover countries in which we have extraterritorial rights — notably China.

He apparently failed to notice Mr. Stimson's brief sketch of the actions taken under those resolutions. Nor did Mr. Conboy point out the fact that in most instances those embargo acts have been applied to help the recognized government to put down the rebellion.

President Taft used the joint resolution of 1912 shortly after its passage to help the recognized government of Mexico and to keep supplies from going to the rebels. In 1914 President Wilson raised the embargo when he found that it hampered the Carranza government from getting arms across the American border while his opponent, Huerta, controlling the Atlantic ports, was able to import them freely from Europe. This is a clear analogy to the present Spanish situation in which Franco, controlling the coast, imports his arms from Italy and Germany.

Under President Coolidge the United States sold arms to the Mexican Government while forbidding shipments to the Mexican revolutionists. Secretary Hughes declared that "the refusal to aid the established government would have thrown our moral influence upon the side of those who were challenging the peace and order of Mexico and we should have incurred a large responsibility for the consequent disturbances. We were . . . exercising our undoubted right to sell arms to the existing government." Secretary Kellogg followed a like course.

In 1926 President Coolidge, when civil war broke out in Nicaragua, first embargoed all shipments to that country, but when he found that the revolutionists were obtaining arms from other countries, he informed the recognized Nicaraguan Government that licenses would be issued for shipments of arms to it. "It would be thoroughly inconsistent," he told Congress, "for this country not to support the government recognized by it while the revolutionists were receiving arms and munitions abroad."

In 1930 the United States followed the same policy in regard to Brazil, Secretary Stimson declaring that it was "our regular action under similar circumstances. . . . We are acting according to general principles of international law. Those principles declare that where we are in friendly relations, through diplomatic channels, with a government which has been recognized as the legitimate government of a country, that government is entitled to the ordinary rights of any government to buy arms in this country; while the people who are opposing and trying to overthrow that government and are not yet recognized as belligerents are not entitled to that right."

This action was justified by the Pan-American Treaty signed at Habana in 1928 and since ratified by the United States. This treaty is not mentioned by Mr. Conboy, although it was mentioned by Mr. Stimson. Spain, to be sure, is not a party to it and it therefore does not control the action of the United States with respect to Spain but it is nonetheless a convincing illustration of our policy on this subject.

By the treaty we agreed "to forbid the traffic in arms and war material, except when intended for the government, while the belligerency of the rebels has not been recognized, in which latter case the rules of neutrality shall be applied."

To summarize, it may be said that the policy of the United States in foreign civil wars has been —

When the civil war was in Europe, to do nothing in the way of restricting the commerce in arms;

When the civil war was in Latin America, to prevent arms from reaching the rebels but to help the recognized government to obtain them.

Why, then, did Congress pass the Spanish arms embargo resolution of January 8, 1937? Secretary Hull has authoritatively stated the reason in his letter to Senator Pittman on May 12, 1938. In that letter he referred to the formation in Europe of the Spanish nonintervention committee. The law of January 8, 1937, was designed to enable the United States to assist in this policy of nonintervention. As Mr. Stimson pointed out, the nonintervention agreement was "flagrantly violated" by Italy and Germany and "at once became a mockery and a failure." The specific reason for passing a law contrary to our historic policy has therefore ceased to exist.

Mr. Conboy also takes up the joint resolution of May 1, 1937, commonly miscalled the Neutrality Act. Mr. Stimson, in his letter, gave his opinion that this general law, which provides for all cases of civil strife that may affect the peace and safety of the United States, superseded the specific resolution of January 8, which applied only to the Spanish civil war.

This opinion Mr. Conboy sweeps away by invoking a canon of statutory construction that a general law does not repeal a special law "in the absence of an express repeal or absolute incompatibility." But canons of construction are not absolute rules of law; they are only generalizations designed to aid courts in determining legislative intent. Moreover, the canon invoked by Mr. Conboy cannot be stated in such sweeping terms.

The Supreme Court of the United States has said that "if the latter act covers the whole subject of the first, and embraces new provisions, plainly showing that it was intended as a substitute for the first act, it will operate as a repeal of that act" (*United States v. Tynen*, II Wall. 88).

The standard treatise on statutory construction quotes the following as a summary of the general principle touching implied repeals: "Where the later or revising statute clearly covers the whole subject matter of antecedent acts, and it plainly appears to have been the purpose of the legislature to give expression in it to the whole law on the subject, the latter is held to be repealed by necessary implication" (Sutherland, vol. I, p. 465.)

It seems clear that the law of May 1, 1937, did cover the whole subject of civil strife in foreign countries which had been dealt with in a particular way in the preceding law of January 8.

The Supreme Court has also declared that "As a general rule it is not open to controversy, that where a new statute covers the whole subject matter of an old one, adds offenses, and prescribes different penalties for those enumerated in the old law, that then the former statute is repealed by implication; as the provisions of both cannot stand together" (*Norris v. Crocker*, 13 How., 429.)

The law of May 1, 1937, changes the penalties prescribed in the law of January 8 by adding to them a provision for the forfeiture of the property exported in violation of the law and of the vessel or vehicle containing the same. It also, by section 6, makes it a penal offense for an American vessel to carry the arms, etc., enumerated in the President's proclamation. Furthermore, the law of January 8 empowers the President to put an end to the embargo only when he finds that "the state of civil strife now obtaining in Spain" has "ceased to exist." On the other hand, the law of May 1 authorized the President to repeal the embargo if he finds that a state of civil strife still exists but that the character of that strife has changed.

What is the evidence of the intent of Congress? The so-called Neutrality Acts of 1935 and 1936 dealt only with international wars, not with civil wars. When the Spanish War broke out, therefore, our statutory law was not applicable and for the reason already stated Congress passed the Spanish Embargo Act of January 8, 1937.

In reporting to the Senate the bill which became the so-called Neutrality Act of May 1, 1937, the Senate Foreign Relations Committee said that the new bill "does extend the provisions of the existing law to foreign states wherein civil strife exists of such a magnitude and conducted under such conditions that the export of arms, ammunition, and implements of war from the United States to said foreign state would threaten and endanger our peace."

The provisions of the resolution of May 1, 1937, were evidently designed to prescribe the rules to be followed in all cases of civil strife and those rules were different from those in the resolution of January 8. The President must have assumed that this law of May 1, 1937, superseded and repealed the law of January 8. That earlier law had itself imposed an embargo on shipments of arms to Spain and had specified the articles embargoed. Yet on May 1, the day the later act was passed, the President issued his proclamation under the law of that date. The proclamation declares that:

"Whereas section 1 of the joint resolution of Congress approved May 1, 1937 . . . authorizes him to proclaim an embargo when civil strife in a foreign state is of such character as to make it necessary to preserve the peace of the United States, therefore, he finds that the civil strife in Spain was of the character contemplated by the law, and accordingly he proclaimed an embargo. He specifically enumerated, as required by the law of May 1, the articles which were covered by the proclamation.

If the embargo imposed by the law of January 8, 1937, was still in force after May 1, why should the President proclaim another embargo? And if the law of January 8 still controlled the situation regarding exports to Spain, how could the President add many new articles which that law did not ban when that law gave him no authority to change the lists?

The conclusion is inevitable that the President believed that the law of May 1 superseded the law of January 8, as Mr. Stimson claims that it did. No congressional voice was raised in opposition to that conclusion thus publicly evidenced. Great weight, says the Supreme Court, "will be given to the contemporaneous construction by department officials, who were called upon to act under the law and to carry its provisions into effect" (*United States v. Hill*, 120 U. S. 169). The President's action was contemporaneous and outweighs the contrary position publicly announced 10 months later by Secretary Hull.

One further point: The law of May 1, 1937, provides that "whenever, in the judgment of the President, the conditions which have caused him to issue any proclamation under the authority of this section have ceased to exist he shall revoke the same. . . ."

As already pointed out, the conditions which caused him to issue his proclamation were the existence of the Nonintervention Committee in Europe and the belief that the United States might become involved if it stood out against that cooperative effort and thus caused its defeat.

The effort has been defeated by Mussolini and Hitler; the basic conditions have changed and the revocation of the embargo by the President would be fully in accord with the statute. It would further mark a return to our historic policy of avoiding intervention in European civil wars by following a strict hands-off policy instead of taking affirmative action which, as events have demonstrated, inevitably affects the outcome of a struggle in which we profess not to be concerned.

Charles C. Burlingham

Philip C. Jessup

New York, January 30, 1939.

DOCUMENT NO. 4

(From the *New York Times* of February 2, 1939)

TEXT OF REPLY OF CONBOY TO BURLINGHAM'S AND JESSUP'S LETTER

To the Editor of the *New York Times*:

In their letter to the *New York Times*, published in your issue of today, Charles C. Burlingham and Philip C. Jessup seek to dispose of an enactment of Congress by the pronouncement that "the conclusion is inevitable that the President believed that the law of May 1 superseded the Law of January 8, as Mr. Stimson claims that it did."

If the conclusion is inevitable, one would expect the Secretary of State so to regard it. If the belief of the President had been as stated, how could the Secretary of State have expressed the contrary belief?

And yet Secretary Hull is publicly on record with an unqualified declaration that if the proclamation of the President of May 1, 1937, were to be revoked, the act of Congress of January 8, 1937, would still remain in effect.

Secretary Hull wrote this in a letter to Raymond Leslie Buell. The letter was published in the *New York Times* of March 23, 1938. The following quotations from the Secretary's communication will suffice to dispose of the unwarranted assumption indulged in by Messrs. Burlingham and Jessup as to the President's belief. Secretary Hull writes:

"After careful consideration of all the facts, I am of the opinion that there has been no change in the situation in Spain such as to warrant the President in revoking his proclamation of May 1, 1937, prohibiting the exportation of arms, ammunition, or implements of war to that country.

"Furthermore, I desire to call your attention in this connection to the provisions of another joint resolution of Congress, approved January 8, 1937, which is likewise still in force."

And later in the same letter:

"Even if the proclamation of the President of May 1, 1937, were to be revoked, the prohibition upon the export of arms, ammunition, and implements of war to Spain laid down in the joint resolution of Congress approved January 8, 1937, would still remain in effect."

Therefore, we have Messrs. Burlingham and Jessup urging the President to revoke the proclamation of May 1, 1937, on the assumption that there then will be no Spanish embargo, despite the unequivocal declaration of Secretary of State Hull that in case of such revocation the joint resolution of January 8, 1937, "would still remain in effect."

In matters of foreign affairs the Secretary of State is at least the adviser of the Executive. The Department of State exists for the guidance of the President. The State Department prepares what proclamations the President signs. To the President's signature is added the official signature of the Secretary of State under the words "By the President," and the seal of the United States is affixed by the Secretary.

The Secretary of State has to be aware of the obligations and the restraints to which he, as well as the President, is subject under law.

As between the responsible authority of Secretary Hull, resting as it must on scrupulous concern for law and facts, and the detached, informal, and unofficial opinion of these gentlemen as to what was in the mind of the President, there is no difficulty of choice.

Martin Conboy

New York, January 31, 1939.

Appendix B

The following information was reported in the *New York Times* on the date indicated:

LOYALIST

1936: July 26, Spanish Workers Club sponsors demonstration for Loyalist Government at sailing of liner *Christobal Colon;* July 29, United Committee in Support of Struggle Against Fascism in Spain plans demonstration; July 31, International Garment Workers Union, contributes toward fund for Spanish workers; August 1, United Committee in Support of the Struggle Against Spanish Fascism holds demonstration; August 4, Central Council of Trade Unions, contributes toward fund for Spanish workers; August 5, D. Dubinsky to help raise funds among U. S. organized labor for Spanish workers; August 9, International Ladies Garment Worker's Union appeals to U. S. trade unions and organized labor for funds for Loyalist victims of the war; August 13, N. Y. State Committee of Communist party donates sum toward support of People's Front in Spain; August 15, Local 144 of Cigar Makers International Union of America appeals to workers in industry to support war against fascism in Spain; August 19, N. Y. State District of Communist party sponsors Madison Square Garden meeting for fund raising purposes for Loyalists; August 20, Communist party of N. Y. sends sum to Spanish Government; August 21, American Federation of Teachers votes to raise funds for Spanish Workers Red Cross and Relief Association; September 19, American Friends of Spanish Democracy holds meeting to collect funds; September 21, Committee for Defense of Spanish Republic holds benefit; September 26, Bishop R. L. Paddock announces formation of Friends of Spanish Democracy to aid in Loyalist cause; October 5, public meeting held by Supporters of Spanish Democracy; October 10, Union Square rally in behalf of Madrid Government; October 20, reception in Town Hall for Friends of Spanish Democracy; October 27, $15,000 raised for Loyalist cause at mass meeting in Madison Square Garden; November 9, American League Against War and Fascism announces cargo of food, clothing, and medical supplies sent to Spain; November 4, American Friends of Spanish Democracy plan conference to launch national campaign in U. S. to send medical aid to Loyalists; November 7, Trade Union Committee appointed to promote financial support in American organizations for Loyalist Government; November 14, American League Against War and Fascism stage demonstration against invasion of Spain by Italian Fascists before Italian Consulate; November 21, North American Committee to Aid Spanish Democracy sends shipload of food, clothing, and medical supplies to Loyalists; November 22, women representatives of N. Y. C. civic and social organizations attend conference sponsored by American League Against War and Fascism — pledge aid to Loyalist Government; November 27, North American Committee to Aid Spanish Democracy plans benefit concert to aid civil war victims; November 29, Communists parade to German Consulate in protest against Nazi assistance to Rebels; December 4, United Cloakmakers Branch of American League Against War and Fascism pledge garments for Loyalists; December 4, CCNY students burn effigies of Franco, Hitler, and Mussolini in drive for funds to aid the Loyalists; December 6, North American Committee to Aid Spanish Democracy gives benefit concert; December 7, N. Y. State Socialist party protests against U. S. neutrality policy; December 13, League of American Writers vote to hold International Conference for Defense of Culture in Madrid; December 21, Italian Anti-Fascist Committee in N. Y. meets to raise funds to send recruits for Loyalists; December 24, Socialist party seeks to form Eugene V. Debs column for International Brigade; December 27, Socialist party conducts campaign for Loyalist writers; December 27, formation of American Society for Technical Aid to Spanish Democracy announced. Society plans to send Americans to Spain to release factory workers for the front; December 30, American Anti-Nazi Committee contributes ambulance for Loyalists.

1937:   January 5, American Friends of Spanish Democracy presents four ambulances to representatives of the Spanish Government at Madison Square Garden mass meeting; January 11, relief expedition to sail for Spain to set up hospital in Madrid; January 12, Ernest Hemingway named chairman of Spanish Ambulance Committee; January 15, farewell dinner for members of medical unit preparing to depart for Spain; January 17, medical unit sails; January 31, medical unit arrives in Barcelona; January 23, North American Committee to Aid Spanish Democracy protests collection of funds for Rebels in N. Y. C.; January 5, United Spanish Socialists hold mass meeting in Madison Square Garden; January 3, samples of garment gifts by Trade Union Committee to Manufacture Clothing for Spain to be presented to Ambassador de los Ríos; January 9, Socialist party pickets Italian and German consulates in protest against presence of their troops in Spain; February 9, North American Committee to Aid Spanish Democracy announces fund collection drive for Loyalists; February 21, CCNY faculty members collect funds to aid Loyalists; March 14, second American medical unit under auspices of American Friends of Spanish Democracy to sail; March 6, Rev. J. A. MacKay blames Archbishop of Toledo for religious issues in Spain; March 7, Rev. H. F. Ward defends support of Loyalists by American League Against War and Fascism; March 19, $50,000 sent by Labor's Red Cross for hospital in Madrid; March 22, Italian Anti-Fascist Committee meets to protest Italian invasion and to raise funds for the Garibaldi Battalion of the International Brigade aiding the Loyalists; April 15, meeting of Socialists in observance of Spanish Republic anniversary; April 6, American Friends of Spanish Democracy donates art award; April 6, Medical Bureau to Aid Spanish Democracy 3rd medical unit arrives in Spain; April 12, fourth medical unit sails; April 2, North American Committee to Aid Spanish Democracy ships flour to Loyalist Spain; April 19, North American Committee to Aid Spanish Democracy sponsors mass meeting; April 2, United Youth Committee to Aid Spanish Democracy ships canned milk to Loyalists; April 2, United Youth Committee to Aid Spanish Democracy and American Musical Alliance sponsor concert for Loyalist funds; April 4, American Student Union collects funds to send food ship to Loyalist Spain; April 11, Swarthmore College memorial fund to honor J. Selligman, Jr., a student who died in the Spanish War. Fund to be used for medical aid to Loyalists; April 15, Socialists hold meeting and express faith in Loyalist cause; April 25, Rev. M. O. Flanagan appeals for medical funds for Basque Catholics and Loyalists; April 27, mass meeting in tribute of Ben Leider — American killed in action with the Loyalists; May 2, fight against fascism in Spain featured in May Day parades; May 6, Medical Bureau to Aid Spanish Democracy announces formation of Workers Committee to Aid Loyalist Spain; May 10, German-American Relief for Spain Committee desires to bring refugee Basque children to the U. S.; May 22, American Board of Guardians for Basque Refugee Children formed; May 31,

Medical Bureau to Aid Spanish Democracy sends 4th ambulance detachment to Valencia; June 26, fund drive for Basque Children planned; June 8, Rabbinical Assembly of America endorses Loyalists; June 11, Socialist party sponsors meeting to raise funds for orphans and ambulance unit; June 13, Friends of Abraham Lincoln Battalion form second group; June 15, Medical Bureau to Aid Spanish Democracy holds meeting to raise funds to send 3 ambulances; June 18, Trade Union Relief for Spain opens fund drive; June 24, Friends of Abraham Lincoln Battalion entertain relatives of Americans fighting for Loyalists in Spain; June 30, International Coordinating Committee for Aid to Spain plans benefit recital; June 30, Spanish Child Feeding Mission seeks funds; July 1, Medical Bureau to Aid Spanish Democracy Unit sails for Spain; July 2, mass protest at the Italian Consul's office against Italian military forces in Spain; July 2, concert to aid Basque children; July 4, three members of Friends of Abraham Lincoln Battalion sail for Spain; July 10, praise N. Y. negroes hurt fighting for Loyalists; July 20, mass meeting at Madison Square Garden for Loyalists' benefit; July 22, Medical Bureau to Aid Spanish Democracy dinner; July 5, International Coordinating Committee for Aid to Spanish Republic holds memorial meeting and concert; July 5, North American Committee to Aid Spanish Democracy sends letter to Roosevelt asking embargo be extended against Germany, Italy, and Portugal; August 3, Medical Bureau to Aid Spanish Democracy holds fiesta; August 10, Rockland County Spanish Milk Fund Chapter holds fiesta; August 19, Musician's Committee to Aid Spanish Democracy formed; August 22, concert planned by Musician's Committee to Aid Spanish Democracy; September 25, Young Communists League sponsors rally for Spain; September 30, City Projects Council gives serum to Dr. Barsky for Loyalist fighters; October 7, North American Committee to Aid Spanish Democracy gives benefit dinner; October 17, forty-eight local labor unions vote to aid Americans fighting for Loyalists; October 15, Medical Bureau to Aid Spanish Democracy Dental Division benefits by concert; October 21, Columbia University Faculty Committee for Aid to the Spanish People holds meeting; November 5, Musician's Committee to Aid Spanish Democracy to hold music contest; November 26, local chapter of National Lawyers Guild urges embargo on munitions to Germany and Italy and lifting of trade restrictions with Spanish Government; December 7, National Maritime Union dedicates ambulance for Loyalists; December 18, American Artists Congress condemns Fascist intervention in Spain; December 15, Medical Bureau to Aid Spanish Democracy plans fiesta.

1938:   January 29, Medical Bureau to Aid Spanish Democracy benefits by dance performance; February 7, Musician's Committee to Aid Spanish Democracy conducts prize contest; March 26, North American Committee to Aid Spanish Democracy aided by manuscript sale; March 18, Friends of Abraham Lincoln Battalion collect funds; March 24, Medical Bureau to Aid Spanish Democracy donates funds to Loyalists; April 5, benefit performance held for Spanish children; April 15, pro-Loyalist rally held at Madison Square Garden; April 25, YWCA plans fast day to aid Loyalist relief group; April 1, Medical Bureau to Aid Spanish Democracy holds luncheon; April 6, Medical Bureau to Aid Spanish Democracy gives benefit dinner; April 13, Medical Bureau to Aid Spanish Democracy gives benefit dinner; May 1, Spanish War veterans to march in May Day parade; May 9, Social Democratic Federation asks Hull to lift embargo; June 5, Medical Bureau to Aid Spanish Democracy appropriates sum for wounded Americans; June 10, lift the embargo rally held at Madison Square Garden; June 28, plan village fair for Spanish children's milk fund; July 2, benefits to aid repatriation of Americans wounded in Spain; July 7, film showing to benefit Loyalist wounded soldiers and refugee children; July 13, U. S. groups start drive for Loyalist relief ship; July 24, American Communications Association meeting passes resolution backing Loyalists; July 17, Rev. M. O. Flanagan plans lectures on behalf of Loyalists; July 20, Madison Square Garden rally to observe war anniversary; September 15, funds raised for relief ship for Loyalist Spain; September 16, Theodore Dreiser defends Loyalist Government against anti-religious charges at benefit for American relief ship for Spain; September 23, meeting of Trade Union Relief for Spain Committee; September 25, gifts sent from American children to Spanish children; September 29, BOR President Isaacs and F. P. Adams join in opening Loyalist Day Week for American relief ship to Spain; September 15, Medical Bureau and North American Committee to Aid Spanish Democracy artists paint pictures to raise money for Spanish relief ship; September 16, League of American Writers benefit to aid Spanish Loyalists; September 18, Spanish Children's Milk Fund benefits by concert; November 19, Spanish Children's Milk Fund sculpture exhibit benefit held; November 22, mass meeting urges lifting of embargo to Spain; November 22, Spanish Children's Milk Fund concert benefit held; November 29, Spanish Child Welfare Association benefit held; November 18, North American Committee relief ship arrives in Barcelona; November 22, Harlem and Musician's Committee present concert; November 30, North American

Central Conference of American Rabbis backs Loyalists; May 9, Committee plans theater program; December 8, Spanish Child Welfare Association and American Friends Service Committee hold benefit; December 18, Friends of Abraham Lincoln Brigade ask Roosevelt to lift embargo; December 18, plan fund drive to build children refugee cities in Spain; December 18, Spanish Children's Milk Fund benefit held; December 28, relief collections given to Loyalists; December 27, Hunter College plans benefit play for Loyalists.

1939: January 6, mass meeting urges lifting of embargo; January 24, Communist rally urges lifting of embargo; January 25, Protestant and Jewish clergy groups urge lifting of embargo; January 25, Times Square demonstrators urge lifting of embargo; January 31, Medical Bureau to Aid Spanish Democracy urges lifting of embargo; January 11, local theaters to aid milk fund; January 22, Medical Bureau to Aid Spanish Democracy ships clothes to Loyalists; January 26, Medical Bureau to Aid Spanish Democracy cables funds to Spain for refugees; February 2, paraders urge lifting of embargo; February 8, Negro Committee to Aid Spanish Democracy asks end of embargo; February 26, American Law Students Association Convention urges lifting of embargo against Spain; February 25, National Student Union sponsors protest against embargo; February 5, Abraham Lincoln Brigade members receive royal welcome upon return from Spain; February 12, Worker's Alliance welcomes members returned from Spain; February 6, Medical Bureau to Aid Spanish Democracy holds benefit dance; February 10, Medical Bureau to Aid Spanish Democracy seeks additional funds; March 5, American Women's Committee for Spanish Republic seeks funds to aid Loyalist children; March 17, Emergency Committee to Aid Spanish Republic plans fund campaign; March 20, American Friends of Spanish Democracy issues statement opposing recognition of Franco; March 16, Medical Bureau and North American Committee to Aid Spanish Democracy sends funds to aid refugees; March 26, Medical Bureau and North American Committee to Aid Spanish Democracy — Secretary Ickes accepts relief campaign chairmanship; March 20, Friends of Spanish Democracy opposes recognition of Franco; April 8, Medical Bureau and North American Committee to Aid Spanish Democracy together with Musician's Committee gives benefit concert.

REBEL

1936:   September 10, Mrs. A. J. Pack obtains medical supplies for Insurgents; October 20, Rev. E. L. Curran scores aim of Loyalists and praises Rebels at a meeting of the International Catholic Truth Society; November 21, Portuguese Radio Club sends supplies to Rebel wounded; December 1, International Catholic Truth Society organizes young women in fund drive for medical supplies to aid Nationalists; December 1, Rev. E. L. Curran charges Manhattan and Brooklyn press with unfairness to anticommunist group in Spain.

1937:   January 23, Brooklyn R. C. Diocese establishes fund to aid Catholics in Spain; February 28, Fordham University Alumnae Association collects funds to send to the Bishop of Toledo to aid sufferers; March 20, Alumnae Association of Fordham University announces support of Franco — opens fund drive to aid the victims of communism; April 10, American Committee for Spanish Relief defies political bias; April 20, Bishop F. J. McConnell criticized for presiding at a celebration of Loyalist victories; May 6, American Committee for Spanish Relief takes over relief efforts of the *Commonweal;* May 15, Cardinal Hayes urges Catholics attend pageant of the American Committee for Spanish Relief; May 20, American Committee for Spanish Relief holds mass meeting and pageant in Madison Square Garden; May 21, American Committee for Spanish Relief plans rallies; May 13, Rev. L. K. Patterson urges united front against Leftists in Spain; May 23, Catholic Press Association announces sympathy for Franco; July 22, American Spanish Relief Fund benefit sponsored by magazine *America;* August 21, *Catholic News* criticizes fiesta held by Medical Bureau to Aid Spanish Democracy; September 30, National Council of Catholic Women express sympathy to women and children of Spain; November 11, Notre Dame Club endorses Franco campaign; December 30, Father J. F. Thorning scores *New York Times* editorial policy and correspondents for being biased in reporting the Spanish Civil War.

1938:   February 6, Spanish American Relief Fund announces expansion; March 13, Catholic students aid Spanish American Relief Fund; September 5, Franco partisans protest showing of film "Blockade;" December 24, National Council of Catholic Men oppose lifting the embargo.

1939:   January 9, Knights of Columbus urge retaining of Spanish arms embargo; January 10, mass meeting urges retaining of embargo; January 17, Assemblyman Devaney offers New York Legislature Resolution memorializing Congress to retain embargo;

January 26, mass meeting cheers Rebel gains; January 28, American Union for Nationalist Spain formed; January 28, American Union for Nationalist Spain urges Roosevelt to recognize Franco government *de facto* and *de jure;* February 21, American Union for Nationalist Spain publishes message received from Franco; March 2, pro-Rebel meeting; March 22, Father Thorning asks Roosevelt to recognize defeat of U.S.S.R. in Spain.

Appendix C

GERMANY AND THE SPANISH CIVIL WAR, 1936-1939

Preface

Immediately following the Second World War the British Foreign Office and the United States Department of State agreed to publish jointly documents from the captured archives of the German Foreign Ministry and the Reich Chancellery. The third volume of this series, *Germany and the Spanish Civil War, 1936-1939*, appeared in 1950, and the documents for this appendix were selected from that publication. They first make clear the German attitude toward the revolt against the Spanish Government; they also describe German military aid to the Franco regime as well as assistance rendered to both sides in Spain by other Great Powers. In addition, the documents are important because they illustrate German reaction to the Spanish policy of the United States Government.

DOCUMENT NO. 36

THE AMBASSADOR IN THE UNITED STATES TO THE FOREIGN MINISTRY

Washington, D. C., August 11, 1936.
zu Pol. III 1587.

No. 1044

With reference to my telegraphic report No. 200 of August 7.
Subject: Disorder in Spain.

Submitted herewith is a collection of American press comments on the Spanish disorders and on Germany's alleged intentions to intervene.

The extent of the agitation directed against Germany on this score is shown by the great number of protesting telegrams that the

245

Embassy has been receiving in the last few days from pacifist and Communist organizations. An assortment of such telegrams is also enclosed.

Luther

————————

DOCUMENT NO. 115

THE AMBASSADOR IN TURKEY TO THE FOREIGN MINISTRY

(Telegram)

Istanbul, November 6, 1936.

Very Secret
No. 16 of November 6

With reference to your inquiry I have learned reliably of the following shipments: October 22, on the *Karl Lepin,* Russian, Odessa to Alicante, 20 trucks and tanks, 4 cannons, 500 tons of ammunition, 1,000 tons of food; October 22, on the *Transbalt,* Russian, Odessa to Cartagena and Barcelona, 40 trucks, 12 tanks, 10 cannons; October 23, on the *Shahter,* Russian, Odessa to Alicante and Barcelona, 6 trucks, 8 cannons 500 tons of ammunition, 2,000 tons of grain; October 24, on the *Kuban,* Odessa to Barcelona, 2,500 tons of grain, 1,200 tons of food; October 25, on the *Varlaam Avasanov,* Russian, Odessa to Barcelona, 8,500 (tons) of Diesel oil; October 25, the *Aldecca,* Spanish, Barcelona to Nikolayev, for the account of the Spanish Government; October 25, the *Cabo Palo,* Barcelona to Odessa, the same; October 27, on the *Kurak,* Russian, the Black Sea to Barcelona and Alicante, 40 trucks, 12 armored cars, 6 cannons, 4 planes, 700 tons of ammunition, 1,500 tons of food; October 28, on the *Blagoyev,* Russian, Black Sea to Cartagena and Alicante, 20 trucks, 8 cannons, 4 tanks, 500 tons of war matériel, 150 tons of clothing, 1,500 tons of grain; October 31, on the *Komsomol,* Black Sea to Barcelona, 50 trucks, 5 planes, 8 tanks, 2,000 tons of war matériel and ammunition, 1,000 tons of food, 100 tons of medicines.

November 3, the *Darro* and the *Segarra,* both Spanish; November 4, the *Georgi Dimitrov* left Alicante with 17 Spanish soldiers, 3 of them wounded and 3 of them women disguised as soldiers; these were put ashore at Istanbul and sent on to Odessa on the *Jan Rudzudak* the same day. Further names of ships, the cargo of which could not be ascertained, will follow.

Keller

DOCUMENT NO. 130

THE AMBASSADOR IN ITALY TO THE FOREIGN MINISTRY

(Telegram)

Rome, November 27, 1936 — 2:15 p.m.
Received November 27 — 5:30 p.m.

No. 266 of November 27

1. Ciano informed me yesterday evening that he was sending Anfuso, who had just returned, again to Franco. In view of the situation in Spain, Italy was determined to send to Spain a whole division of Black Shirts, of whom 4,000 men were already organized in four battalions; but first Italy had to have certain guaranties as to the future course of Spanish policy. Anfuso would therefore submit a written statement to Franco in which Franco was to obligate himself to conduct future Spanish policy in the Mediterranean in harmony with that of Italy, of course without Italy's making territorial demands; but the transit of French native troops through Spanish territory, for example, must be barred. Spain also was to obligate herself to build certain airports. He would communicate further details to me in a few days.

In yesterday's conversation Mussolini confirmed to me his intention to keep to his course unswervingly in the Spanish question. To be sure, one was tempted to say with Faust: "Cursed above all be patience"; he was certain of gradual success, however. Moreover, after the naval review that went off splendidly yesterday he expressed the conviction that the Italian fleet was in the best possible condition today and was in the process of constant organic development.

2. Ciano informed me that upon final consideration Grandi had been sent back to London without the agreement having been put into written form after all. The matter was therefore still in a nebulous preliminary stage, so to speak.

Hassell

DOCUMENT NO. 143

MEMORANDUM BY THE ACTING STATE SECRETARY

Berlin, December 5, 1936.

The American Ambassador called on me today and expressed his grave concern about the general situation. He had had word from Washington, too, that they viewed the European situation with great concern and were reckoning with the possibility of war. Great influence was being exerted on President Roosevelt from many sides, especially by the peace organizations and the churches, to present the world with a proposal for limiting armaments or for disarming, and it was to be expected — Mr. Dodd intimated that he had been informed to this effect by the State Department — that a resolution to this effect might be debated even now, during the present conference in Buenos Aires. I told the Ambassador that I did not quite see why people in America were so particularly worried. Certainly the Spanish situation contained many elements of risk, but this was due only to Russia's outrageous violation of the embargo. Germany would place no great hopes on a big disarmament conference, in view of the experience gained in Geneva; on the other hand, the German stand in the disarmament question, so far as I knew, was still the same as that laid down in the Führer's speech of May 21, 1935.

The Ambassador then brought up the following: The American Government had learned from Rome and Latin America that a secret agreement had recently been concluded between the Italian Government and the Government of General Franco, whereby Franco granted the Italian Government far-reaching privileges in the future. If Franco won and this agreement went into force for all of Spain, Spain's sovereignty would be at an end; Spain would, as it were, assume Albania's position and be under a kind of Italian suzerainty. The Latin American countries, which had so far been much in sympathy with Franco, were watching this development with concern; the force of tradition played a part in this (Spain, the mother country). The Ambassador asked whether we had any knowledge of this agreement. I answered Mr. Dodd that I knew nothing about it. He knew, of course, that during Count Ciano's visit to Berlin the integrity of the national and colonial territory of Spain had been recognized explicitly by the Italian Government. Under these circumstances his information seemed improbable to me.

Dieckhoff

DOCUMENT NO. 178

MEMORANDUM BY THE HEAD OF THE EXTRA-EUROPEAN SECTION OF THE
POLITICAL DEPARTMENT

Berlin, December 31, 1936.
c.c. Pol. III 42.

The First Secretary of the American Embassy, Mr. Lee, called on me and on instructions from his Government read to me a communication by the American Department of State.

According to this communication, the American Government was unable to reject the application of the Robert Cuse firm to ship airplanes and engines to Bilbao in the amount of $2,775,000, since the joint resolution of Congress called for an embargo on the shipment of weapons and war matériel to belligerent nations only and did not apply to the case of civil war. During the Spanish conflict the American Government had received many applications from exporters with regard to the shipment of war matériel to Spain. For patriotic reasons, however, they had all, with the exception of the aforesaid firm, given up their plans, in view of the non-intervention policy of the American Government.

The State Department, which sincerely regrets the contravention of the non-intervention policy of the American Government in the present case, further states that most of the planes intended for export in this case are not new and first have to be repaired, so that their shipment cannot begin in less than two months and cannot be completed in less than six months.

v. Erdmannsdorff

DOCUMENT NO. 188

THE CHARGÉ D'AFFAIRES IN THE UNITED STATES TO THE FOREIGN

MINISTRY

Washington, D. C., January 7, 1937.
Received January 26.
Pol. III 446.

With reference to our report No. 2 of January 4.

Subject: Deliveries of American war matériel to the Socialist Government in Spain and activity of American fliers.

Enclosed I have the honor to submit more newspaper reports, concerning the shipment of war matériel, particularly of planes, to the Socialist Government in Spain. Immediately after the opening of Congress, as has already been reported, a joint resolution was introduced in the Senate providing for a ban on all deliveries of war matériel to Spain and also to third countries, in case delivery to Spain is intended. This resolution was passed unanimously in the Senate, and in the House of Representatives with one dissenting vote. The text of the resolution is enclosed. Meanwhile the firm of Mr. Cuse in great haste had loaded planes and other war matériel on the Spanish ship *Mar Cantábrico* lying in the harbor of New York, and a race reminiscent of a detective story started between the parties interested in this cargo of arms and the Congress. Because of a technical error made in the Senate, the resolution could not enter into force before the 8th. On the afternoon of the 6th the *Mar Cantábrico* consequently left the three-mile zone, and thus the territorial limits of the United States, without interference. We still lack details of the connections between the firm of Vimalert and Amtorg, that is to say, the Soviet Government. No great significance should be attributed in this connection to the denial issued by Ambassador Troyanovsky here.

The airplane purchases made by the Ambassador of the Spanish Leftist Government in Mexico through an agent in San Francisco, who likewise received his license from the State Department, have been confirmed. The list of purchases made by him is enclosed. The Mexican Government, on the other hand, as the State Department announced, had pledged itself to prohibit the reexport of war matériel purchased in the United States.

Finally the publications of the Department of Commerce show that in the last 6 months a considerable number of airplanes have been sold to the Central American countries.

Because of the impossibility of preventing the export of war matériel for Spain until the new embargo law is enacted, the State Department was in a very embarrassing position because it had to expose itself to the reproach of seriously disturbing the efforts of the European powers to prevent further intervention in the Spanish Civil War. This confusion in the State Department is said to explain the contradictions in which that Department has become involved in the last few days. For example:

1. In the note to the powers in which it explained the granting of the license to Cuse, the State Department asserted that the planes and engines would not be ready for shipment for several months. This assertion has already been refuted by the sailing of the *Mar Cantábrico* on the 6th of this month with a portion of the shipment in question.

2. The State Department denied that the planes sold to Central American countries in the last few months have been or would be exported to Europe. This is contradicted, among other things, by the published reports of exports of American war matériel from Mexico.

3. It was stated in an official American quarter that no American planes of any kind were being used in the Spanish Civil War. This claim, too, was proved to be false by the reports of the American fliers who have reported the use of Douglas and Curtiss planes.

I also enclose two more very illuminating reports by the American transoceanic flier, Acosta, who served on the Spanish front for the Leftist Government, as well as some reports of American correspondents regarding the participation of German Communists on the side of the Spanish Socialists, which give a detailed picture of the dominant role played by Russian officers and Russian fliers in the Spanish Civil War. The Hearst press has, moreover, published material on the recruiting activity of agents of the Spanish Socialists among the fliers here. I also enclose this.

Finally, I enclose some newspaper clippings regarding the activities of the Ambassador of the Socialist Spanish Government here de los Ríos, who, in the last few days especially, has again been making intensive efforts to win over public opinion in the United States for the Spanish Socialists.

Thomsen

DOCUMENT NO. 207

THE CHARGÉ D'AFFAIRES IN SPAIN TO THE FOREIGN MINISTRY

Salamanca, January 18, 1937.
Received January 22.
Pol. I 338 g.

Secret

Sa. 3-459

Subject: Report on the general situation.

According to a statement by Mancini, about 20,000 Italians with two battalions of heavy artillery and 1,800 trucks are to be ready for action by the end of January in the vicinity of Seville. As a result of this prompt and powerful assistance the crisis that existed in December may be regarded as definitely overcome. Our latest deliveries cannot take effect until much later since the units to be equipped with them must first be trained and organized.

On the whole, the prospects of military success are far more favorable now. Nevertheless, even if operations proceed smoothly, months will probably still pass before the borders of Catalonia proper are reached.

Mancini told me that Italy had thus far put about 800 million lire into the Spanish enterprise; he anticipated an additional 200 million lire. I am reporting these figures with all due reservations. Furthermore, Mancini states that in return for this Italy has thus far got virtually nothing out of Spain. If this is true, we have obtained far more in this respect through Hisma. . . .

Faupel

DOCUMENT NO. 274

THE AMBASSADOR IN THE UNITED STATES TO THE FOREIGN MINISTRY

(Telegram)

Washington, May 31, 1937 – 5:25 a.m.
Received June 1 – 3:30 a.m.
Pol. III 2765.

Urgent

Secret

No. 137 of May 31

For the Foreign Minister.

Mr. Hull today urgently requested me to call on him at his hotel and spoke to me with visible anxiety about the Spanish situation. He first expressed his heartfelt sympathy for those who had been killed and wounded on the *Deutschland*, then went into the details of the Iviza incident, mentioned the bombardment of Almería, expressed the hope that it might not be necessary for us to take further action, and concluded with a friendly, rather vaguely phrased statement to the effect that Germany could presumably be counted on to continue doing everything possible to preserve the peace.

I first explained to the Secretary of State that it was only in response to the urging of the other powers that we had permitted units of our fleet to participate in the patrol of the Spanish coasts; these ships were performing a difficult international task there in the interest of localizing the Spanish Civil War as far as possible. If attacks were now made on these ships by planes of the Valencia Government, the action was downright criminal. The attack on the *Deutschland* was the third assault of this kind, since both a

British and an Italian ship had recently been attacked in the same manner. It was all the more criminal since the *Deutschland* had been lying peacefully in the harbor, resting from patrol duty; the crew had been eating in the mess. No shot had been fired by the Germans; the attack by the planes had been entirely unprovoked. The result of this outrageous attack had been 23 dead and more than 80 wounded German sailors. As for the bombardment of Almería, I had no official report on it, but it was evidently the natural German counteraction against the attack on our ship. Whether we would take still further action, I did not know; that would presumably be determined chiefly by the attitude of Valencia. Our further participation in the activities of the Non-Intervention Committee and in the coastal patrol would also probably depend on this attitude, since we could not continue exposing our ships and men to such attacks without some guaranty. That the German Government would do nothing to increase the tension, unless it should be absolutely compelled to do so, was self-evident and hardly needed any proof, in view of everything that the Secretary of State knew about our attitude in the Spanish question — a remark with which Mr. Hull immediately agreed. The further developments depended less, in my opinion, on Germany than on the attitude of the Non-Intervention Committee and, naturally, on the attitude of the Government in Valencia. As far as the latter was concerned, however, I had considerable doubt whether it even wished to contribute at all toward lessening the tension; in the very difficult situation in which it found itself, militarily and politically, it was probably more interested in complicating matters, and in the last analysis this was very likely the reason for these air attacks . . . [group garbled] warships.

Dieckhoff

DOCUMENT NO. 276

THE AMBASSADOR IN THE UNITED STATES TO THE FOREIGN MINISTRY

(Telegram)

Washington, June 2, 1937 — 5:53 p.m.
Received June 3 — 1:55 a.m.
Pol. III 2820.

Confidential
No. 144 of June 2

Yesterday (Monday was a holiday) General Bötticher had an opportunity to speak with leading Army and Navy authorities. He gave an exact description of the incidents at Iviza and Almería, emphasizing in particular that the German pocket battleship had the right to anchor off Iviza, that she lay there peaceably, and did not fire a shot either before or after the airplane attack. This information was very enlightening to the Army and the Navy in the face of the propaganda according to which the German ship opened fire first and had no right to anchor off Iviza. In view of the widely circulated suspicion that Germany acted irresponsibly and that she had warlike intentions, Bötticher spoke of the need for immediate reprisals, for which there was full understanding when the true facts of the case were explained. Of particular importance was the explanation that our measures were directed against a fortified city, since propaganda here . . . [group incomplete] that the shelling was a particularly harsh measure against the population. A well-informed person from the General Staff stated confidentially that there were exceedingly bad reports concerning the Red Government and conditions in Red Spain. In the armed forces they regard the situation and . . . [group garbled] in part authoritative assertions of certain American political figures calmly; they do not believe the newspaper reports that a threat of war exists, and they say they would be grateful for any more detailed information. A reassuring influence emanates from the armed forces, which has all the more political effect the less it is evident to the public. For this reason, and also because of the valuable position of confidence which Bötticher possesses personally, please treat this telegram as confidential. Request transmission to the War Ministry.

Dieckhoff

DOCUMENT NO. 444

THE AMBASSADOR IN ITALY TO THE FOREIGN MINISTRY

(Telegram)

Rome, October 19, 1937 — 8:35 p.m.
Received October 19 — 11:05 p.m.

Secret

No. 292 of October 19

For the Foreign Minister.

Mussolini told me today that he had received a telegram from Franco this morning asking for the dispatch of one more division with which to accomplish the final liquidation of the Asturian front. Mussolini expressed his pained astonishment; he said the Spaniards were very good soldiers but had no idea of modern warfare and were making exceedingly slow progress in Asturias. He had instructed the War Ministry to dispatch a division and to do this as soon as possible, naturally, in view of the political situation. He said in reply to my question that the militia involved had been organized into units for the purpose and was adequately trained and ready for action; he apparently wished to stress the difference between this and the militia originally sent.

Hassell

DOCUMENT NO. 580

THE AMBASSADOR IN SPAIN TO THE FOREIGN MINISTRY

(Telegram)

San Sebástian, May 4, 1938 — 2:30 p.m.
Received May 4 — 4:15 p.m.
Pol. III 1426.

No 2 of May 4

The Foreign Minister confirmed to me that lately the amount of war matériel reaching Red Spain via France was really tremendous and was the only thing that made further resistance by the Reds possible; he hoped that the French Ministers had been prevailed upon in London to limit deliveries of war matériel across the French frontier.

French diplomatic circles in St. Jean de Luz say that this was the case but that the French Government had to proceed carefully, one step at a time, because of the threat of a general strike.

Stohrer

DOCUMENT NO. 585

THE AMBASSADOR IN THE UNITED STATES TO THE FOREIGN MINISTRY

Washington, D. C., May 16, 1938.
Pol. III 1650.

No. 853

With reference to previous reports.

Subject: Lifting of the arms embargo against both parties in the Spanish Civil War.

Within the scope of the most recent move to lift the arms embargo against the Red Spanish Government, the enclosed bill for lifting the embargo and amending the neutrality act was introduced by Senator Nye on May 3. Senator Pittman, the Chairman of the Foreign Relations Committee of the Senate, before submitting it for open debate, sent the bill to Secretary of State Hull with a request for his opinion. The Secretary of State waited until the President's return before giving his opinion and has now made it known in the form of a letter of reply to Senator Pittman. The reply is a flat no to Nye and his supporters with respect to the lifting of the embargo. As to the amending of the neutrality act, which is considered inevitable by ever-growing sectors of the American public, Mr. Hull simply said in his reply that the question was too serious to be discussed profitably in the closing weeks of this session of the Congress. I am also enclosing the text of the letter.

At the recommendation of Hull, the Senate Foreign Relations Committee with unusual speed (17 votes to 1) postponed consideration of the Nye resolution for an indefinite time. The fate of the resolution is thereby sealed.

This development shows that the Administration is still not inclined to take a step which, as it was planned, would have benefited only the Red Spanish Government — though perhaps only in the form of moral support. Decisive for the attitude of the Administration on this question is the British attitude; strong internal political factors to which I have repeatedly referred in my reports on this matter also play a considerable role.

Dieckhoff

DOCUMENT NO. 630

MEMORANDUM BY THE AMBASSADOR IN THE SOVIET UNION

Moscow, July 5, 1938.

No. A 965

The attitude of the Soviet Union in the Spanish Civil War.

The Ambassadors of Britain and France have of late repeatedly approached People's Commissar Litvinov in order to induce the Soviet Government to adopt a more conciliatory attitude in the Non-Intervention Committee and to accept the latest British proposals.

Twice the British Ambassador, Lord Chilston, has discussed with Litvinov the question of the Soviet Union's participation in defraying the expenses occasioned by the withdrawal of foreign volunteers from Spain. At first Litvinov rejected any Soviet participation on the ground that the Soviet Union could not be expected

to pay for removing Germans and Italians. He at first did not
want to concede Lord Chilston's objection that Soviet volunteers,
too, were in Spain. Finally Lord Chilston proposed to Litvinov
that the Soviet Union obligate itself to assume the costs arising in
case Soviet volunteers were found to be in Spain and had to be
removed. Litvinov agreed to this proposal.

The French Ambassador, Coulondre, called on Litvinov repeatedly, especially before the session of the Non-Intervention Committee on June 21, in order to induce the Soviet Government to give
in. Litvinov personally, so M. Coulondre told me, had shown himself entirely ready to comply with the French wishes, but he had
encountered opposition in the Politburo to his proposals in this
sense. Finally, however, Litvinov had been able to prevail with
his view in the Politburo.

Concerning the attitude of Litvinov as well as of the Politburo
on the Spanish Civil War and the differences of opinion existing
between the two, Coulondre gave the following account — probably
on the basis of the impressions gained from his talks with Litvinov:

At the beginning of the Spanish Civil War Stalin and the
Politburo had kept aloof. Only upon the urging of the foreign
Communist parties, especially the French Communists, had the
Kremlin considered itself obliged to support Red Spain to an increasing extent, chiefly for fear of a defection of the foreign Communists. After Stalin and the Politburo had decided upon intervention — even though perhaps against their wishes — they wanted
to see their intervention crowned with success. It was understand-
able that, if only for reasons of prestige, they did not wish to see
a defeat of the Reds. While the Politburo was guided more by
considerations of ideology and sentiment in its evaluation of the
Spanish Civil War, Litvinov's attitude was politically realistic and
took into account the interests of the Soviet Union as a Great
Power. From the standpoint of Soviet policy, Litvinov considered
it best to withdraw from the Spanish venture without overly great
losses. Under certain conditions, above all under the condition
"L'Espagne pour les Espagnols," Litvinov apparently was ready to
accept an agreement between the two Spanish combatants.

M. Coulondre seemed to be of the opinion that Litvinov
would have further success in gaining acceptance in the Politburo for his realistic views.

M. Coulondre's judgment is confirmed to some extent by Litvinov's statements concerning the Spanish question in his well-
known speech of June 23 on foreign policy. Litvinov stated that
vital interests of England and France were being threatened in

Spain by Germany and Italy. It therefore had to be expected of England and France that they would defend their threatened positions in Spain against Germany and Italy. The Soviet Government had accorded the Spanish Government only the "modest" help which the League of Nations had recommended.

Litvinov's remarks concerning the activity of the Non-Intervention Committee are also meant to leave the impression that no power interests are at stake in Spain for the Soviet Government, in contrast to England and France. From the manner in which Litvinov depicts the Spanish problem *sine ira et studio* as a question which does not affect the Soviet Government directly, it may be concluded that the Soviet Government believes a victory of the Red Spaniards rather improbable and therefore considers it better to prepare the public for such an outcome and for a disentanglement of the Soviet Union.

Count von der Schulenburg

DOCUMENT NO. 737

THE AMBASSADOR IN GREAT BRITAIN TO THE FOREIGN MINISTRY

(Airgram)

London, February 16, 1939.
Received February 17 – 4:50 p.m.
Pol. III 703.

No. 41 of February 16

The British Government intends to let the French take the lead in the question of recognizing Franco. This is to be done out of consideration for American public opinion, which the British feel will not be so much aroused if the French have recognized Franco first. The French are said to have indicated plainly here that they are indifferent to American sensitivity in this question which is of vital importance to France.

According to reliable reports, General Jordana has again assured Senator Bérard that the foreign volunteers will be sent home immediately after the last remnant of Red Spain is subdued. Bérard had received instructions to try to influence Jordana to make this a definite commitment.

Bérard is also instructed to obtain from Franco a precise statement of his attitude on the question of an amnesty. With this concession the French Government intends to bring about the surrender of Negrín. Should Negrín even then continue to offer resistance France would recall its diplomatic mission from Red Spain and recognize Franco's as the only legal government in Spain.

Dirksen

DOCUMENT NO. 803

THE AMBASSADOR IN SPAIN TO THE FOREIGN MINISTRY

(Telegram)

San Sebastian, May 22, 1939.
Received May 23 — 12:40 a.m.

No. 541 of May 22
Telephoned from Burgos:

The farewell parade of the Condor Legion in León went off splendidly; among those present were Franco, all of the Spanish generals, including General Kindelan, the Italian Ambassador, the Italian Commander, the Italian General of the Air Forces.

After reviewing the troops, Franco made them a brilliant speech; General Baron von Richthofen answered in Spanish. Next, Baron von Richthofen announced a large donation by the Condor Legion to the families of the men killed in the Spanish Air Force, amounting to one million pesetas. Then came the parade, with both the troops and the instructors making an excellent impression.

Next there was a joint luncheon in a cordial, comradely spirit; there were expressions of friendship between the Spanish, Italian, and German comrades at arms. I proposed a toast to Franco.

Details are being published by DNB, which will also report, according to instructions, on the announcement of Reichsleiter Ley's large gift to Franco (your telegram of May 20, No. 347). Publication in the Spanish press has been arranged.

Stohrer

EDITORS' NOTE

In a discussion with Ciano on September 28, 1940 (F6/0404-09), of a possible role for Spain in the European war, Hitler delivered the following judgment on Germany's intervention in the Spanish Civil War:

"When the Civil War broke out in Spain, Germany supported Franco on what was for her situation at the time a very extensive scale. This support, moreover, had not been without risk. It had not been confined merely to the delivery of matériel, but volunteers had also been provided and many Germans and Italians had fallen in Spain. He did not wish to reckon this sacrifice of blood in economic terms but regarded it as an absolute gift to Spain.

"Economically, Germany had expended many hundreds of millions for Spain. He (the Führer) had taken the position at the time that the repayment of this debt should not be discussed during the war but must be taken up after Franco's victory. When Germany now requested payment of the 400 million Spanish Civil War debt, this was often represented by the Spaniards as a tactless mixing of economic and ideal considerations; as a German one found oneself appearing to the Spaniards almost like a Jew who wished to do business in the most sacred human values. Therefore, in all agreements with the Spaniards the position must be made clear in advance; if Germany was to provide grain, the question of compensation must be clarified at once.

"Italy and Germany had done a great deal for Spain in 1936. Italy had just been through her Abyssinian enterprise, and Germany was in the middle of her rearmament. Without the help of both countries there would be no Franco today."

Ciano replied that Mussolini shared Hitler's reservations about Spanish participation in the European war and added:

"Italy had not forgotten the experiences of the Spanish Civil War either. Franco had declared at that time that, if he received 12 transport or bombing planes, he would win the war in a few days. These 12 planes had grown into more than 1,000 planes, 6,000 dead, and 14 billion lire. With all their sympathy for Spain this had nevertheless given them pause, and the Duce feared that now also great sacrifices would be demanded of Germany and Italy without compensation. In addition it was to be feared that, after the pattern of the Spanish Civil War, the demands now put forward by Spain would be constantly increased in the further course of events. Therefore, caution was indicated. . . ."

Bibliography

I. GOVERNMENT DOCUMENTS

A. United States

1. Unpublished

Diplomatic Correspondence in the Department of State Archives, Washington, D. C. Includes: consular reports, communications between the Department of State and Foreign Service Officers abroad, and memoranda by the Secretary of State and other high officials within the Department. File Nos:

124.52/116a	.... /6	.... /2629
.... /116b	.... /17	.... /2660
.... /116c	.... /1582	.... /2692
.... /135a	.... /1716	.... /2741a
.... /135b	.... /52/15	852.00/2741b
.... /135c	.... /52/38	.... /2742
.... /142a	800.51W89/1058	.... /2938
.... /142b	852.00/232a	.... /3728
.... /168	.... /1624a	.... /3796
.... /225	.... /1624b	.... /3890
.... /425	852.00/2175	.... /3918
352.1115/5	.... /2190a	.... /3922
.... /45	.... /2190b	.... /3928
.... /136	.... /2296	.... /3937
.... /201	.... /2300	.... /3960
.... /346	.... /2325	.... /4062a
.... /999	.... /2348	.... /4144
352.1115/1017	.... /2395	.... /4179
352.1121/72	.... /2430	.... /4235
.... /74	.... /2489	.... /4248
.... /117	.... /2510a	.... /4327
711.00111/1	.... /2574	.... /4772
.... /5	.... /2589	.... /4989

.... /5051
.... /5118
.... /5392
.... /5839
.... /5885
852.00/5890
.... /5906½
.... /5931
.... /6122
.... /6132
.... /6178
.... /6216½
.... /6760
.... /6771
.... /6955
.... /7254
.... /7671
.... /7683

.... /7803
.... /8554½
.... /8623
.... /8654½
.... /8747
852.24/108
.... /109
.... /349
.... /351
.... /370
.... /379
.... /379a
852.24/631
.... /708
852.48/123
.... /253
.... /Relief/4
852.2221/5

.... /10
.... /39
.... /61
.... /72
.... /190
.... /198
.... /311
.... /435½
.... /468
.... /493
.... /769
.... /785
.... /806
.... /1131
.... /1302
.... /1323
.... /1384

2. Published

Congressional Record, LXXXI-LXXXIV. 75 Cong., 1 Sess. — 76 Cong., 1 Sess. Washington, 1936-1939.

Hull, Cordell. Our Foreign Relations and Our Foreign Policy. United States Department of State, Publication No. 925 (Address by Cordell Hull before the Good Neighbor League, New York City, September 15, 1936). Washington, September, 1936.

————————. Order in International Relations. United States Department of State, Publication No. 1082 (Address at the University of Toronto, Canada, October 22, 1937). Washington, October, 1937.

————————. Our Foreign Policy. United States Department of State, Publication No. 1146 (Address at the National Press Club, Washington, D. C., March 17, 1938). Washington, March, 1938.

————————. International Relations and the Foreign Policy of the United States. United States Department of State, Publication No. 1225 (Address over the Red Network of the National Broadcasting Company, August 16, 1938). Washington, August, 1938.

National Munitions Control Board. Annual Reports, 1937, 1938, 1939. Washington, 1937-1940.

United States Census Bureau. Religious Bodies, 1936. Washington, 1941.

United States Congress, House, Committee on Foreign Affairs. *Hearings Before the Committee on Foreign Affairs; American Neutrality Policy, 1937.* H. J. Res. 147, 75 Cong., 1 Sess. Washington, 1937.

——————, House. *Fascism in Action.* House Document No 401, 80 Cong., 1 Sess. Washington, 1947.

United States Department of State. *Press Releases,* XV-XX. Washington, 1936-1939.

——————. *Bulletin,* I. Washington, 1939.

——————. *Foreign Relations of the United States.* 1936, II; 1937, I; 1938, I. Washington, 1954-1955. Many of the unpublished documents previously listed have since been included in this series.

——————. *Peace and War: United States Foreign Policy, 1931-1941.* Washington, 1943.

——————. *The Spanish Government and the Axis: Official German Documents.* Publication No. 2483. Washington, March, 1946.

——————. *Documents on German Foreign Policy, 1918-1945,* III, *Germany and the Spanish Civil War, 1936-1939.* Washington, 1950.

Welles, Sumner. *Our Foreign Policy and Peace.* United States Department of State, Publication No. 946 (Address before the Foreign Policy Association, New York City, October 19, 1936). Washington, October, 1936.

B. Spanish Republican Government

Spanish Foreign Office. *The Italian Invasion of Spain.* Washington, 1937.

Spanish Information Bureau. *News of Spain.* New York, Biweekly, February 19, 1937–March 19, 1938; Weekly, March 26, 1938–February 23, 1939.

C. Spanish Nationalist Government

Oficino de Informacíon Española. *Las Brigades Internacionales; La Ayuda Extranjera a Los Rejos Espanoles.* Madrid, 1948.

Spanish Embassy. *Report on Spain.* Washington, 1946.

D. League of Nations

League of Nations Assembly, Sixth Committee. *Situation in Spain and Connected Questions.* Geneva, 1937.

II. MANUSCRIPTS AND SPECIAL COLLECTIONS

Roosevelt, Franklin Delano, "Official Files." Boxes 422A, 422B, 422C, 1124, 1504; Sumner Welles File, Cordell Hull File, R. Walton Moore File, President's Secretary's File, Roosevelt Library, Hyde Park, New York.

White, David McKelvy, Collection. "Material on the Spanish Civil War Collected by the Veterans of the Abraham Lincoln Brigade." Includes: fifteen bundles of pamphlets; files of the *Volunteer for Liberty*, May, 1937–November, 1938; three bundles of pamphlets in Spanish; and six bundles of miscellaneous material comprising press releases, speeches, telegrams, letters, and congratulatory messages. New York Public Library, New York, New York.

III. COLLECTIONS OF PUBLISHED DOCUMENTS

American Federation of Labor. *Proceedings of the Annual Convention, 1936-1939.* Washington, 1936-1939.

Jones, S. Shepard and Myers, Denys P. (eds.). *Documents on American Foreign Relations,* I, January, 1938–June, 1939. Boston, 1939.

Padelford, Norman J. *International Law and Diplomacy in the Spanish Civil Strife.* New York, 1939.

Rosenman, Samuel I. (ed.). *The Public Papers and Addresses of Franklin D. Roosevelt,* I-IX. New York, 1938-1941.

Wheeler-Bennett, John W. (ed.). *Documents on International Affairs, 1936-1938.* London, 1936-1938.

IV. NEWSPAPERS

Catholic Action of the South (New Orleans), July, 1936-May, 1939.
Christian Science Monitor (Boston), July, 1936-June, 1939.
Los Angeles Examiner, July, 1936-June, 1939.
Los Angeles Times, July, 1936-June, 1939.
Louisville Courier-Journal, January, 1937-February, 1937.
New Orleans Times-Picayune, July, 1936-June, 1939.
New Orleans States, July, 1936-June, 1939.
New York Times, July, 1936-June, 1939.
New York Post, March 16, 1939.
New York American, February 1, 1937.
San Francisco Chronicle, January 2, 5, 15, 1937.
Socialist Call (New York), February, 1936-August, 1939.

Times (London), July, 1936-June, 1939.
Wall Street Journal (New York), July, 1936-June, 1939.
Washington Post, January 8, 28, 1939.

V. PERIODICALS

A. Editorials

Advance, CXXVIII (July, 1936)-CXXXI (June, 1939).
America, LVI (January, 1937), 314.
Catholic Action, XVIII (July, 1936)-XXI (May, 1939).
Catholic World, CXLIII (September, 1936)-CXLIX (May, 1939).
Christian Century, LIII (July, 1936)-LVI (June, 1939).
Commercial and Financial Chronicle, CXLIII (July, 1936)-CXLVIII (June, 1939).
Commonweal, XXIV (July, 1936)-XXIX (June, 1939).
Current History, XLVI (November, 1937), 25-28.
Editor and Publisher, XIX (January 16, 1937), 14.
Nation, CXLIII (July, 1936)-CXLVIII (June, 1939).
New Masses, XXVI (January 26, 1937), 7.
New Republic, LXXXVII (July, 1936)-XCV (June, 1939).
Public Opinion Quarterly, I (January, 1937)-IV (January, 1940).
Publisher's Weekly, CXXXI (November 26, 1938), 1893-1896.
Science News Letter, XXXIII (May 7, 1938), 298.
Tidings, XX (July, 1936)-XXIII (August, 1939).
Time, XXVIII (July, 1936)-XXX (June, 1939).
Volunteer for Liberty, I (May, 1937)-II (November, 1938).
United Nations Bulletin, I (December 24, 1946), 21-24.

B. Articles Dealing with the War in Spain

"A Blackshirt in Spain," *Living Age,* CCCLII (June, 1937), 299-305.
Baroja, Pio. "The Mistakes of the Spanish Republic," *Living Age,* CCCLI (January, 1937), 422-427.
Bouscaren, Anthony T. "Spanish Republic Reviewed," *Catholic World,* CLXX (October, 1949), 43-49.
Buell, Raymond Leslie. "U. S. Neutrality in the Spanish Conflict," *Foreign Policy Reports,* XIII (November 15, 1937), 206-216.
Colvin, Ian D. "The Case for Franco," *Atlantic Monthly,* CLXI (March, 1938), 397-402.
Dean, Vera Micheles. "European Diplomacy in the Spanish Crisis," *Foreign Policy Reports,* XII (December 1, 1936), 222.

"Embargo on Arms to Spain," *International Conciliation*, CCCXL-VIII (March, 1939), 117-138.

Enrique, Gil. "Repercussions of the Spanish Crisis in Latin America," *Foreign Affairs*, XV (April, 1937), 547-553.

Eulau, Heinz. "Proselytizing in the Catholic Press," *Public Opinion Quarterly*, XI (Summer, 1947), 189-197.

Fenby, Charles. "British Public Opinion on Spain," *Political Quarterly*, VIII (April, 1937), 248-258.

Fernsworth, Lawrence. "Back of the Spanish Rebellion," *Foreign Affairs*, XV (October, 1936), 87-101.

Finch, George A. "Editorial Comment: The United States and the Spanish Civil War," *American Journal of International Law*, XXXI (January, 1937), 74-81.

Garner, James W. "Questions of International Law in the Spanish Civil War," *American Journal of International Law*, XXXI (January, 1937), 66-73.

Gillis, James M. "What Have We Learned from Spain," *Catholic World*, CXLIX (May, 1939), 129-138.

Godden, G. M. "How Communism Attacked Spain," *Catholic World*, CXLIV (January, 1937), 403-407.

Gordon, J. King. "Fascist Weekend in Montreal," *Christian Century*, LIII (November 25, 1936), 1560-1562.

Hart, Merwin K. "America-Look at Spain," *Vital Speeches of the Day*, V (November, 1938), 57-58.

—————. "Our Position Respecting Spain," *Vital Speeches of the Day*, VI (January, 1939), 187-191.

Holmes, Olive. "New Pressures May Alter U. S. Policy on Spain," *Foreign Policy Bulletin*, XXIX (January 20, 1950), 1-2.

Ickes, H. L. "Heil Franco! Heil Franco! Heil Franco!" *New Republic*, CXXIII (August 28, 1950), 18.

—————. "Insult Added to Injury," *New Republic*, CXXIV (January 22, 1951), 17.

Jerrold, Douglas. "Red Propaganda from Spain," *American Review*, IX (May, 1937), 129-151.

—————. "Spain: Impressions and Reflections," *Nineteenth Century and After*, CXXI (April, 1937), 470-492.

Knoblaugh, Edward H. "The Loyalist Propaganda Machine," *Catholic World*, CXLVI (January, 1938), 479-481.

Krivitsky, W. G. "Stalin's Hand in Spain," *Saturday Evening Post*, CCXII (April 15, 1939), 5-6, 115-122.

Langdon-Davies, John. "The Case for the Government," *Atlantic Monthly*, CLXI (March, 1938), 403-408.

Lehmann, Leo H. "The Catholic Church in Politics," *New Republic*, XCVII (November 16, 1938), 34.

Lerner, Max. "Behind Hull's Embargo," *Nation*, CXLVI (May 28, 1938), 607-610.

Lingelbach, W. E. "Political Crisis in Spain," *Current History*, XLII (June, 1935), 318-319.

—————. "Spain Moves Toward Fascism," *Current History*, XLI (January, 1935), 492-493.

—————. "Franco: Master in Spain," *Events*, V (April, 1939), 279.

—————. "The Spanish Civil War Ends," *Events*, V (May, 1939), 347-348.

Lore, Ludwig. "Intervention in Spain," *Current History*, XLV (November, 1936), 41-45.

Lunn, Arnold. "Red Hecklers Wanted: A Challenge from a Champion," *America*, LIX (April 9, 1938), 22-26.

M—, Mary. "A Catholic Speaks Her Mind," *Nation*, CXLV (December 18, 1937), 683-685.

Manuel, Frank. "Background of the Spanish Revolt," *Nation*, CXLIII (July 25, 1936), 94-97.

Matthews, Herbert L. "Franco's Problems," *Foreign Affairs*, XVIII (July, 1939), 723-727.

Minsky, Louis. "Propaganda Bureaus as 'News Services'," *Public Opinion Quarterly*, II (October, 1938), 677.

Monks, Bernard J. "Franco of Spain," *Catholic World*, CXLVII (September, 1938), 667-674.

Neibuhr, Reinhold. "Arrogance in the Name of Christ," *Christian Century*, LIII (September 2, 1936), 1157-1158.

Newcomb, Theodore. "The Influence of Attitude Climate Upon Some Determinants of Opinion," *Journal of Abnormal and Social Psychology*, XLI (July, 1946), 291-302.

O'Rourke, Vernon A. "Recognition of Belligerency and the Spanish War," *American Journal of International Law*, XXXI (July, 1937), 398-413.

O'Sheel, Shaemas. Letter, *New Republic*, XCIII (February 2, 1938), 367-368.

Padelford, Norman J. and Seymour, H. G. "Some International Problems and the Spanish Civil War," *American Journal of International Law*, XXXI (September, 1937), 364-380.

Padleford, Norman J. "The International Non-Intervention Agreement and the Spanish Civil War," *American Journal of International Law*, XXXI (October, 1937), 578-603.

Peers, E. A. and Buckley, Henry. "Spanish Elections," *Contemporary Review*, CXLIX (April, 1936), 409-419.

Pflaum, Irving. "Russia's Role in Spain," *American Mercury*, XLVII (May, 1939), 9-17.

Pratt, Fletcher. "Propaganda from Spain," *American Mercury*, XLI (July, 1937), 409-422.

——————. "Hot-Air Castles in Spain," *American Mercury*, XLII (April, 1938), 450-461.

Reissig, Herman F. Letter, *Nation*, CXLV (July 24, 1937), 110.

Riegal, O. W. "Press, Radio, and the Spanish Civil War," *Public Opinion Quarterly*, I (January, 1937), 135-136.

Riggs, A. S. "No Surprize in Spain," *Catholic World*, CXLIV (November, 1936), 156-159.

Schuster, George M. "A Catholic Defends His Church," *New Republic*, XCVII (January 4, 1939), 246-248.

Seeley, Evelyn. "Hearst Fights the Spanish Republic," *New Republic*, LXXXVIII (September 30, 1936), 217-220.

Sellers, J. L. "Review of Carlton J. H. Hayes, *Wartime Mission in Spain*," *Mississippi Valley Historical Review*, XXXIII (June, 1946), 140-142.

Sencourt, Robert. "How Spain has Reacted," *Catholic World*, CXLVII (May, 1938), 138-142.

Southworth, H. Rutledge. "The Spanish Phalanx and Latin America," *Foreign Affairs*, XVIII (October, 1939), 148-152.

"Spain: A Case Study," *Propaganda Analysis*, II (July 1, 1939), 1-6.

"Spanish War Ballot: Results," *American Review of Reviews*, XCV (March, 1937), 32.

Stowell, Ellery C. "'Nonintervention' and Personal Freedom," *American Journal of International Law*, XXXI (April, 1937), 313-315.

"The Spanish Constitution," *Current History*, XXXVI (June, 1932), 374-384.

"The Struggle in Spain," *Fortune*, XV (April, 1937), 81.

Thomas, Norman. "Spain: A Socialist View," *Nation*, CXLIV (June 19, 1937), 700.

Thomson, Charles A. "Spain: Issues Behind the Conflict," *Foreign Policy Reports*, XII (January 1, 1937), 246.

————. "Spain: Civil War," *Foreign Policy Reports*, XII (January 15, 1937), 258.

————. "The War in Spain," *Foreign Policy Reports*, XIV (May 1, 1938), 38-48.

Thorning, Joseph F. "Franco's Spain," *Catholic World*, CXLVIII (February, 1939), 568-573.

————. "Why the Press Failed on Spain," *Catholic World*, CXLVII (December, 1938), 289-291.

Vezin, Charles. Letter, *American Review of Reviews*, XCV (April, 1937), 82.

Whiffin, Peter. "A Priest Warns the Church," *Forum*, XCVII (April, 1937), 195-201.

Wilcox, Francis O. "The League of Nations and the Spanish Civil War," *Annals of the American Academy of Political and Social Science*, CXCVIII (July, 1938), 65-72.

————. "Localization of the Spanish War," *American Political Science Review*, XXXII (April, 1938), 237-260.

de Wilde, John C. "The Struggle Over Spain," *Foreign Policy Reports*, XIV (April 1, 1938), 14-17.

Ziffren, Lester. "Correspondent in Spain," *Public Opinion Quarterly*, I (Spring, 1937), 112-116.

C. Articles Dealing with United States Foreign Policy

Baillie, Hugh. "Speech Before the New York State Chamber of Commerce," *Vital Speeches of the Day*, III (February, 1937), 236-238.

Beard, Charles A. "Giddy Minds and Foreign Quarrels: An Estimate of American Foreign Policy," *Harper's Magazine*, CXXIX (September, 1939), 344-349.

Bradley, Phillips. "Storm Warnings of Conflict," *Annals of the American Academy of Political and Social Science*, CXCII (July, 1937), 15.

Buell, Raymond Leslie. "The Neutrality Act of 1937," *Foreign Policy Reports*, XIII (October 1, 1937), 166-180.

Cantril, Hadley. "Public Opinion in Flux," *Annals of the American Academy of Political and Social Science*, CCXX (March, 1942), 136-152.

Dean, Vera Micheles. "Europe's Diplomatic Tug of War," *Foreign Policy Reports*, XIV (July 15, 1939), 110-112.

Dulles, Allen W. and Armstrong, Hamilton Fish. "Legislating Peace," *Foreign Affairs*, XVII (October, 1938), 1-12.

Gallup, George and Robinson, Claude. "American Institute of Public Opinion Surveys, 1935-1938," *Public Opinion Quarterly*, II (Fall, 1938), 373.

Howe, Quincy. "American Foreign Policy and Public Opinion," *Yale Review*, XXXI (December, 1941), 318-324.

Ickes, H. L. "Senator McCarran and the ECA Bill," *New Republic*, CXXI (August 1, 1949), 22.

Kellogg, Paul. "Between Going to War and Doing Nothing," *Survey Graphic*, XXVIII (March, 1939), 16-20.

Kennedy, John E. "Liberal's Defeat — A Case History," *Nation*, CXLVII (November 26, 1938), 564-565.

McCarran, Pat. "Why Shouldn't the Spanish Fight for Us?" *Saturday Evening Post*, CCXXIII (April 28, 1951), 25.

Millis, Walter. "Where the Dangers Lie," *Annals of the American Academy of Political and Social Science*, CXCII (July, 1937), 24-30.

Morgenthau, Jr., Henry. "The Morgenthau Diaries, III: How FDR Fought the Axis," *Colliers*, CXX (October 11, 1947), 20-21, 72-79.

—————. "The Morgenthau Diaries, IV: The Story Behind Lend-Lease," *Colliers*, CXX (October 18, 1947), 16-17.

Newberger, Richard L. "What the Home Folks Say About Events Abroad," *Harper's Magazine*, CXXIX (September, 1939), 411-415.

Roper, Elmo. "Fortune Survey," *Fortune Magazine*, XV (April, 1937), 204.

Street, Wolcott D. (ed.). "Should Our Neutrality Law be Repealed or Revised?" *Bulletin of America's Town Meeting of the Air*, IV (December 26, 1938), 5-16.

Wickware, F. S. "What the American People Want," *Harper's Magazine*, CLXXVII (October, 1938), 550-552.

—————. "What We Think About Foreign Affairs," *Harper's Magazine*, CXXIX (September, 1939), 397-406.

VI. PAMPHLETS

American Friends of Spanish Democracy. *Spain*. New York, n.d.

Azaña, Manuel; Negrín, Juan; Álvarez del Vayo; *et al. Spain's War of Independence*. Washington, 1937.

Azaña, Don Manuel. *Discours prononcé par s. Ex. M. Azaña, Président de la République espagnole, á Valence, 21 Janier 1937.* Switzerland, n. d.

Barrio, Diego Martínez. *Paginas para la historia del Frente Popular.* Madrid, 1937.

Ben Leider: American Hero. New York, n.d.

Catholics Reply to Open Letter of 150 Protestant Signatories on Spain. (Reprinted from *Catholic Mind,* November 22, 1937). N.p., n.d.

Code, Joseph Bernard. *The Spanish War and Lying Propaganda.* New York, 1938.

Espinosa, Aurelio M. *The Second Spanish Republic and the Causes of the Counter Revolution.* San Francisco, 1937.

Fischer, Louis. *The War in Spain.* New York, 1937.

Friends of the Abraham Lincoln Battalion. *The Story of the Abraham Lincoln Battalion.* N.p., n.d.

Gannes, Harry. *How the Soviet Union Helps Spain.* New York, 1936.

Joint Letter of the Spanish Bishops to the Bishops of the Whole World. *The War in Spain.* New York, 1937.

League of American Writers. *Writers Take Sides; Letters About the War in Spain from Four-Hundred Eighteen American Authors.* New York, 1938.

Material Assembled by the Library of Congress. *Spanish Civil War: Miscellaneous Addresses, 1936-1939.* Washington, D. C.

—————. *Pamphlets on Spanish Civil War Relief, 1936.* Washington, D. C.

—————. *Pamphlets on the Spanish Civil War, 1937.* Washington, D. C.

Medical Bureau and North American Committee to Aid Spanish Democracy. *Catholic Evidence on Spain.* New York, 1939.

Merry de Val, Marquis. *Spain's Fight for Civilization, Throwing Light upon the Origin of Spain's Plight.* N.p., n.d.

National Legion of Decency List, June 30, 1938.

Negrín, Juan. *Christianity and Spain.* New York, 1939.

—————. *L'adieu de Président Negrín aux combattants internationaux, Discours prononcé par le Dr. Juan Negrín le 9 octobre 1938, a Barcelone, a L' occasion du départ d' Espagne des volontaires etrangers.* Paris, n.d.

Negro Committee to Aid Spain. *A Negro Nurse in Republican Spain.* New York, 1938.

North, Joseph. *Men in the Ranks: The Story of Twelve Americans in Spain.* New York, 1939.

Paulist Fathers. *One Year of the War, 1936-1937.* New York, n.d.

Smith, Harold. *Attack for Victory.* New York, 1942.

Talbot, Francis X. *Clarifying Spanish Civil War Issues* (Reprinted from the *Catholic Mind,* November 22, 1937), N.p., n.d.

Thorning, Joseph F. *Why the Press Failed on Spain.* New York, n.d.

Veterans of the Abraham Lincoln Brigade, *Is it Subversive to be Anti-Franco?* New York, n.d.

Ward, Harry F. and MacLeod, A. A. *Spain's Democracy Talks to America.* New York, 1936.

VII.   MONOGRAPHS: PUBLISHED AND UNPUBLISHED

Adams, Nicholson B. *The Heritage of Spain.* New York, 1943.

Altamira y Crevea, Rafael. *Historia de España,* 6 vols. Barcelona, 1931.

Álvarez del Vayo, Julio. *Freedom's Battle.* New York, 1940.

————————. *The Last Optimist.* London, 1950.

Bardoux, Jacques. *Lechaos espagnol, éviterons-nous la contagion?* Paris, 1937.

Barea, Artura. *The Forging of a Rebel.* New York, 1946.

Bessie, Alvah Cecil. *Men in Battle: A Story of Americans in Spain.* New York, 1939.

Block, J. R. *Espagne, Espagne!* Paris, 1936.

Borkenau, Franz. *The Spanish Cockpit.* London, 1937.

Bowers, Claude G. *My Mission to Spain. Watching the Rehearsal for World War II.* New York, 1954.

Brenan, Gerald. *The Spanish Labyrinth. An Account of the Social and Political Background of the Civil War.* New York, 1943.

Browder, Earl, and Lawrence, Bill. *Next Steps to Win the War in Spain.* New York, 1938.

Buckley, Henry W. *Life and Death of the Spanish Republic.* London, 1940.

Campoamor, Clara. *La révolution espagnole vue par une républicaine.* Paris, 1937.

Castillejo y Duarte, Jose. *War of Ideas in Spain.* London, 1943.

Cattell, David T. *Communism and the Spanish Civil War.* Berkeley, 1955.

Curran, Edward Lodge. *Franco.* New York, 1937.

Davies, John Langdon. *Behind the Spanish Barricades.* New York, 1937.

Díaz José and Dolores Ibarruri. *España y la guerra imperialista.* Mexico City, 1939.

Díaz, José. *Lessons of the Spanish War, 1936-1939.* London, 1940.

Dimitrov, Georgi. *The United Front.* New York, 1938.

Dundas, Lawrence. *Behind the Spanish Mask.* London, 1943.

Feis, Herbert. *The Spanish Story: Franco and the Nations at War.* New York, 1948.

Foltz, C. *Masquerade in Spain.* Boston, 1948.

Foss, William and Gerahty, Cecil. *The Spanish Arena.* London, 1938.

Gannes, Harry. *Spain in Revolt.* New York, 1936.

Ganzon, Guadalupe F. "The Rise of the Nationalist Government in Spain." Ph.D. dissertation, Stanford University, 1950.

Garcia Pradas, J. *Rusia y España.* Paris, 1948.

Gorkin, Julian. *Canibales politicos, Hitler y Stalin en España.* Mexico City, 1941.

Hamilton, Thomas J. *Appeasement's Child. The Franco Regime in Spain.* New York, 1943.

Hayes, Carlton J. H. *Wartime Mission in Spain 1942-1945.* New York, 1945.

——————. *The United States and Spain.* New York, 1951.

Hericourt, Pierre. *Arms for Red Spain.* London, 1937.

Hoare, Sir Samuel. *Ambassador on Special Mission.* London, 1946.

Hubbard, John R. "British Public Opinion and the Spanish Civil War, 1936-1939." Ph.D. dissertation, University of Texas, 1950.

Hughes, Emmet John. *Report from Spain.* New York, 1947.

Jimenez de Asua, Luis (ed.). *La Constitucion Politica de la Democracia Española.* Santiago (Chili), 1942.

King, G. S. *Heart of Spain.* Cambridge, 1941.

Knoblaugh, Edward H. *Correspondent in Spain.* New York, 1937.

Koestler, Arthur. *Spanish Testament.* London, 1937.

Kutchback, Frances. "A Study of the American Legion With Emphasis on Its Attitude Toward Foreign Affairs." M.A. thesis, Claremont College, 1940.

Loveday, Arthur F. *World War in Spain.* London, 1939.

Lunn, Arnold. *Spanish Rehearsal.* New York, 1937.

——————. *Spain and the Christian Front.* New York, 1939.

de Madariaga, Salvador. *Spain.* New York, 1943.

Mellor, F. H. *Morocco Awakes.* London, 1939.

Mendizábal, Alfred. *The Martyrdom of Spain.* London, 1938.

O'Duffy, Eoin. *Crusade in Spain.* London, 1938.

Oliveira, A. Ramos. *Politics, Economics and Men of Modern Spain, 1808-1946.* London, 1946.

Ortega y Gasset, José. *Invertebrate Spain.* New York, 1937.

Orwell, George. *Homage to Catalonia.* London, 1938.

Parry, Hugh Jones. "The Spanish Civil War." Ph.D. dissertation, University of Southern California, 1949.

Pattee, Richard. *This is Spain.* Milwaukee, 1951.

Paul, Elliot. *The Life and Death of a Spanish Town.* New York, 1942.

Peers, E. Allison. *The Spanish Tragedy.* London, 1936.

——————. *Spain, the Church and the Orders.* London, 1939.

——————. *The Spanish Dilemma.* London, 1940.

——————. *Spain in Eclipse, 1937-1943.* London, 1943.

Perez Salas, Coronel Jesus. *Guerra en España 1936-1939.* Mexico City, 1947.

Plenn, Abel. *Wind in the Olive Trees.* New York, 1945.

Prieto, Carlos. *Spanish Front.* London, 1936.

Regler, Gustav. *The Great Crusade.* Toronto, 1940.

Rocker, Rudolph. *The Tragedy of Spain.* New York, 1937.

Rolfe, Edwin. *The Lincoln Battalion. The Story of the Americans Who Fought in Spain in the International Brigades.* New York, 1939.

Romero, Luis. *Impresiones de un militar republicano.* Barcelona, 1937.

Rust, William. *Britons in Spain, The History of the British Battalion of the XVth International Brigade.* London, 1939.

Salter, Cedric. *Tryout in Spain.* New York, 1943.

Sencourt, Robert. *Spain's Ordeal.* London, 1938.

Smith, Rhea Marsh. *The Day of the Liberals in Spain.* London, 1938.

Stimson, Henry L. *et al. The Embargo on Arms to Spain.* New York, 1939.

Strong, Anna Louise. *Spain in Arms.* New York, 1937.

Summerfield, John. *Volunteer in Spain.* New York, 1937.

Thayer, James R. "The Reaction of American Public Opinion to Certain International Crises, 1935-1947." M.A. thesis, University of Denver, 1947.

Tinker, Frank Glasgow. *Some Still Live.* New York, 1938.

Toynbee, Arnold J. *Survey of International Affairs, 1937,* II, *The International Repercussions of the War in Spain.* London, 1938.

White, David McKelvy. *Franco Spain: America's Enemy.* New York, 1945.

VIII. GENERAL ACCOUNTS

Atwater, Elton. *American Regulation of Arms Exports.* Washington, 1941.

Bailey, Thomas A. *The Man in the Street. The Impact of American Public Opinion on Foreign Policy.* New York, 1948.

——————. *A Diplomatic History of the American People.* New York, 1948.

Beals, Carleton. *The Coming Struggle for Latin America.* New York, 1938.

Beard, Charles A. *American Foreign Policy in the Making, 1932-1940. A Study in Responsibilities.* New Haven, 1946.

Bendiner, Robert. *The Riddle of the State Department.* New York, 1943.

Bloom, Sol. *The Autobiography of Sol Bloom.* New York, 1948.

Borchard, Edwin and Lage, William Potter. *Neutrality for the United States.* New Haven, 1940.

Bradley, Phillips (ed.). *American Isolation Reconsidered.* Washington, 1941.

Bruner, Jerome. *Mandate from the People.* New York, 1944.

Brynes, James F. *Speaking Frankly.* New York, 1947.

Cantril, Hadley. *Gauging Public Opinion.* Princeton, 1944.

Carlson, John Roy. *Undercover.* New York, 1943.

Cave, Floyd A. (ed.). *The Origins and Consequences of World War II.* New York, 1948.

Childs, Marquis W. *I Write from Washington.* New York, 1942.

Churchill, Winston. *The Gathering Storm.* London, 1948.

——————. *Step by Step 1936-1939.* London, 1939.

Connolly, Cyril. *The Condemned Playground.* New York, 1946.

Council on Foreign Relations. *The United States in World Affairs: An Account of American Foreign Relations, 1936-1940.* New York, 1937-1941.

Dodd, Jr., William E. and Dodd, Martha (eds.). *Ambassador Dodd's Diary.* New York, 1941.

Farley, James A. *Jim Farley's Story.* New York, 1948.

Field, Harry W. *American Public Opinion and Foreign Policy.* New York, 1945.

Fischer, Louis. *Men and Politics.* New York, 1941.

Ganthorne-Hardy, G. M. *A Short History of International Affairs, 1920-1939.* London, 1947.

Graves, Robert. *The Long Weekend.* New York, 1941.

Greenwall, Harry J. *Mediterranean Crisis.* London, 1939.

Gunther, John. *Inside Europe.* New York, 1936.

Haines, C. Grove and Hoffman, Ross J. S. *The Origins and Background of the Second World War.* New York, 1947.

Hull, Cordell. *The Memoirs of Cordell Hull,* I, II. New York, 1948.

Johnson, Walter. *The Battle Against Isolation.* Chicago, 1944.

Kain, Ronald Stuart. *Europe: Versailles to Warsaw.* New York, 1939.

Kaltenborn, H. V. *Kaltenborn Edits the News.* New York, 1937.

Krivitsky, Walter. *In Stalin's Secret Service.* New York, 1939.

Langer, William L. and Gleason, S. Everett. *The Challenge to Isolation, 1937-1940.* New York, 1952.

Low, David. *A Cartoon History of Our Times.* New York, 1939.

Matthews, Herbert L. *Education of a Correspondent.* New York, 1946.

——————. *Two Wars and More to Come.* New York, 1938.

Merriman, Roger B. *Six Contemporaneous Revolutions.* London, 1938.

Monroe, Elizabeth. *The Mediterranean in Politics.* New York, 1938.

Perkins, Francis. *The Roosevelt I Knew.* New York, 1946.

Roosevelt, Eleanor. *This I Remember.* New York, 1949.

Rosten, Leo C. *Hollywood: The Movie Colony and the Movie Makers.* New York, 1941.

Seldes, George. *Lords of the Press.* New York, 1938.

——————. *The Catholic Crisis.* New York, 1945.

Sharp, Walter R. and Kirk, Grayson. *Contemporary International Politics.* New York, 1940.

Sherwood, Robert E. *Roosevelt and Hopkins.* New York, 1948.

Thompson, Dorothy. *Let the Record Speak.* Boston, 1949.

Thorp, Margaret Farrand. *America at the Movies.* New Haven, 1939.

Toynbee, Arnold J. *Survey of International Affairs, 1936.* London, 1937.

Van Alstyne, Richard W. *American Diplomacy in Action.* Palo Alto (California), 1947.

Voorhis, Jerry. *Confessions of a Congressman.* New York, 1947.

Welles, Sumner. *The Time for Decision.* New York, 1944.

——————. *Where are We Heading?* New York, 1946.

Wright, Quincy. *A Study of War.* Chicago, 1942.

IX. BIBLIOGRAPHICAL REFERENCES

Hardin, Floyd. *The Spanish Civil War and Its Political, Social, Economic, and Ideological Backgrounds.* Denver, University of Denver, 1940.

Woolbert, Robert Gale. *Foreign Affairs Bibliography, 1932-1942.* New York, 1945.

X. INTERVIEW

Stern, J. David, New Orleans, December 14, 1951.

XI. PERSONAL LETTERS

Bowers, Claude G. to F. Jay Taylor. January 25, 1954.

——————. to ——————. February 15, 1954.

——————. to ——————. July 16, 1954.

——————. to ——————. January 14, 1955.

——————. to ——————. June 6, 1955.

Fishman, Moe. to ——————. January 17, 1955.

——————. to ——————. January 25, 1955.

——————. to ——————. May 17, 1955.

Index